PROFESSIONAL NOMAD

ADVENTURES OF A BUSINESS EXECUTIVE
IN THE GLOBAL COMMUNITY

Maurice E. Marwood

Order this book online at www.trafford.com/08-0776
or email orders@trafford.com

Most Trafford titles are also available at major online book retailers.

© Copyright 2009 Maurice E. Marwood.
Cover Design by Victor J. Crapnell, Art Deptartment Design
www.artdepartmentdesign.com
Edited by: Dr. Patricia Anderson, PhD, query@HelpingYouGetPublished.com &
Mavis Andrews, mavisandrews@shaw.ca
All rights reserved. Except as permitted under the United States Copyright Act of 1976,
no part of this publication may be reproduced, stored in a retrieval system, or transmitted,
in any form or by any means, electronic, mechanical, photocopying, recording, or otherwise,
without the written prior permission of the author.

Note for Librarians: A cataloguing record for this book is available from Library
and Archives Canada at www.collectionscanada.ca/amicus/index-e.html

Printed in Victoria, BC, Canada.

ISBN: 978-1-4251-8035-5

This publication is designed to provide accurate and authoritative information concerning the
subject matter covered. It is sold with the understanding that neither the author nor the publisher
is engaged in rendering legal, accounting, or other professional service. If legal advice or other
expert assistance is required, the services of a competent professional person should be sought.

— From a declaration of principles
jointly adopted by a Committee of
the American Bar Association and a
Committee of Publishers

This book is a work of non-fiction based on my notes, research, observations, and recollections.
Names, places, and incidents are not products of the author's imagination—they are real.
I have done my best to present an accurate picture; however, if any errors or inadvertent
misrepresentations remain in the text, I assume full responsibility for these, as well as for the
book as a whole.

 www.trafford.com

North America & international
toll-free: 1 888 232 4444 (USA & Canada)
phone: 250 383 6864 ♦ fax: 250 383 6804 ♦ email: info@trafford.com

The United Kingdom & Europe
phone: +44 (0)1865 487 395 ♦ local rate: 0845 230 9601
facsimile: +44 (0)1865 481 507 ♦ email: info.uk@trafford.com

10 9 8 7 6 5

DEDICATION

First, I would like to dedicate this book to my wife, Hélène; my son, Dale; my daughter, Pamela; and my two stepsons, Andrew and Lawrence. Posthumously, I would also like to dedicate the book to my first wife, Betty, and our son, Gregory. Collectively, my family has given me many happy moments and tolerated my idiosyncrasies.

This book is also a tribute to the hundreds of colleagues with whom I have had the pleasure of working, and to the millions of business leaders who provide their employees with opportunities to do productive work. That is the greatest humanitarian gesture one can make, an act of greater virtue than a handout given by government or the most benevolent "public servant." Business people do that every day.

As a businessman, I am proud of the contributions made by the organizations that I have led, and I am indebted to the business leaders who gave me the opportunities to both benefit and contribute. I thank you all.

My philosophy, in essence, is the concept of man as a heroic being, with his own happiness as the moral purpose of his life, with productive achievement as his noblest activity, and reason as his only absolute.

—Ayn Rand

CONTENTS

Introduction 1
1 A Geographical Accident (1941 — 1955) 3
2 An Epiphany (1955 — 1959) 13
3 A Tipping Point (1959 — 1966) 19
4 Research and Technology (1966 — 1969) 25
5 Reshaping the Environment (1969 — 1971) 37
6 A Business Education (1971 — 1976) 43
7 A Boiling Caldron (1976 — 1979) 51
8 East Is East (1979 — 1982) 69
9 Namaste (1980) 79
10 Intrapreneurialism (1982 — 1986) 93
11 Another Life (1976 — 1991) 103
12 Trucking Along (1986 — 1989) 109
13 A Turnaround (1989 — 1992) 115
14 Mixing It Up (1992 — 1995) 123
15 A Silk Purse from a Sow's Ear? (1995 — 1998) 129
16 Islands in the Stream (1998 — 2003) 141
17 Warm Winds and Calm Seas (1993 — 2003) 151
18 Kassequa (2003 — 2004) 163
19 Ihla Formosa (2004 — 2008) 177
20 A Capital Idea (2004 — 2008) 203
21 Ethics, Morality, and Social Responsibility 215
22 Mysticism: A Worldwide Epidemic 223
23 As I See It 233
24 Life Is for Living 247
Acknowledgments 257
About the Author 261

INTRODUCTION

A journey of a thousand li begins from under one's feet.
—Lao-Zi, The Tao and Its Virtue

Surviving the small family farm; escaping destitution; altering the environment; immersion in mysticism; mountaineering in Europe; discovering Asia, Africa and the Middle East; marathoning; trekking Nepal; turbulent restructuring; exploring the beautiful Bahamas; diving with sharks; cruising the waterways; enjoying friendly Taiwan; achieving spiritual relief; and learning about relationships...

This is the story of my tumultuous life as a professional nomad. It is a union of both observations and reflections, and recounts a wealth of eclectic experiences, memories, beliefs, and opinions gathered while living, working, and traveling in over 80 countries during about 50 years. I spent 20 of those years working for Caterpillar* proper and another 10 working within the Caterpillar dealer organizations.[1] A variety of restructuring assignments for organizations in Canada occupied an additional 12 years of my career. Firsthand involvement in a wide range of events and diverse situations shaped my values, opinions, and philosophy about life and living, and formed the basis of this story.

I have not tried to be comprehensive and have deliberately avoided telling much about my private life with my family and friends—although I have included a few selected anecdotes, personal experiences, and adventures. I was educated as an engineer but gradually, and somewhat inadvertently, developed a specialty in management and leadership of business organizations, particularly those that needed to reverse performance from decline and failure to recovery and success. Much of the story relates to my experiences and impressions while applying that specialty. What I portray represents my own personal views and

---

[1] Caterpillar Inc. is the world's leading manufacturer of construction and mining equipment, diesel and natural gas engines, and industrial gas turbines. The company also is a leading services provider through Caterpillar Financial Services, Caterpillar Remanufacturing Services, Caterpillar Logistics Services, and Progress Rail Services. More information is available at http://www.cat.com.

INTRODUCTION

is not a corporate matter.

Mr. E. B. White, author of the well-known *Elements of Style*, instructs writers not to inject opinions into their writing. To do so is to imply that the demand for them is brisk. I am certain the demand for my opinions is not brisk; however, we all live in a storm of opinions, most of which are way off the mark for successful living. Therefore, I freely express mine, thinking, naively perhaps, that they might provide guidance and provoke thought in making better choices for better living. Like most, I am careful not to let my lack of knowledge of a subject deter me from expressing an opinion.

The world is full of educated derelicts, and a scholarly education and lengthy pedigree do not necessarily validate one's beliefs or opinions; only the quality of the logic behind them can determine their value. The reasoning should be robust; it should not be based on trite, commonly accepted clichés that merely happen to be popular. In addition, consider whether an opinion is based on a morality of life that promotes living well, or on a morality of death that promotes self-sacrifice, deprivation, and suffering. The accomplishments of the Universe are great and wondrous for us to appreciate, marvel at, and enjoy. Each of us is a rare and unique human being who should be able to flourish as a proud, independent, sovereign individual with inalienable rights. I challenge you to weigh my opinions according to these criteria.

In the 21st century, success in business will require a global perspective and the mind-set to communicate and interact with people from many different societies and cultural backgrounds. Even small local businesses must communicate closely with multinational partners in order to thrive and grow. To build successful careers, younger generations will need to work effectively in a multinational environment. That will become increasingly important as the century unfolds. I hope that my experiences and reflections will provide some insight into the challenges and opportunities to be encountered along the way. Perhaps they will be an inspiration, especially to younger nomads who aspire to careers in international business, as well as to those who simply wish to live flourishing lives and to understand more about the global community in which they live.

And I would be particularly pleased if it helped someone resolve a few of the many contradictions about life and living that we all encounter every day.

Enjoy the journey. Flourish. Live well. Do not submit.
Avoid becoming a passenger in life.

1

A GEOGRAPHICAL ACCIDENT

MELBOURNE, ONTARIO, CANADA
(1941 — 1955)

In the final analysis, it is not what you do for your children but what you have taught them to do for themselves that will make them successful human beings.

—Ann Landers

Edward Mulcaster was a 26-year-old orphan when he stepped off the boat and onto Canadian soil in 1828. He already missed his home in the parish of Carlisle, a border town between England and Scotland, but he was ambitious and heard that Canada offered many opportunities. Edward was determined to take advantage of those opportunities and make a life that mattered. He married Esther Cottrell, made a home, and raised his family near Goderich, Ontario. They were both suited to working the land and were happily building a life together when Esther died two weeks after the birth of Thomas, their fourth child. Esther was only 39 years old.

Distraught, Edward moved to Essex County and subsequently bought some farmland and lived with his three sons and a daughter in a shed that is recorded as being "approximately three logs high and no bigger than 12 square feet." Although he was widowed at a young age, he never wanted another wife and never remarried. Edward worked hard to be a good father and provided for his family until he died in 1878 at the relatively old age of 73.

Their first son, Richard, was 24 years old when he married Rebecca Sergeant in 1868. They were enjoying a busy and happy life in Windsor with their nine children when Rebecca tragically died shortly after the birth of their 10th child. Rebecca was only 49 years old. Richard needed help with his large family and eventually fell in love and married his second wife, Eliza. Due to the demands

A GEOGRAPHICAL ACCIDENT

of an already large family, they avoided having more children. Giving birth in those years was a very risky business, since health care services were primitive and not readily available. Consequently, it was not at all uncommon for men to be married several times—usually to much younger women, of course.

Richard and Rebecca's fifth son, Albert Mulcaster, married Gertrude, and their second child, Ruby—my mother—was born in 1908 near Windsor, Ontario. She grew up in the country and dropped out of school after grade eight to help her father work the farm. It was a struggle, but she loved the outdoors and the peace and quiet of country life. Mother regretted not being able to finish her formal education and continued self-study whenever possible.

Mother's family. She is front left.

On my father's side, my great-great-grandfather, William Job Marwood, arrived in Canada about 1860 from the town of Moretonhampstead in Devon, England. Three generations later, my father was born on August 7, 1910, in Calgary, Alberta; however, for most of his life he lived in Ontario. My father was mechanically inclined, became an auto mechanic, and drove fast and reckless. At an age when all young men think they are immortal, he tried racing a train across a local crossing, and lost. He lived, but barely, and for the rest of his life walked with a limp because his left leg was an inch shorter than his right. During the roaring '20s, when not trying to break speed records in his car, he flew the De Havilland Gypsy Moth acrobatic airplane for fun.

A GEOGRAPHICAL ACCIDENT

Mother and Father, circa 1940

When the depression hit in 1930, my father walked the country roads looking for work in return for room and board and 50 cents a day in spending money—as many other young men did in those days. He found work on the Mulcaster farm for a while, and eventually, on April 20, 1935, married my mother. They made their first home in Riverside, near Windsor, where father was a machinist at the Ford Motor Company. Stories and many smiling photographs of them suggest that they were happy in those days—Father had a decent income doing what he was good at, and Mother enjoyed life at home raising the children, staying active in the local church, and visiting her family. Father was exempt from having to join the army in World War II, presumably because of his leg injury and his work manufacturing military hardware at Ford.

I took my first breath as a citizen of the world in Windsor, Ontario, Canada, on Wednesday, April 23, 1941.[2] I was one of the few fortunate enough to have been born to parents living in a mostly peaceful and civilized region of the world.

---

2   It was St. George's Day. St. George was the brave knight who, according to legend, killed the dragon that was about to devour the king's daughter. Due to his chivalrous behavior, he became a symbol of the eternal struggle between good and evil. Mother nearly named me George and I thanked her profusely for exercising better judgment—I am definitely not a George.

A GEOGRAPHICAL ACCIDENT

Considering all the possibilities of the parents to whom I could have been born, and the many political, economic, cultural, and belief systems into which I could have been born, I judge my birth to have been a very fortunate geographical accident. Having seen the desperate lives of so many who were not so fortunate, I am very thankful and careful not to take that huge advantage for granted. It is what made my life experiences possible.

The world was in great turmoil in 1941: Hitler ravaged Europe and launched the battle for Moscow—the greatest battle of all time[3] (2.5 million were killed, taken prisoner, or severely wounded in the short period of about seven months); the German ship *Bismarck* sank the HMS *Hood* (all but three crewmen died); the Royal Navy sank the *Bismarck* (2,300 sailors died); the German plan for the Holocaust was developed as a "final solution to the Jewish question"; and the Japanese Navy launched a surprise attack on Pearl Harbor, in Hawaii (2,400 killed and 1,178 wounded). It was as if three 9/11s happened in one year.

A few trivial firsts also occurred: Walt Disney's movie *Dumbo* was released to theaters, the breakfast cereal Cheerios was introduced by General Mills, and the first FM radio station began to broadcast from Nashville, Tennessee. Life expectancy was 63 years, a new car cost $850, gasoline was 12 cents a gallon, a movie ticket cost 30 cents, a new home could be bought for $4,100, and tuition to Harvard University cost $420 per year. The only memory I have of Windsor is of blacking out the windows at night in case the German bombers saw the lights of the city and let loose. It seems a strange thing to remember, as I was only three or four years old at the time.

Although details are sketchy, it seems that near the end of the war my father had an opportunity to move to Ottawa to work on a special military project that Ford had been awarded. It may have been a good career opportunity, but the pending disruption, cost, and intimidation of the big city would have been too much for Mother, so they did not go. Instead, they quit the city life in 1945 and bought a farm near the town of Melbourne, Ontario. This was prime farming land, with fertile soil, a long growing season, warm climate, and many good neighbors willing to help each other during the busy seasons. Life was good at first, even though it required long hours working the land and pinching pennies to make ends meet.

Many men returning from the war in the 1940s became farmers because they had no other prospect of making a living. That scenario did not apply to my father; there had to have been another reason, and I believe it was in response to my mother's encouragement. The home in the country; the small family farm; the proper place to raise a family; the genuine values of the rural life as opposed

---

[3] Andrew Nagorski, *The Greatest Battle* (2007).

A GEOGRAPHICAL ACCIDENT

to the noisy, hectic, tempting, and hazardous life in the city; the spirituality of living close to the earth and the animals, and the pleasure of handling them; the joy of putting seeds in the ground and watching them come to life; the birds in the sky and the gentle rain and the bright sunshine—that is what farming meant to my mother. She saw it as an achievement of fundamental satisfaction. It is the only reason I can think of that would have caused my father to leave a secure job with a good company in a pleasant location—and for what? A profession he did not understand or enjoy, a big mortgage, and a life of drudgery.

Throughout my nomadic life roaming the world, my mother always encouraged me to come back home, buy a piece of land, and settle down and raise my family in the country, as she felt they should be raised, instead of tearing up their roots every few years, again and again, like gypsies. Her admonitions added veracity to my speculations on how and why my parents took up farming. It is strange how we make decisions at times. Of course, the benefit of hindsight is a wonderful thing, and no one knows what the outcome might have been had their decision been different.

Perhaps father did not really like working in the factory, taking orders from an autocratic supervisor. Nevertheless, he was not cut out to be a farmer and spent most of his time fixing whatever machinery was broken—most of it was, most of the time—and working a full-time job at the Pond Mills hydro substation, and later at the Kelvinator factory in London. That is what he did best. My most vivid memories of my father, during the few hours he was home on the farm, are of watching him repair a piece of machinery, cursing in frustration at whatever step of the process proved difficult. However, he always persisted and completed the job. Occasionally, I would hand him a screwdriver or a wrench and he would take a few moments to show me what he was doing, but not often. Meanwhile, Mother drove the tractor, working the fields, or did other farm chores. Everyone helped with feeding and tending the livestock, and working in the fields. I began driving the old Fordson tractor as soon as I was heavy enough to push the clutch pedal down when I stood on it.

A GEOGRAPHICAL ACCIDENT

*With Father on the farm in Melbourne, 1947;
Back row: Curtis, Father, and author;
front row: Everett and Francis.
This was the year the author entered Longwood Public School.*

I was four years old when we moved to Melbourne, and I remember those years fondly. Two years later, I entered Longwood Public School, a small one-room facility with four or five students in each of the first eight grades. Longwood was surely the smallest locality in the world, with only the school and a post office, each located on opposite sides of the main railroad tracks. The school was a sturdy brick structure surrounded by farmland. Most days, we walked, or rode our bicycles, about a mile to school—there was no bus, but we never considered it a hardship to walk. In fact, I usually looked forward to it in good weather.

A GEOGRAPHICAL ACCIDENT

Longwood Public School—1955. Thirty students from grades one to eight, in one room and with one teacher. The author is in the middle of the back row.

Our teacher was only about 18 years old. During the 1950s, a high school senior could take a teacher's course during the summer after graduation, and immediately begin to teach grade school the following September. Our teacher's father drove her to school every day, and in the winter, he fired up the wood-burning stove in the morning to take the chill off. She was a great teacher who continuously balanced her time between all eight grades, coaching each student with patience and kindness as she focused on the basic skills of reading, writing, and arithmetic. We memorized the multiplication tables, learned sentence structure, vocabulary, grammar, and the rules of good spelling as we built our linguistic skills. We also studied Canadian geography—memorizing the provinces and their capital cities—along with a bit of world geography and history. Many years later, I drove by the place and discovered the school had been converted into a house after all the small local one-room country schools had been consolidated.

It was at Longwood where I met my first true love, Barbara. She was in the same grade and lived about a mile from the school in a small wooden shack. Barbara was a wisp of a girl, a waif really, but she was the only girl who smiled at me, and that was all it took—she melted my heart. We rode our bikes home together, if we could avoid attracting too much attention. I hope she lived a flourishing life, but it seemed to me at the time that the odds were against her.

Only twice in my entire life have I shown serious anger. The first occurred, quite unexpectedly, in grade seven when I was fed up with being harassed. Walter, the school bully, had failed a few grades and was three or four years older and much taller than I was, as I recall. After taking his abuse for several minutes, something snapped, and I became a killing machine. Eventually, a few kids were able to pull me off him; subsequently, I got a lot more respect from Walter. He began treating the teacher with a bit more respect, too. The only other time I snapped was during a similar situation in high school after being harassed by a group of local hoodlums.

Although my mother tried to teach me to play the piano, I much preferred to be outside, running in the woods, or playing cowboys and Indians with my older brother Curtis, or with Ron, my friend who lived across the street. We carved toy guns, made crude bows, arrows, and slingshots, and threw our bowie knives at the trees. I loved to read the Zane Grey novels of adventure in the Wild West and then relive those adventures by running through the woods with our toy guns and vivid imaginations.

Television was not yet part of our lives but we had a set of *Encyclopaedia Britannica*, some *Popular Science* and *Mechanics Illustrated* magazines, as well as a few wholesome comic books. We spent hours learning magic tricks, or reading about how things worked and how to build a variety of gadgets. We played with the ubiquitous Erector Sets and almost-indestructible wooden toys. The best part was assembling balsa model airplanes from kits, spending hours huddled over the many small pieces, holding them in place one by one until the glue did its job. That usually resulted in losing a layer of skin from my fingers, and, after I had gone to bed at night, the walls moved in and out, and the ceiling moved up and down in waves. It felt quite pleasant, and I never said anything to Mother for fear she might rush me off to the doctor. Many years later, I realized I had been high from sniffing glue all afternoon.

At an early age, I showed a desire to climb whatever looked interesting. First, it was the walnut trees in our backyard. When the spring winds blew, I would scramble to the top of the tall spruce trees and sway back and forth with them. During one daring ascent, at age six, I bounced off several large branches as I fell out of a tree to the ground—that resulted in having a hernia repaired. While the doctor had me under the knife, he decided he might as well go ahead and remove my tonsils and adenoids—it was the custom in those days to do that, whether you needed it or not. I was under the knife again when I got my index finger caught in the corn shredder and removed the top half inch of it, my finger, that is. We found it and the doctor was able to sew it back on—you can hardly notice it now.

Once the hernia healed, I was climbing up the corner of our house, using the small handholds and toeholds formed by the overlapping bricks. From there, it was up the rafters of the barn to steal eggs from the pigeons' nests. (It may be no surprise to learn that I later took up mountain climbing.) When I turned 12, Father taught me to use his .22 rifle, and at every opportunity, I would sneak through the woods looking for rabbits (or anything else that moved) or target the pigeons nesting high up in the barn. None of them was in great danger from my marksmanship, but it was no wonder my mother prematurely developed gray hair.

One day, Ron and I decided it was time to try smoking. We found some dried corncobs and fashioned them into workable pipes; a bit of dried corn silk and a few maple leaves substituted for tobacco. After about 30 minutes of puffing and swallowing the smoke, we turned green and started to feel nauseous. After another 30 minutes or so of heaving our guts out, we decided we had enjoyed about all we could stand of it. Fortunately, Mother never discovered our experiment with smoking. I never again put a pipe or cigarette in my mouth; the closest I ever got to smoking was the occasional cigar when somebody had a baby, or something else to celebrate—and I was always careful not to inhale. Father smoked on the sly, not wanting to set a bad example for us or incur Mother's disappointment. Of course, I knew about it, and I strongly suspected she did too, but she never let on. Mother hardly ever raised her voice and never said an unkind word about anybody that I recall, although she did have an intense argument or two with one of the "inmates" at the assisted living residence when she was about 90.

Shortly after recovering from filling our lungs and stomachs with acrid smoke, we decided to make Molotov cocktails—minus the ingredient of gasoline, fortunately. We lit firecrackers, dropped them in Coke bottles and then tried to throw them before they exploded in our hand. At first, it was easy because we did not hold them long. As we got more proficient, of course, the game became one of seeing who could hold them the longest. I won, but not before a small piece of glass had punctured my lower lip. Mother never learned about that little incident either.

Occasionally, during the hot days of summer, we splashed around in the farm pond. It was only about 30 feet across, and as stagnant as only a farm pond can get. The water was about 18 inches deep in the middle, and to get there we had to walk through mud and cow dung almost up to our knees. It was fun trying to catch the frogs sitting on the lily pads, but we never really did much swimming; we seemed to know instinctively not to get our faces too close to the water. Later, my brother Curtis caught a mild case of polio, which was spread through contaminated food and water—that filthy pond was likely the culprit. It was only good luck that we did not all die of something. Growing up on a farm either kills you or strengthens your immune system. There is no doubt I benefited from the latter—I never once got sick during the many years traveling through remote places in Asia, Africa, the Middle East, and South America—knock on wood.

A GEOGRAPHICAL ACCIDENT

During those years, my parents always set Sunday aside for worship, relaxation, spending quality time with family, and, during the summer months, visiting the many aunts, uncles, and cousins. In hindsight, I can see that those formidable years provided a good environment for a young boy coming of age and discovering life and living, and the basic virtues that were to serve me for the rest of my life were instilled then. As my life unfolded, I often looked to the past to understand the present, and agree with what Robert Fulghum said: "All I really need to know I learned in kindergarten."[4]

History identifies the 1950s as a very prosperous decade. The war was over and the excess productive capacity from the war effort was converted to making domestic goods such as televisions, telephones, refrigerators, vacuum cleaners, and washing machines. For some reason, our family did not benefit from all that prosperity. By the mid-'50s, my parents had four hungry, growing children to feed and clothe, and the combined income from the farm and Father's job at Kelvinator was insufficient to make the mortgage payments on the farm. Rather than face foreclosure, Father convinced Mother that they had to sell and move north where, allegedly, land was cheaper and opportunities greater. His cousin was "successfully" operating a small cattle ranch near Matheson, far up in Northern Ontario, and encouraged Father to come north. During the summer of 1955, Father auctioned off everything on the farm, packed what would fit into a small truck, and we headed north to Matheson.

Mother was not happy with the decision; she hated to leave her community of friends in Melbourne for the cold, harsh climate of the north. Her unhappiness likely spilled over to me because I have no memories of the move. No doubt financial pressures contributed to the decision to move, but I am quite certain my father's adventurous spirit and his desire to try new things were also factors—traits he passed on to me. Father was a high-strung Type-A personality with a strong work ethic and an intense ambition to succeed. He worked hard—too hard—trying to hold down two jobs, and often three. I felt sorry for him because he sincerely tried to give us a comfortable life. I believe he would have done so, had he not abandoned the work he knew.

Let a man practice the profession that he best knows.
—CICERO

---

4   Robert Fulghum, *All I Really Need to Know I Learned in Kindergarten* (1989).

2

AN EPIPHANY

MATHESON, ONTARIO, CANADA
(1955 — 1959)

The Law of the Efficacy of Prayer

In a dangerous world, there will always be more people around whose prayers for their own safety have been answered than those whose prayers have not.

—Nicholas Humphrey

After arriving in Matheson, Father moved a small house onto the piece of land he had acquired and began to establish a new home in a very inhospitable part of Canada. The house was too small for decent comfort or any privacy—very different from the spacious home we had just left. We had no running water, no indoor washing facilities or toilet, no central heating, no insulation, no storage room, and only an ancient wood stove for cooking. Dead poplar trees were hauled out of the forest, cut up, split into manageable sizes and stacked to dry so that Mother could cook. A bathtub in the corner of the kitchen provided the means to have a quick and simple sponge bath once a week—whether we needed it or not. Water was carried from a well, located at the bottom of a steep ravine.

The winters were harsh and bitterly cold, and it was a daily task to keep a hole in the pond free of ice, using an axe, so the livestock could drink. Most days I got up early to help milk the cows before walking into Matheson for the 45-minute bus ride to Iroquois Falls High School. In the winter, when my sister attempted to wash the kitchen floor, the water froze before she could mop it up. Mother extinguished the coal-burning stove in the living room every night before going to bed to avoid the risk of carbon monoxide poisoning, and in the morning, the bucket of drinking water would be frozen. The outdoor toilet was

AN EPIPHANY

a challenge, especially during winter at -20°F. I was in and out in a couple of minutes or less—that habit stayed with me all my life, and the idea of reading in the bathroom is an anathema to me.

Within a few months, Father had to work at the local John Manville asbestos mine to supplement the meager income from the farm, and he often held a third job, driving the local school bus or the county snowplow, to make ends meet. Life was hard for everyone, but mainly for my mother. Her life was only work—all day, every day—doing farm chores, taking care of four teenagers, and trying to make a home. She chose to sacrifice her life for her children, and for that, I will be forever grateful. Nevertheless, it was painful to watch her continually struggle with no choice but to accept the meager portions of enjoyment and pleasure that came her way.

The image of her struggling up the ravine with a bucket of water is still vivid. I see her working in the fields as hard as any man could; milking the cows with cracked and bleeding hands; shoveling manure out of the barn; driving the tractor late at night to get the crops in before it rained; heaving bags of fertilizer and seed onto the planter; cooking in the kitchen with her winter clothes on, waiting for the wood stove to heat up enough to take off her hat; not having clothes good enough to attend her beloved church on Sunday; having to stick a hypodermic needle into her stomach for several days to receive the vaccine that protected her from contracting rabies after a fox attacked the cows; and nursing Curtis through a bout of rheumatic fever. I think that for a time I resented him for being sick because of the added burden he put on my mother, as if he got sick on purpose—a remarkably stupid attitude. Mother's love for and commitment to her family were her motivation, and they were apparently strong enough to make her choice an easy one.

Farm life provided a variety of unusual experiences. A few events dealing with the livestock left an indelible impression on me: castrating the young pigs, artificially inseminating the cows, arranging natural insemination of the hogs. Occasionally Mother asked us to get a chicken for dinner. I would tie one string around its feet and another around its neck. Curtis and my younger sister Frances would hold the strings and turn their heads away as I brought the axe down across its neck, which was stretched over a block of wood. We would then all run like hell to avoid being sprayed with blood as the chicken ran around with its head cut off.

Occasionally, the cows broke through the fence along the railroad tracks to enjoy the lush green grass. Freight trains came by once or twice a day and the cows hardly raised their heads, but cows are the dumbest animals on the face of the Earth. One particular day, Betsy heard the sound and looked back at the advancing train just in time for it to take her head almost off. That meant an im-

AN EPIPHANY

mediate butchering to salvage the meat—guess who did much of the cutting.

Despite all the work and chores to be done, I always seemed to find time for play. One day a young man in the community gave me an old pair of seven-foot wooden jumping skis with leather thong bindings that secured the boots to the skis so there was no possibility of them releasing during a fall. I managed to learn to ski with him at the local ski hill. It was a small hill, but an old Model T Ford car was set up to power a rope tow so that we did not have to walk up the hill after every run. Since the days were short, lights were installed so we could ski in the evenings after school. Skiing was an escape from the winter drudgery of the farm and I enjoyed it at every opportunity, and thanks to the generosity of my friend, it became a passion and a lifelong sport.

We always looked forward to the arrival of spring and warm weather, especially since summer only lasted a few short weeks. It would arrive suddenly—and in a couple weeks the snow disappeared, the grass turned green, and it was time once again to cultivate the fields to see if they would yield something useful. The land was not very fertile and seemed to consist mostly of rocks. Since the seasons were short, the only crops worth growing were used as fodder for the cattle and pigs. Each spring, Mother planted a garden of fresh vegetables to enjoy in the summer and preserve for the cold winter months. When not at school or attending to chores, I hunted the forest, paddled our canoe on the river, and fished near the river rapids to supplement the food supply. The fish were so numerous that within about 30 minutes I would have enough. That experience of easy fishing took away the challenge; thereafter, I never seemed to have enough patience to enjoy fishing as a sport. My single-shot 410-gauge shotgun accompanied me everywhere I went and the crows would scatter, mainly to avoid the noise.

Despite the hardship, those were happy times. Nevertheless, it became obvious to me during those years that I was on my own—my destiny was up to me and me alone. Of course, there was plenty of moral support from my parents, and they encouraged me to get an education as the only way out of the desperate life we were living. As soon as I was old enough, I sought work during the summer months. Young, strong, and eager, I worked for the Department of Lands and Forests, scaling logs, and as a laborer on various construction projects in the community—usually on the end of a shovel. One day, while I was working hard at the bottom of a trench, the boss came by, smiled, and quietly watched me for a few moments. I was sweaty, muddy, tired, and in need of a drink, but I was glad for the work and smiled back.

"What are you going to do with your life?" he asked.

"I'm going to be an engineer," I impulsively blurted out.

"Go for it," he said encouragingly as he smiled and walked away.

AN EPIPHANY

It was an epiphany. My conscious focus had been on survival, not introspection about future career aspirations, yet, in an instant, I had set myself a goal and been given a challenge. The way was not clear but, suddenly, the goal was. Eventually I came to learn that success is a journey—not a destination—and if one is on their chosen journey, they are successful. Unknowingly, at that moment, I became successful. Success also requires a desire to win and the belief that you can win. I could not verbalize it at the time, but I had both—driven by a fear of being destitute and getting trapped into living the kind of life my parents were living.

Then, as if Mother had to be tested further, my father took sick and died suddenly on January 4, 1958, at the young age of 48. His blood pressure was off the scale and caused his kidneys to fail—they had already been damaged in the car/train accident many years before. Mother was left with no money and four teenagers to support. Other than a small "Mother's Allowance," there was no safety net in those years, and people had to depend on each other. It was a traumatic time. Fortunately, friends and relatives came to our aid, especially her brother Blake. He offered to share his home on the old family farm where she had grown up and met my father. During the summer of 1959, we gladly returned to the warmer climate of southern Ontario, near the hospitable lakeside environment of Kingsville.

The summer after my father died, I managed to get a good job working for a prospector who was exploring for gold around Timmins, Ontario. I carried his seismic receiver while he walked 100 yards behind with the seismic generator. Every few minutes, when he signaled, I planted the receiver on the ground, and he took a reading and made notes in his little book. Each day we covered about 15 to 20 miles along the many logging roads winding through those rugged northern Ontario forests. He drove me home every night, exhausted but happy, and paid me $100 cash for a seven-day workweek, an exorbitant sum at the time. In addition, it was clean work in the fresh air, which was much better than being on the end of a shovel at the bottom of a dirty trench.

I managed to complete four years at Iroquois Falls High School, in Iroquois Falls, Ontario, and at the end of the following summer, I bought my first car, a 1949 Mercury that Curtis and I drove to our new home in Kingsville. The engine had a tendency to overheat, and even though it was a hot day in August, we had to leave the heater on so as to keep the needle out of the red zone. I decided to take a chance and save money by not buying insurance. Fortunately, it was an uneventful trip and we arrived with a small cash reserve.

Curtis and I attended grade 13 together at Kingsville District High School. Being a more diligent student, Curtis was accepted into the University of Western Ontario—he wanted to become a teacher. Unfortunately, my grades

AN EPIPHANY

were not good enough for me to be accepted anywhere; I had obviously spent too much time playing football instead of studying.

Now I had two fundamental choices—quit school and find a job or repeat grade 13, improve my marks, and hope to qualify for university the following year. My first inclination was to find work. That summer I tried a variety of backbreaking jobs—construction, picking tomatoes in the hot sun, painting barns while balancing on a ladder 50 feet off the ground, and helping my uncle do chores on his farm. As September approached, I concluded there must be an easier way to make a living, so in 1960 I returned to Kingsville District High School to repeat grade 13.

Luck was with me. When I showed up in the classroom, my favorite teacher and football coach—Charlie Campbell, an alumnus of the Ontario Agricultural College (OAC) in Guelph, Ontario—expressed surprise that I was there. He got on the phone, called in a couple of his markers at the school, and got me accepted immediately with his promise that I had potential and would do well; I will be forever in his debt. Although registration had already closed, I scrambled to fill a suitcase with a few essentials and headed off to Guelph.[5]

---

5   John Kenneth Galbraith (1908—2006) graduated from the Ontario Agricultural College (OAC) and became an influential Canadian-American economist. After becoming famous, he was quoted in *Time* magazine as saying OAC was probably the worst school in the English-speaking world. The college became its own university in 1965 and went on to be rated one of the best universities in Canada for several years in a row.

3

A TIPPING POINT

GUELPH, ONTARIO, CANADA
(1959 — 1966)

The only purpose of education is to teach a student how to live his life—by developing his mind and equipping him to deal with reality. The training he needs is theoretical, i.e., conceptual. He has to be taught to think, to understand, to integrate, to prove. He has to be taught the essentials of the knowledge discovered in the past—and he has to be equipped to acquire further knowledge by his own effort.

—Ayn Rand

The aim of education should be to teach us rather how to think, than what to think—rather to improve our minds, so as to enable us to think for ourselves than to load the memory with the thoughts of other men.

—Bill Beattie

There was no money for college but I was not deterred by such details. Charlie Campbell arranged a small bursary, and I scraped up enough money for tuition and room and board for the first semester. What more did I need? I was on my journey and a whole year ahead of plan. Education would unlock the door to a better life, and it was happening—a tipping point.[6] Destitution, get thee behind me!

Life at university was busy and exciting, although it was a challenge to keep up with the course work while enjoying a little social life and playing sports—squash, varsity football, skiing, and wrestling. In the spring, the final grades were posted on the student bulletin board, ranked in descending order. A red line,

---

[6] A tipping point is defined as a small thing that can have a big effect—a dramatic moment when everything can change all at once. See Malcolm Gladwell, *The Tipping Point* (2002).

A TIPPING POINT

drawn about halfway down, showed the cutoff between those who passed and those who did not. I was relieved to see that my name was the third one above the red line. At that moment, I gave thanks and resolved not to cut it quite so close the next year. Fortunately, my grades became progressively better as the years went by.

My years at Guelph were some of the happiest. Life was unfolding, the future was promising, opportunity beckoned. Mother was happier, being back to her roots, surrounded by family and old friends. Her children were growing up and successfully making their own way in the world, and destitution was no longer knocking at her door. She eventually fell in love again, with a kind man who gave her a few more happy years as a married woman, and she lived to the ripe old age of 92, with a clear mind and many memories.

In 1964, I graduated with a Bachelor of Science degree in Agricultural Engineering, conferred by the University of Toronto. There were only eight people in our class. I was finally an engineer and wished I could talk to my old boss in Matheson, and thank him for being the catalyst for my epiphany six years earlier.

In 1963, I fell in love with Betty, and we were married on September 12, 1964, shortly after I graduated. She still had one more year to complete before finishing her studies at McDonald Institute, so we decided that I should stay at Guelph and earn my Master's degree, instead of seeking immediate employment elsewhere. We were invited to housesit a professor's home during his sabbatical, and I found a part-time job as a research assistant for Professor Peter Southwell. He was my faculty advisor during graduate studies, and taught me much about thinking and writing. He became a good friend, mentor, and father figure, and I owe him a great debt. In 1965, OAC became a fully accredited, independent university and Betty received one of the first degrees conferred by the new University of Guelph. A year later, I received my Master's and it was finally time to get a real job, pay off our student loans, and make a life.

I don't mean to suggest that the sole purpose of an education is to prepare one to make a good living—it is not, although that was my focus at the time. My engineering curriculum concentrated on the hard sciences. There was little time to "waste" on the other branches of learning (such as literature, psychology, sociology, philosophy, and history), which did not seem pertinent to the real world. That was certainly my attitude, so those disciplines were pushed into the distant background of my education, and I did not object. Today, of course, the situation is different. Students frequently have more choices in what they can learn, and that is good. The modern generation often does not place earning power at the top of the hierarchy, choosing instead to pursue the social

A TIPPING POINT

sciences in order to "deepen their knowledge and understanding of the world" in which they live, as if the two choices were dichotomous and contradictory. It is unlikely that these students have ever faced the prospect of destitution, or even much of what could be called hardship. Some even become professional students for as long as possible, simply to escape the world in which they live, often at the expense of someone other than themselves.

*Graduating class in Mechanical Engineering—1964.
A motley crew. The author is second from the left in the back row.*

One of my most interesting courses at Guelph involved the study of internal combustion engines. A training aid for the course was an old Caterpillar single-cylinder test engine that had somehow found its way to the school. Those engines were originally designed specifically to help develop and test various lubricating oils that would stand up to the rigorous demands of Caterpillar's diesel engines. It was important that the oil be properly formulated so as to contribute to reliability, durability, and long life. The test engine at Guelph was cut away to show all the internal working components—which made it a great training aid. In Canada, during the mid-1960s, Caterpillar and its products were well known and highly respected for their performance and quality. That single-cylinder engine was my first exposure to the company, and a favorable one.

A few months before my graduation, I wrote Caterpillar and inquired about employment opportunities. The Vietnam war was raging, and many young men had already been drafted, creating a dire shortage of engineers. In fact, the shortage was so severe that many American companies were actively recruiting at schools across Canada; I was fortunate to be in a sellers' market. The interviews at the head office in Peoria, Illinois, USA, went well, and I received an offer of

A TIPPING POINT

employment—$790/month plus good benefits—to begin as soon as possible after graduation. That was significantly more than the going rate in Canada at the time, and, in addition, the idea of moving to the USA and "seeing the world" was a big attraction. Little did I know then how real that opportunity would become. Caterpillar expedited the immigration process, and the magic Green Card arrived six months after the application was submitted.

In early February 1966, Betty and I loaded all our worldly possessions in a four-by-six trailer, hooked it behind our Volkswagen Bug, and headed to Peoria, Illinois; and on February 16, I became employed by the Caterpillar Tractor Co.

A TIPPING POINT

Married Betty Brownhill, September 12, 1964.

4

RESEARCH AND TECHNOLOGY

CATERPILLAR TRACTOR CO.
PEORIA, ILLINOIS, USA
(1966 — 1969)

The professional manager is a servant. Rank does not confer privilege. It does not give power. It imposes responsibility.[7]

—PETER F. DRUCKER

In the early 1870s, Daniel Best was frustrated with the amount of manual work involved in harvesting, cleaning, and hauling the grain on the vast wheat farms in the north-central part of California. He set about making grain cleaners, which became very popular, and in 1871, he formed the Best Manufacturing Company. Subsequently he developed a grain harvester, the forerunner of the modern grain combine, and steam tractors to pull the machines.

Meanwhile, the Holt family business, Stockton Wheel Company, was building wooden wheels for the conveyances used to haul the logs out of the woods to the lumber mills in northern California. Eventually, the business expanded into manufacturing steam tractors, threshing machines, and streetcars. Several of these products were in direct competition to the Best Manufacturing Company. After many years competing with each other, the Holt Manufacturing Company and C. L. Best Tractor Co. amalgamated in 1925, to form the Caterpillar Tractor Co.[8]

Neither Holt nor Best can take credit for inventing the use of tracks instead of wheels to spread the weight of the machine over a larger area and reduce

---

[7] Peter F. Drucker, introductory comments to Alfred P. Sloan Jr., *My Years with General Motors* (1990).
[8] Sources for the historical information include Caterpillar Tractor Co., *Century of Change* (1984); Robert N. Pripps, *The Big Book of Caterpillar* (2000); and Caterpillar Inc., *The Caterpillar Story* (1990), and *Caterpillar—75 Years: All in a Day's Work* (2000).

ground pressure. In fact, about 50 years earlier, in 1825, a chain-belt track system was patented in England by George Cayley. Later, in 1858, Warren Miller successfully demonstrated a tracked machine in California, and various inventors in North America subsequently built several other versions. Benjamin Holt examined a number of these designs and in 1904 tested his first track-type tractor near Stockton, California. It is reported that a spectator commented, "She crawls along like a caterpillar," and Benjamin Holt replied, "Caterpillar she is!" The name has since become one of the most recognizable trademarks.

On arriving in Peoria, we rented a small house, bought some furniture, and set up our first home. Betty was four months pregnant and the first order of business was to become established with a local family doctor. Several other new Caterpillar employees with young families and mothers-to-be had also just arrived in the community, and we quickly became acquainted. At the time, Caterpillar was a paternalistic company that provided a lot of good support as we settled into the area. Within a few months, we had established a circle of close friends with whom we shared frustrations and joy for many years to come. Although we did not fully realize it at the time, we had joined the "Caterpillar family." It was not long before I had met employees who had joined the "family" before I was born. It was not uncommon to read about employees who had worked 40 years or more for Caterpillar, and a few years later, I worked with an employee who eventually retired after 50 years with the company.

By the mid-1960s, the Vietnam War had stressed and polarized the entire country. All able-bodied young men were required to register for the draft; then they waited anxiously, hoping they would not be called up. As a "Resident Alien" with a Green Card, I also had to register six months after entering the country, even though I was a Canadian citizen. Of course, unlike American men, I could legally cross back over the border if drafted, but there was little risk of that because a hierarchy protected me. As I recall, single young men with little education were the first to go, then young married men with no children, followed by educated young married men, and, finally, educated young married men with children. Being older, educated, and married with a child, I was at the bottom of the hierarchy. In addition, working in the Research Department entitled me to a "Critical Skills Deferment," which seemed a bit of a stretch, but I did not protest; those working in sales and marketing were not entitled to a deferment.[9]

Our first son, Dale, arrived on June 24, 1966. He was a healthy and lively baby, and brought a new joy to our lives. Betty was a natural-born mother and accepted her role with complete satisfaction, doing the many things necessary to ensure he was raised with love and care. She did not complain that I was

---

9   Tragically, over 50,000 young men and women did not return from that unfinished war.

busy at work most of the time, and often doing work-related tasks while at home; a work/life balance was not a high priority in those days. Caterpillar shut down for two weeks during the summer, and we took vacations then (whether we wanted to or not) and went camping, exploring, or home to visit family in Canada. Life was good.

As a Canadian who has spent many years living and working on both sides of the border, I can confirm that many of us suffer from an inferiority complex vis-à-vis Americans. Indeed, it has been said that the entire country suffers from that syndrome. We Canadians tend to be critical of Americans without ever getting to know them—a reflection of our own insecurities and envy of America's self-confidence, independence, courage, success, and can-do attitude. For example, in those days, if you said to the average Canadian, "Let's develop a rocket ship and go to the moon!" our answer would be, "Why would you ever want to waste money on a foolish venture like that?" If you asked the average American, he would answer, "Great idea, let's do it."

In 1966, I certainly suffered from that inferiority syndrome. I was fearful of having to compete with graduates of the prestigious American Ivy League schools. How could an education from a small and marginalized agricultural college in a sleepy Canadian farming community ever match up? I figured my only hope was to be diligent about doing the simple things well—come early, stay late, do an honest day's work, don't take unnecessary time off, know the rules, follow the rules, be respectful of others, get along, listen carefully, follow instructions, think before speaking, don't interrupt, don't complain, and always demonstrate a positive attitude—all the things we learned in kindergarten.

Woody Allen said, "80 percent of success is showing up." Throughout my career, I have noticed that those who consistently practiced the simple traits mentioned above usually stand above the crowd, regardless of their innate abilities and intelligence. Consistently practicing those simple habits demonstrates reliability and instills trust—two characteristics of paramount importance in any organization—and also invariably results in better job performance. It soon became obvious that an Ivy League education was no threat to me, and that the syndrome had no substance; there was no need to worry. My education since grade school had prepared me for the challenge.

Starting in the early 1960s, Management by Objectives (MBO) was the hottest topic in management development, and George S. Odiorne was its best-known proponent. Odiorne considered MBO to be a systematic way "of figuring out where you are going before you commit resources and time." His famous book, *Management Decisions by Objectives*, was Caterpillar's bible. William Blackie, Caterpillar's newly appointed Chairman, thought that Odiorne had something special to offer. Shortly after joining Caterpillar in 1966, I was taught the MBO theory according to Odiorne—management by objectives and judgment by results. Odiorne's process of solving management problems was straightforward, methodical, and simple (although not necessarily easy). There were six basic steps to the process: define the problem, gather the facts, analyze and evaluate the facts, pick the best available alternative, implement it, and follow up on it. Of course, Mr. Odiorne made a career out of explaining how each of these steps was to be carried out.

The concept was new to me and I thought it was the most fantastic stuff that I had ever heard (remember that I was trained as an engineer). Eventually, the Odiorne problem-solving method became embedded in my brain, perhaps to a fault. My wife often complained: "Why do you have to be so rational all the time, so logical, so methodical, so challenging, and so skeptical? Why can't you just *be?*" Despite my wife's complaints, that decision-making tool has been a consistently reliable methodology for solving all kinds of problems. Over the years, it has survived the more recent methodologies that have been promoted as panaceas that will suddenly break down barriers to progress and achieve dramatic, far-reaching results. In fact, as I evaluated them, most were simply reworked variations of Odiorne's original concept with a few "bells and whistles" added.

By the time I joined Caterpillar Tractor Co. in 1966, it had become a multinational company with sales revenue of $1.5 billion, employment in excess of 55,000 people, and manufacturing plants around the world. The company had expanded rapidly during the 1950s, with new plants, expansions, or acquisitions being announced almost every year. The vast United States interstate highway construction program fueled much of the growth and spawned the addition of several new products. The company was rapidly becoming a multinational one, and the need for a new worldwide headquarters had become evident during the early '60s. By 1966 when I joined the company, the construction of the building was well underway, in a two-block area of downtown Peoria.

A large portion of Caterpillar's sales was overseas and so there were opportunities to work in several foreign locations. Working overseas sounded enticing, but first I wanted to be an engineer, which is what I had said during the interview process. That was the journey I was on and the goal that had brought me thus far. Consequently, I entered a 12-month training program that most new hires went through to learn the policies, procedures, products, and organization. There were about 15 other young recruits in the program and we moved through several areas of the company during those first 12 months, including the Peoria Proving Grounds, Mossville Technical Center, various product design groups, and a variety of manufacturing facilities scattered throughout the Midwest. When the training period ended, I was assigned to work in the

RESEARCH AND TECHNOLOGY

Vehicle Research Department, first at the Peoria Proving Grounds and later at the Mossville Technical Center, testing new components and prototype products.

First job at Caterpillar Tractor Co. in the Vehicle Research Division. The author is second from the left in the back row. In those days, you could always tell who was boss because they wore white shirts, ties, and jackets and sat in the front row.

The Mossville Technical Center was a large campus-like complex completed in 1961, with several buildings devoted to different types of basic research and development activities. The word "research" is often confusing because it can be used to denote scientific discovery, advanced engineering work, or even routine product improvements (although that is generally considered an abuse of the term). How basic does a project have to be to be called "basic research?" The scientific community generally agrees that basic research is the pursuit of knowledge for its own sake. During the 1960s, Caterpillar's research laboratories were devoted to both high-level applied research and basic research on systems and processes, such as combustion, soil dynamics, and materials development. From time to time, we were asked to help solve design and manufacturing problems such as noise, vibration, and structural defects; and periodically, creative engineering improvements emerged from those troubleshooting activities. However, it seemed to me that too many resources were devoted to esoteric research, and not enough to product development.

"How long have you worked for the company?" I asked Len Carlson one day. Len was an experienced research engineer with whom I had worked on a variety of projects. He was a quiet, unassuming, and friendly fellow who "knew the ropes" and was happy to share his knowledge and experience.

"About 15 years here in research," he replied. "When I joined, things were much different because we were a much smaller company, and there were not so many policies and procedures and standards to worry about. In fact, we used to

RESEARCH AND TECHNOLOGY

bring our own cars into the shop here and work on them during the weekends … no more."

"So what have you worked on that eventually got into production and made a fortune for the company?" I asked.

"None that I know of. The work we do here is really not product development, it is more like pure research; in other words, we investigate new materials and design concepts that might help us keep ahead of competition sometime in the future, but nobody seems to worry much about that," he responded.

I was quite surprised. A whole career and nothing he worked on ever got to production—and nobody cared! For the next several months, I was very observant and questioned others about the nature of the work we were doing and its application. Although we always worked on the products being developed, many of the specific projects were concerned with pursuing somebody's new bright idea, or with minute design modifications that were subsequently tested, changed, and tested again, ad infinitum.

As the months rolled by, I began to doubt whether I wanted to be a research engineer; that new awakening occurred after about three years in the Vehicle Research group. I decided that my journey needed a new direction. I wanted to work in the real world where products were designed, tested, manufactured, and then sold to customers; and I wanted to see the results of my work in the marketplace, making money for the business that had created them. Six months later, after much discussion, negotiation, and hard talk, I was finally able to arrange a transfer out of research, and into a marketing group that supported the dealer organization—closer to the customers.

❧

So far, it seemed, my entire life had been immersed in science and technology in one way or another, and I was comfortable dealing with tangible, quantitative issues. As my career unfolded, I gradually moved away from technology, although experiences throughout my life have continually underscored the importance of science and technology to our well-being.

Recently, a medical report stated that a child born in North America today has a life expectancy of over 75 years. Out of curiosity, I checked the same statistic for 1908, the year my mother was born; at that time, her life expectancy as 49.5 years. She beat the odds by living well until she died peacefully at 92. But think of it—my new granddaughter has 25 more years in the bank than my mother did when she opened her eyes to the world. That 25-year bonus is a factual testimony to the many advances brought about mainly by discoveries and developments in science and technology during the last century—in my

RESEARCH AND TECHNOLOGY

mother's lifetime.

My first face-to-face encounter with technology came at a young age while riding home from school on my bicycle. The chain suddenly broke and my face had a close encounter with the gravel on the country road. The simple bicycle was an important technology that improved the quality of my life. Living on a farm forced us to deal with technical devices every day—mostly making sure they functioned as intended. Acquiring my first car at 17 was a rite of passage, like experiencing your first love or buying your first home. That old '49 Mercury required constant maintenance and tender loving care, and taught me much about technology—I became intimately acquainted with the Ford flathead V8 engine. In subsequent years, I witnessed the construction of the interstate highway system, which launched the automobile industry to a significant extent, changing society and our way of life forever—for the better.

Later, while studying for my engineering degree in 1963, I encountered another technical challenge. It came in the shape of an IBM 360 mainframe computer and the punched cards that were used to give instructions to the beast, using FORTRAN code. It was a monster, but it did finite element analyses, which until then had not been practical because of the massive number of calculations involved. Years later, in 1982, I acquired my first home computer—an Osborne. It was state of the art at the time because it had 64K RAM with two floppy disk drives and was considered portable—light-years ahead of the old IBM 360. One floppy disk was for the application program and the other was to store data—hard drives were not yet commercially available. The Osborne Company soon went out of business, having been surpassed by one of the great entrepreneurs, Stephen Jobs and his Apple Computer Company. Today there is more computing power in the average cell phone than in that first Osborne computer. Technology continues to open up a completely new world of opportunities to control our environment and enhance our standard of living.

The information highway—the Internet—is taking us much further and faster than any interstate highway system ever could. Its growth has been phenomenal. Almost everyone is signing on, surfing, browsing, emailing, and putting up a blog site. The Internet is flattening the world. However, for many, the Internet raises questions: "How can I use that thing to achieve meaningful progress? What does it deliver and how will it improve my life? What does it all mean?" No one knows the answers because we are discovering them as we go along. Fortunately, we can access the Internet for a pittance without even leaving the comfort of our home.

But are all these new technologies any different from what our parents, and their parents, experienced? They lived through invention of the automobile, the airplane, the light bulb, the radio, television, and many other technical advances

RESEARCH AND TECHNOLOGY

that brought as many changes to their way of life as the computer age is bringing to ours. Many were put out of work by the automobile age (certainly those making buggies and buggy whips), but many more new jobs were created to replace those lost. That trend has been ongoing since the Industrial Revolution. I remember when TV was first introduced to the public; now it is almost considered a necessity. During my university days, Gordon Gould invented the laser[10], without which we could not play our CDs and DVDs. Now the laser has been surpassed by digital microchip technology that allows us to store a thousand songs on a device smaller than a credit card.

Technology always brings change, and we should learn to welcome and embrace it. Still, many express fear of the unknown future that this new technology will bring. They argue that all these technological devices are destroying our "traditional way of life"—suggesting that the traditional way was better. Ogden Nash made that suggestion when he said, "Progress might have been alright once, but it has gone on too long." Someone else once remarked, "The only thing wrong with the future is that it is getting too close." Ever since mankind moved out of caves and invented the wheel, technology has been "destroying" our traditional way of life—thank goodness!

Some people, however, long for the "good old days," but were they that good? A professor at Carnegie Mellon University has given us a glimpse of the "good old days." His research reveals that, in 1908, there were 120,000 horses in New York City. The removal of horse dung was a major logistical problem; the most challenging problem, however, was the disposal of horses that dropped dead in the heavy traffic. A survey in 1910 showed that over 15,000 carcasses were hauled away by street crews. Moreover, because of the horses, hordes of flies infested all of our cities, contributing to a far greater spread of diseases than what we experience today. A report from 1908 recorded that about 20,000 New Yorkers were dying each year from cholera, typhoid, dysentery, and infant diarrhea. The "good old days" were not so good. It was new technology—the internal combustion engine—that helped to overcome those problems.

As recently as 50 years ago, the North American farmer, with the highest productivity in the world, could feed himself and 11 other people. Today, thanks to the miracle of scientific advances, that same farmer is able to feed more than 50 people. Many other proud achievements in technology have eased the hunger pains of countless millions of people in nations around the globe.

---

10   LASER: From the acronym Light Amplification by Stimulated Emission of Radiation, a laser is a device that utilizes the ability of certain substances to absorb electromagnetic energy and re-radiate it as a highly focused beam of synchronized single-wavelength radiation. Although many credit Charles Hard Townes and Theodore H. Maiman for the invention of the laser, Gordon Gould filed the first patent application in 1959, and, after a lengthy legal battle, was finally awarded the patent in 1987.

RESEARCH AND TECHNOLOGY

Yet there are those who seek to ban the use of pesticides, fertilizers, and genetic engineering—and return to the "good old days" when all produce was organic, and subsistence farming practices were the norm throughout most of the world. Proponents of pesticide banning ignore the fact that DDT saved over 5 million lives and prevented serious illnesses for over a 100 million more. In India, it cut the malarial death rate from about 1 million annually to less than 2,000. Then, under pressure from environmentalists, it was banned in 1972, for political reasons, by the administrator of the EPA, William Ruckelshaus (who reportedly did not even attend any of the many hearings during which DDT was determined to be safe).[11]

Today, because of that tragic decision, malaria afflicts a half-billion people and kills over one million of them each year; 75 percent of them are pregnant African women and African children under five years of age.[12] Despite the months of hearings that examined the scientific evidence in detail and determined DDT to be safe, environmentalists were responsible for getting DDT restricted. Consequently, millions of people have suffered and died, most of them young children. DDT is a perfect example of how science can save lives when allowed to do so. In 2007, the World Health Organization (WHO) conceded that they would once again start encouraging the use of DDT to fight malaria. Perhaps science will win in the end; however, hysterical and irrational opposition from the environmentalists remains intense.

One of the more exciting scientific developments today is in the area of embryonic stem cell research, which holds the promise of rescuing millions from life-threatening diseases and injury. Unfortunately, it is being attacked by those who consider a few unconscious cells more important than living, breathing, thinking human beings. Those of us who value human life must stand up and defend cloning and embryonic stem cell research. It holds immense promise for healthier and more fulfilling lives, perhaps even more promise than any previous medical breakthrough. Recently, there has been scientific progress in making human embryonic stem cells without destroying human embryos.[13]

In 2007, the journal *Science* reported a good-news story from the National Cancer Institute. Dr. Steven Rosenberg and his colleagues applied a new therapy, using genetically modified versions of the patient's own white blood cells to eradicate cancer from two men who were facing certain death from the disease. At a time when science and reason are under attack, magnificent achievements such as that should remind us of the power of the human mind to unveil

---

11 Roger Bate, "The Rise, Fall, Rise and Imminent Fall of DDT" (American Enterprise Institute Short Publication, no. 14, November 2007), http://www.aei.org; Bate is a resident fellow of AEI.
12 *Wall Street Journal*, August 22, 2006.
13 *Economist*, November 24, 2007, 85.

RESEARCH AND TECHNOLOGY

the secrets of nature and create new life-giving technologies. It is morally and ethically imperative that stem cell and gene therapy research continue to move forward.

In one generation, science and technology have defeated or controlled diphtheria, smallpox, typhoid, measles, tuberculosis, and pneumonia; and more hospitals, schools, colleges, and libraries have been built than during all previous generations. More scientists, doctors, surgeons, dentists, teachers, and engineers have graduated during the past few decades than during the past thousand years. Moreover, technology has brought more opportunity to more young people than to any other generation since the dawn of history.

Despite that progress, there are still challenges to be met, hopes to be realized, and goals to be achieved. However, none of them will be achieved by opponents of progress, nor by teachers and preachers of despair. Rather, they will be achieved by workers who can dream; by entrepreneurs who have faith in science, technology, and the free enterprise system; and by those who believe in a better and brighter future and apply their creative intelligence to the challenges and opportunities we face. Fortunately, human ingenuity has no limitations.

Think of it! Perhaps, when my great-great-granddaughter is born, she will enjoy another 25-year bonus.

※ ※ ※

On August 31, 1968, our second son, Gregory, was born at St. Francis Hospital in Peoria, Illinois. At first, he appeared to be completely healthy, but within a few weeks, he was listless and obviously not developing normally. Soon thereafter, he was diagnosed with chronic myelocytic leukemia (CML)—a rare form of the disease that the doctors said was present at birth. After many months of treatment in Peoria and at the St. Jude Hospital in Memphis, Tennessee, the disease took his life.[14] He was nine months old—a happy, smiling child up to the end. The doctors explained that they knew little about the disease, except that it seemed to occur in clusters around the country and then they showed us a map with a cluster of pins representing other victims of the same disease in the Peoria area.

Gregory had the Philadelphia chromosome, which is a hereditary abnormality associated with CML. Our local Peoria pediatrician pointed out that due to the hereditary transmission of the Philadelphia chromosome there could be a risk of a recurrence of the disease in subsequent children. Therefore, he did not recommend future pregnancies. However, the pediatrician at St. Jude's Children's Research Hospital disagreed, saying there was "no evidence to sub-

---

[14] St. Jude is the patron saint of lost causes.

stantiate familial occurrence of that chronic type of myelocytic leukemia" and advised us to go ahead and have another child if that was our desire. Despite their differing opinions, they both agreed that the medical community knew very little about that particular form of leukemia and the hereditary risk.

We grieved. The only other death that I had experienced of someone close to me had been that of my father. Since he had to travel far away to Toronto for treatment, I was not near him when he died and was unable to attend the funeral. My memory of him is simply of his going away and not returning. Therefore, I have never grieved his death. In fact, for a time, I resented him for disappearing and leaving my mother destitute. However, for Gregory, we grieved. The loss of a child may be experienced, but the personal impact cannot be explained. Fortunately, we had Dale, and he gave us much joy and happiness that, in time, mitigated our loss. In addition, we decided to adopt a daughter as soon as it could be arranged.

5

RESHAPING THE ENVIRONMENT

CATERPILLAR TRACTOR CO.
TEXAS AND MINNESOTA, USA
(1969 — 1971)

The folks at Microsoft have a saying about their research center in Beijing, which, for scientist and engineers, is one of the most sought after places to work in all of China. "Remember, in China when you are one-in-a-million there are 1,300 other people just like you."[15]

—Thomas L. Friedman

SINCE 1925, the leaders at Caterpillar focused on establishing first-class engineering and manufacturing operations that were committed to quality, durability, and reliability. That was their strength—it did not include sales, marketing, or distribution. Therefore, they sought the support of an exceptional group of aggressive and independent entrepreneurs to manage customer relations at the local level, to sell the benefits of Caterpillar products, and to provide superior customer service. Those entrepreneurs were to be well connected to their communities and skilled at building lasting relationships with their customers. Although Caterpillar and its dealers are not partners in the legal sense, they maintained a close working relationship and depended on each other for success—"Working as One" in a unique association—and still do. Over the years, it has become recognized as perhaps the best distribution system in the industrial world: "Ours is a partnership like no other, an enduring family relationship founded on trust, respect, mutual performance, unsurpassed quality and a relentless desire to lead by helping Cat customers succeed."[16]

The Service Department, to which I was transferred in 1969, was responsible

---

15 Thomas L. Friedman, *The World Is Flat* (2005), 265.
16 Caterpillar, *Working as One: The Enduring Partnership of Cat Dealers and Caterpillar* (2006)

RESHAPING THE ENVIRONMENT

for carrying on that tradition, and reinforcing the partnership by helping the dealers with technical training, facility planning and development, service tools and equipment, warranty administration, and, from time to time, solving technical problems.

By the mid-1960s, Love Field, the airport in downtown Dallas, Texas, could no longer handle the volume of air traffic necessary to adequately serve the burgeoning metropolitan areas. Therefore, a new Dallas-Fort Worth Airport Project was launched. The first task was to level an 18,000-acre field, using about 150 Caterpillar machines, working around the clock. As I was already familiar with the application and operation of the products, Caterpillar asked me to assist Darr Equipment Co. to support the equipment doing the work on the new airport, so, in late 1969, we moved to Dallas. My job was to function as a technical service representative and support both Darr Equipment Co., in Texas, and Riggs Tractor Co., in Arkansas.

Supporting the Dallas-Fort Worth airport project was my primary responsibility. The time constraint was tight; the contractor worked two 10-hour shifts seven days a week, and demanded immediate parts support and fast, reliable service. Darr Equipment responded and met all their expectations—as did the Caterpillar equipment. I visited the site almost everyday, inspected the condition of the equipment between shifts, and helped the dealer with maintenance problems. Reports were sent to the engineers at the factory, so that product improvements and modifications could be made as necessary. Suggestions and improvements were fed back to the customer, for which he was grateful. Together, we helped the customer keep the project on schedule and under budget.

One day, shortly after arriving in Dallas, I was riding to the job site with Lee White, the Vice President of Parts and Service for Darr Equipment Co.

"So, how long do you expect to be here?" he asked me. Mr. White seldom asked a question to which he did not already know the answer.

"Depends on how good a job I do," I responded, not intending to be facetious. "May seem strange perhaps, but if I screw up, I'll be here forever. If I do a decent job, they will likely promote me out, in a couple years or so."

The turnover of field reps was very high in those years, partly because of the growth of the company, but mostly because management could never settle on how territories and functions should be organized. Therefore, they kept trying something new all the time.

Mr. White laughed, because he knew it was true. He had helped train a whole crop of newly assigned Caterpillar reps over the years, and I was just the latest of the bunch. Mr. White was a hands-on manager who had earned his stripes at the school of hard knocks during his many years in the business. He was respected by Caterpillar as one of the very best to teach new field reps how the job was supposed to be done. According to Lee White, there was only one way to learn the business—put on a pair of coveralls, travel with the field service technicians, learn to operate the equipment, crawl under the machines and get covered in dirt and grease, skin your knuckles, sweat in the heat, take abuse from customers, work around the clock until the job was done, and don't complain.

One day I went out on a service job with Joe, an experienced field service technician, to help him fix a leak on a D8 tractor working in the desert. My job was to remove the leaking hydraulic hose while Joe smoked a cigarette and "supervised." After I had positioned myself under the machine, ready to get busy, he told me not to move. Then he reached in with a stick and chased away a couple of big rattlesnakes that were resting above me nearby on the warm transmission. They dropped down right beside me, glanced over briefly, and slowly crawled away as my heart resumed beating. It gets cool at night in Texas, so the rattlesnakes like to crawl up on the machines to stay warm. Of course, Joe knew where they were when he told me to crawl under there and get busy. He figured it would be a good lesson for the day—one I might not forget. He was right. Fortunately, I passed my initiation into the business and earned Lee White's respect. We became good friends, and he helped me whenever he could. It was all a great learning experience, and I hold him in high esteem to this day.

That first field assignment, helping to build a modern airport and to improve the infrastructure of the region, provided a lot of satisfaction. It was productive work—the purposeful use of our minds to reshape the environment to sustain and improve our lives. In the past 40 years, that airport has enhanced the lives of countless millions of people by providing jobs for many families, and easing the travel burden of many others, thereby improving their productivity. It has strengthened the airlines and supported many ancillary companies serving the industry. That assignment provided me an opportunity to make a contribution—an opportunity to be productive and to do the kind of work I enjoyed. That is what business does, perhaps the greatest of all possible contributions to social responsibility. Productive work is one of the greatest virtues.

Soon after moving to Dallas, Betty and I had contacted an adoption agency in San Antonio and submitted our application for a new daughter. Our specifications were tight—a girl who was healthy, as young as possible, and, to the extent to which it could be controlled, one who came from good parents. About a year later, we got a call saying that our needs had been met, and on July 31, 1970, with eager anticipation and a good portion of anxiety, we drove to San Antonio to receive our new daughter. Pamela was six days old, had all her toes and fingers, and was the most beautiful thing you ever saw. The nurse handed her to Betty and we immediately knew that she was ours. Dale was only four at the time, but we carefully let him hold her, briefly. He smiled and looked up at us, and we knew he had accepted his new sister. It was, without a doubt, the best decision that Betty and I ever made, and I can say categorically that Pamela has given me more joy for more time than has any other person. She still does.

A few months later, I was asked to be a service operations representative. Service operations required close communications with the dealer principal, to discuss long-term strategic issues: growth plans, organization structure, facility development, marketing programs, and system improvements. It was no longer necessary for me to work on the equipment or get dirty and greasy. It was considered a promotion, because rising above the strictly technical work into the lofty realm of operations allegedly presented greater responsibility, authority, and strategic consequences. That may be, but it is critical not to diminish the importance of dealing face-to-face with customers and with the product where the business actually takes place—service people do that more than anyone. I never tire of visiting job sites and watching the equipment being used to alter and improve the natural environment.

My new territory included the north-central part of the country, and our moving from Dallas to Minneapolis, in January of 1971, was a shock to the system—from year-round warmth and sunny weather to a long, cold, and snowy winter. In Minneapolis, winter would arrive one weekend and stay for about seven months. Still, we enjoyed living there. There was plenty of sunshine, and we settled in, dressed for the cold weather when necessary, and enjoyed the dry snow and crisp fresh air. Unlike many city administrations, Minneapolis knew how to deal with the snow. We awoke early in the morning after a major snowfall to discover that the street and sidewalks had already been plowed. Spring would arrive, usually over a weekend in April, and we would know winter was finished for another year. That was a pleasant experience compared to the Midwest, where the transition between winter and spring lasted several weeks; just when we thought winter was over, a blizzard would come through and cover up all the spring flowers that were just beginning to emerge.

Ziegler Inc., the dealer in Minneapolis, Minnesota, had always been considered one of the more progressive dealers in terms of leading-edge thinking and a willingness to try new ways of doing the business. Consequently, Caterpillar often used Ziegler as the "guinea pig" for testing new concepts and programs. The firm always had an intense focus on the customer and enjoyed a good share of the market, and set a good example of how a dealer ought to be—a template for others. Over the years I came to appreciate that the quality of its people was generally better than average.

The dealer in North Dakota, Butler Machinery Company, was a smaller or-

RESHAPING THE ENVIRONMENT

ganization, struggling to cover a large, sparsely populated territory. Matt Butler was a joy to work with, and we spent many hours discussing a variety of subjects—some of which were actually related to the job I was supposed to be doing. Matt was a pilot and flew his own airplane around the territory as a way to accumulate hours and save time. He was a very active, energetic individual with a busy mind that always seemed to be well ahead of mine. I think that today he might have been diagnosed with ADHD; he certainly was hyperactive. The best time for us to have a discussion was while he was flying, and he often invited me to ride along as his copilot and conduct our meetings in the sky. I did not mind, since it was the best time to get his focused attention. In addition, he showed me how the controls caused the plane to behave.

During the years immediately preceding my assignment to Minnesota, Vince Lombardi had established himself as a football icon. He was one of the most successful head coaches in the history of American football and the driving force of the Green Bay Packers from 1959 to 1967, leading them in their capture of five NFL championships during his nine-year tenure. Mr. Lombardi is famous for many quotations and was often unfairly criticized for saying, "Winning is everything." In fact, what he really said was, "Winning isn't everything; the desire to win is everything. In fact, it's the only thing." Vince Lombardi was an inspiration to me, and I always rooted for the Packers over the Vikings, much to the consternation of my friends and colleagues in Minnesota.

I had only begun to earn the dealers' trust and confidence when the phone rang again. In their infinite wisdom, the managers in Peoria had another inspiration about how the territories should be organized. Consequently, they wanted me to come back to head office and take on a new assignment in Service Engineering. I had been in Minneapolis only nine months; no wonder the dealers complained about high turnover of field reps.

6

A BUSINESS EDUCATION

CATERPILLAR TRACTOR CO.
PEORIA, ILLINOIS, USA
(1971 — 1976)

Capitalism has a long history of positive accomplishments for the betterment of mankind. It has increased the world's wealth enormously, it has encouraged the arts and sciences, it has sustained liberal values and it has strengthened democratic institutions. We are a great country today, in large part because we have been a capitalist country. Capitalism is our orthodoxy. It is what the Founding Fathers believed in, and it is the basis of our politics today. It is, in short, probably the best means ever devised by man for ordering a free and prosperous society.[17]

—Henry Ford II

THE hydraulic excavator became a popular machine in Europe during the 1950s, and by 1970, thousands of excavator machines were being sold in North America—but not by Caterpillar. There was a lot of buzz in the industry about when Caterpillar would introduce an excavator, and a special fast-track project was launched in 1970. When I was asked to join the project team in late 1971, several prototypes had already been built, and it became my task to coordinate final pre-production testing under actual field conditions. A New Product Introduction (NPI) process was carefully followed to ensure a smooth introduction to dealers and customers. At some point, every department of the company is involved in the NPI process, and my role provided a unique opportunity to get up-close-and-personal with most of them.

---

17 From a text delivered as a speech at the University of Chicago Graduate School of Business Management Conference, April 26, 1979.

A BUSINESS EDUCATION

The NPI Team with Caterpillar's first Hydraulic Excavator, Model 225. It was first introduced in 1972. The author is sitting with his feet on the tracks.

Caterpillar was often not the first to introduce a new product, preferring to wait until dependable technology caught up with the innovations; however, by the time they eventually introduced a new product it was generally on the leading edge of performance. In the case of the excavator, Caterpillar was definitely late with its introduction. That made it even more critical that the first models exceed market expectations and set a new standard for performance and efficiency. Testing of the prototypes under real-life working conditions was the final confirmation. Several new prototypes were sent to the field and monitored carefully for several weeks to check performance, productivity, fuel consumption, and a multitude of other metrics. All defects were carefully recorded—no matter how minor—as well as comments from customers and operators. The data was compiled and summarized regularly, to keep the NPI team fully apprised of how well the machines were doing.

Fortunately, the design was good; the prototypes performed well and, in 1972, Caterpillar entered the hydraulic excavator market with the Model 225. I stayed with the excavator team for a couple more years, to help expand the family of products and support the introduction. The team went on to introduce the model 235 in 1973, the 245 in 1974, and the 215 in 1976. Being part of the team that introduced a new family of hydraulic excavators provided much satisfaction, especially considering the significant contribution that the excavator product line has since made to the growth of the business.

Being part of the NPI team that introduced the first hydraulic excavator was one of the best learning experiences of my entire career with the company. I learned about business—a subject not included in my engineering education.

A BUSINESS EDUCATION

It was a revelation. I suddenly felt very ignorant and decided that it was time to shed my engineering mentality, and learn to think as a businessperson—in other words, to rise up from amongst the trees and look down on the forest—to see, and understand, the organization as a whole.

Bookshelves are filled with volumes on management science programs that promise innovative solutions to a wide variety of business problems. Those solutions are usually aimed at improving product and process quality, and designed to excite and motivate the business community to adopt the latest panacea. Each one remains popular until the next one comes along. The one I was first exposed to in the early 1970s was Joseph Juran and Edwards Deming's quality control methodology. Joseph Juran applied the Pereto Principle ("the vital few and the trivial many"), and Deming applied various statistical methods, such as analysis of variance and hypothesis testing. Those two men had become famous for helping the Japanese solve their quality crisis after WWII. Deming, more than any other individual not of Japanese heritage, is considered to be the most important person to have had an impact on improving Japanese manufacturing and business quality. Most management staff at Caterpillar received training on Joseph Juran's quality management methods, and subsequently applied them on the job. Once again, that kind of professional business knowledge was all new, interesting, and stimulating to me.

Unfortunately, it was not clear whether our new knowledge made any significant difference to the quality of our collective work. During the next couple of years, Juran's methodology slowly fell by the wayside at Caterpillar as its champion moved on to another position or lost interest. I was later to discover that this was a behavioral pattern—the initial excitement over the latest panacea was soon followed by disillusionment and abandonment. Eventually, an enterprising manager would latch on to a new program and take the organization through the cycle again. Usually something of value would be gained each time as the organization struggled to improve quality, efficiency, and management effectiveness, but not since the work that Juran and Deming did in Japan about 60 years ago, have I noticed any major breakthroughs in quality improvement. However, small incremental improvements occasionally appeared, and that may be a better way to maintain consistent progress than seeking major breakthroughs.

Early in 1974, I was approached by a senior manager who asked if I would be interested in attending the Executive MBA Program at the University of Chicago, along with two other Caterpillar employees. I had periodically given passing thought to getting an MBA, but it was not a priority with me and there was no clear path to making it happen. However, my recent experience as a member of the excavator NPI team clearly illustrated that there was much to learn if I was to become a businessperson in the true sense of the word.

A BUSINESS EDUCATION

Although an engineering education teaches the scientific method of thinking—a good foundation for any type of work—it does not teach either management skills or leadership acumen, and it certainly does not teach the fundamentals of finance and accounting, or the importance of mastering interpersonal skills. Timing is everything, and that opportunity seemed to come at an ideal time to fill those voids in my understanding of business. Of course, I would be pleased to attend.

About the same time, I was asked to take on a different assignment and work in the Products Control Department. This department monitored and controlled all product prices, costs, margins, and production schedules; it was also responsible for overall administration of the NPI process. The department conducted regular design review meetings to monitor the progress of product development projects and the capital budgets associated with those projects. Consolidated sales and demand forecasts from the various marketing organizations were scrutinized, evaluated, and combined with a variety of other factors—such as inventory, capacity constraints, and labor issues—to establish worldwide production schedules. Plant managers were usually given an opportunity to make their case; however, during that era, all key production, pricing, and budget decisions were made right at the top of the company. The Products Control Department answered directly to the Executive Office; no one else was empowered to make these critical business decisions.

Following the scientific method of decision-making, everything started with facts and hard data. My assignment entailed crunching the numbers and analyzing the data so that it became meaningful information. That information was then studied and evaluated, after which it became knowledge. Alternatives were tested, and the division managers applied their broad business experience and wisdom to make a selection. After the homework was completed, a report was presented to the executive office, with recommendations. Thus, I came to understand the hierarchy of decision-making: data > information > knowledge > wisdom. It all started with facts and data—there was no room for wishful thinking, gut-feel, intuition, emotion, and/or mystical revelations. That particular decision-making process became embedded in my brain, and it has served me well over the years.

The human mind, with its ability to reason and choose, is a unique and profound attribute that allows us to exercise significant control over our lives. Our very survival depends on our ability to think, evaluate, identify alternatives, and make life-altering choices. The refusal to use that all-important mental ability to reason, to think, and to live well is to reject the supreme quality that makes us human. Choices and decisions should follow a structured process: 1) define the problem or situation that requires a decision, 2) carefully assess the facts,

A BUSINESS EDUCATION

3) evaluate the available alternatives, and, finally, 4) select the best one. When a decision is made according to that process, it will be a good decision, regardless of the outcome—good because the correct processes were followed. If the outcome happens to be different from what was expected, then it was the *wrong* decision, even though it was a *good* one because the correct decision-making process had been followed. On the other hand, decisions based on gut-feel, intuition, premonitions, mystical revelations, superstitions, or emotions are inherently *bad* decisions, regardless of the outcome. In those latter instances of decision-making, if the outcome meets expectations, it must be attributed to good luck rather than to good management—therefore it is still a *bad* decision, since the decision-making process was wrong.

> *Nothing is more difficult, and therefore more precious, than to be able to decide.*
>
> — NAPOLEON BONAPARTE

My assignment in Products Control Department aligned perfectly with my extracurricular task of attending the University of Chicago's MBA program. Business travel did not interfere with class schedules, and my full-time job was such that it could be managed along with the demands of the MBA program. The program's duration was two years, with classes at the university one day a week on alternate Fridays and Saturdays. Five students from Peoria attended the program and each week we commuted between Peoria and Chicago to attend classes. Homework assignments required hours of study, in the evenings and on weekends. Each student in the class was a member of a team that would meet once or twice during the week to discuss the assignments and help each other to understand the subject matter; those of us from Peoria formed a study team. Fortunately, there was an exceptionally good cross section of strengths among us. Some of us were strong in the hard sciences, others in the soft sciences; the assignments required that we understand both, and we all worked well together. We experienced a wide range of emotions—fear, frustration, anxiety, and joy—which we shared with each other from time to time as we got to know each other well. The team members represented a broad array of experience, talent, and skills, and provided excellent support for one another, as well as being a "relief valve" in times of need. For two years, our social activities were quite sparse, and my family deserves much gratitude for their support and understanding during that busy and challenging period.

During my second year of the program, I concluded that, although it was a demanding program, the only way one would fail was to do nothing. By attending all classes, paying attention, participating, working well with other team members, putting forth effort on assignments, and having them in on time, one was ensured of success, because it demonstrated that learning was taking place. The quality of the work, the brainpower one demonstrated, and the ease with which one was able to find a solution—all were secondary. Once again, doing the easy stuff well was critically important.

The program was an enlightening, mind-opening experience that enriched many areas of my life and contributed significantly to my understanding of business and to whatever degree of success I have been able to achieve over the years.

During the University of Chicago MBA program, I became familiar with the *Ten Pillars of Economic Wisdom*. Although simple, the concepts represented an important part of my business education. There are no new "theories" in the *Ten Pillars*—only new arrangements of established thoughts and new phraseology consisting of simple words having one clear meaning, and no other. The research laboratory from which it came was the American Economic Foundation's weekly, coast-to-coast public service radio debate, *Wake Up, America!* From 1940 to 1947, that program exposed the American people to honest, but vigorous, differences of opinion. It was out of the fan mail that the words and phrases emerged. It was the audience—the "man on the street"—who wrote the first drafts. The decisive test of mass acceptance was made in the Foundation's Hall of Free Enterprise, at the 1964 World's Fair in New York City, where the *Ten Pillars* were inscribed on 10 bronze plaques and exposed to 25 million visitors from all over the world. As well, 1.5 million visitors entered the pavilion to witness dramatic demonstrations of the *Ten Pillars*, and pressed buttons (3 million times) for answers to economic questions.[18]

The Ten Pillars of Economic Wisdom

1. Nothing in our material world can come from nowhere, nor can it be free; everything in our economic life has a source, a destination and a cost that must be paid—by someone.
2. Government is never a source of goods. Everything produced is produced by the people, and everything that government gives to the people, it must first take from the people.

---

18 *The Ten Pillars* was originally co-authored by Fred G. Clark, and Richard Stanton Rimanoczy, then Chairman and President, respectively, of the American Economic Foundation. In 1980 the organization moved to Cleveland, Ohio; however, according to the *Encyclopedia of Cleveland History*, by 2003, the organization ceased to exist, maintaining neither a web presence nor a Cleveland phone book listing: http://ech.case.edu/ech-cgi/article.pl?id=AEF.

3. The only valuable money that government has to spend is that money taxed or borrowed from people's earnings. When government decides to spend more than it has thus received, that unearned extra money is created out of thin air, through the banks and/or the printing presses, and when spent, takes on value only by reducing the value of all other money, savings and insurance.

4. In our modern exchange economy, all payroll and employment come from customers, and the only worthwhile job security is customer security. If there are no customers, there can be no payroll and no jobs.

5. Customer security can be achieved by the worker only when he/she cooperates with management in doing the things that win and hold customers. Job security, therefore, is a partnership problem that can only be solved in a spirit of understanding and cooperation.

6. Because wages are the principal cost of everything, widespread wage increases without corresponding increases in productivity, simply increase everyone's cost of living.

7. The greatest good for the greatest number means, in its material sense, the most goods for the greatest number, which, in turn, means the greatest productivity per worker.

8. All productivity is based on three factors: (a) natural resources, whose form, place and condition are changed by the expenditure of (b) human energy (both muscular and mental), with the aid of (c) tools.

9. Tools are the only one of these three factors that man can increase without limit, and tools come into being in a free society only when there is a reward for that portion of their earnings that people must temporarily channel into new tools of production as opposed to purchases that produce immediate comfort and pleasure. Proper payment for the use of tools is essential for their creation.

10. The productivity of the tools—that is, the efficiency of the human energy applied in connection with their use—has always been highest in a competitive society in which the economic decisions are freely made by millions of progressive-seeking individuals, rather than in a state-planned society in which those decisions are made by a handful of all-powerful people, regardless of how benevolent, sincere and intelligent those people may be.

7

A BOILING CALDRON

CATERPILLAR OVERSEAS SA
GENEVA, SWITZERLAND
(1976 — 1979)

Regrettably, we live in an age when many—even some businessmen—have become apologists for profit. Not us. We need say no more in defense of profit than to note that it has been our chief incentive toward achievement and excellence; and it has been by far our principal source for the capital needed to finance growth and protect Caterpillar jobs. It has been rightly said that a company must do well to do good.[19]

—Lee L. Morgan, former President of
Caterpillar Tractor Co.

Shortly after completing the MBA program, I was asked to relocate to Geneva, Switzerland, and join the team managing the Southern Division of Caterpillar Overseas SA (COSA). Although there was some indication an overseas assignment might develop, that opportunity came as an exciting surprise. We knew it would require major adjustments to a new language, culture, and lifestyle, but we looked forward to the adventure with eager anticipation. Most colleagues who had lived the experience spoke of it positively and indicated that living in Switzerland was a high point in their lives and careers.

COSA was established in 1960 as the administrative and marketing division for distribution of products in Western and Eastern Europe, Africa, and the Middle East. The Southern Division included Africa and the Middle East. Although the headquarters were in Geneva, representative offices were located in Rome, Athens, Jeddah, Abidjan, Nairobi, and Johannesburg. Several Caterpillar representatives specializing in various functions (sales, service, parts,

---

19   Lee L. Morgan, speech to the Rotary Club of Peoria, Illinois, September 29, 1972.

and finance) worked out of those offices. Other members of the Southern Division management team included Larry Wallden (Sales), Bob Petterson (Finance), and Rick Reeder (Parts). I was responsible for Customer Service. That was perhaps the best functioning team of individuals with whom I had the privilege of working during my career with Caterpillar. We were a close-knit group, focused on a common goal to capture business by developing the dealers' ability to provide superior sales coverage and service support to customers throughout the region.

During the early 1970s, oil exploration in the Middle East and Nigeria was rapidly expanding, and production and refining facilities were being installed. Saudi Arabia's five-year government budget from 1969 to 1974 was $9.2 billion; during the next five years, while I was there, it was $142 billion. The country was in the throes of massive expansion and oil revenues gushed into every area of the kingdom.[20] The demand for Caterpillar's products was very strong. Zahid Tractor, in Saudi Arabia, had recently been accepted into the family of Caterpillar dealers, and struggled to develop their capabilities and respond to the growing demand for products and services. Today, Zahid Tractor has over 30 facilities, supporting the sale and service of Caterpillar products in the Kingdom of Saudi Arabia. One of Zahid's earliest and largest customers was the Bin Laden Group, a strong supporter of Caterpillar products.

The Bin Laden Construction Group, founded by Mohammed bin Laden in the Saudi Red Sea port city of Jeddah in the 1950s, was a highly respected construction company and a good customer. The group grew into one of the major firms in the oil-rich kingdom of Saudi Arabia when it was entrusted by the royal court with the task of expanding Islamic holy sites in Mecca and Medina. The Bin Laden Construction group also built several palaces in Riyadh and Jeddah for members of the Saudi Royal Family and carried out restoration work on Jerusalem's Al-Aqsa Mosque, following an arson attack in 1969. Mohammed bin Laden left 54 sons and daughters from several marriages. Salem bin Laden, Mohammad's eldest son, ran the financial empire left behind by his father, until he died when his private plane crashed in Texas, in 1988. Thirteen of Mohammad's sons sit on the board of the family's firm, which has since extended its reach to several Arab countries and employs tens of thousands of people. The infamous Osama bin Laden, the 17th son, was disowned by the family after he was stripped of his Saudi citizenship in 1994 for suspected terrorist activities and for criticizing the Al Saud ruling family.[21]

Large oil reserves had been confirmed in Saudi Arabia, and Arabian American

---

20 The government statistics are from the *Economist*, March 23, 2002. Of course, since then, the revenues from oil have continued to increase massively, especially with the price of oil over $100 per barrel.
21 http://www.rense.com/general19/business.htm .

A BOILING CALDRON

Oil Company[22] (ARAMCO) was building huge refining and distribution facilities in the country to expand daily production—most of which was destined to go to the United States. Money flowed like water, and it was being spent with little regard for frugality.

I was in Zahid's office one day, when a Saudi contractor came in to buy a new D8 tractor. He paid cash up front by dumping a suitcase full of money on the desk. A few weeks later, he came back wanting to buy another D8.

"What happened to the D8 you bought a few months ago?" we inquired.

"Oh, the tracks wore out, running in the sand, so we need another one," he answered.

"Well, if you brought it in we could replace the undercarriage and it will be as good as new again, for a fraction of the cost of a new tractor."

"Can't."

"Why?"

"Well, it also had a couple of other problems, so I just dug a hole in the sand, pushed it in and covered it up."

That kind of waste and mismanagement was not uncommon. The dealer was selling as many tractors as Caterpillar would send them, and still it was not enough to satisfy the demand.

Nigeria was also expanding its oil exploration, and production facilities and demand for equipment was strong. Much time was spent in traveling throughout Nigeria to visit customers and help the dealer develop capabilities to serve them. Libya was another country with large oil reserves. Like Saudi Arabia, they were expanding their exploration and production facilities and utilizing large numbers of Caterpillar products. Most other African countries did not experience the same kind of growth, but demand was steady, and we made regular visits to keep the market development programs on track and support the dealers' sales and service activities. The South African diamond mines were going strong and it was interesting to visit those operations and see firsthand how Caterpillar equipment took over the hard manual labor that would otherwise have been required. Employees were strip-searched each day to prevent pilfering, but, reportedly, a few rough diamonds still managed to get out.

During one of our trips to Johannesburg, Larry Wallden and I got a call from the dealer principal in Zambia.

---

22 Saudi Aramco, the state-owned national oil company of Saudi Arabia, is the largest oil corporation in the world and the largest in terms of proven crude oil reserves and production. Headquartered in Dhahran, Saudi Arabia, Saudi Aramco also operates the world's largest single hydrocarbon network, the Master Gas System. It was formerly known as just Aramco, an acronym for Arabian American Oil Company: http://www.wikipedia.com (accessed July 15, 2007).

A BOILING CALDRON

*Visiting customers in the Empty Quarter of Saudi Arabia, 1977.
This feat takes serious practice.*

"I know you guys are busy, but, since you're in the area, I would like you to pass through Lusaka on your way back north and see me. We have some important issues we need to talk about," he said.

"Sorry, wish we could, but the flight connections are poor. We'll have to organize another visit," Larry responded.

"Not good enough," he said. "Get to the airport and I will pick you up first thing tomorrow morning. We can meet for a couple of hours and you can keep to your original schedule without a problem."

We were not sure what arrangements he was going to make, but if it happened as he said, it would be workable. Early the next morning, a tall, beautiful, blond young woman met us at the airport. She proceeded to escort us out to a Lear Jet that was waiting on the runway. We knew, of course, that she was the flight attendant on the plane that, apparently, the dealer had chartered to pick us up. We entered the jet and were surprised to discover we were the only passengers—no pilot, no copilot, and no crew at all. Then the young woman followed us on board, took the controls, made a quick taxi to the runway, and took off at full throttle, straight up—and I mean straight up—without ever contacting the control tower. Larry and I tightened our seatbelts, looked at each other in astonishment, and never said a word. At about 40,000 feet, she suddenly leveled off, engaged the autopilot, and came back to serve us coffee and chat. Less than two hours later, we landed smoothly in Lusaka and had a productive meeting with the dealer principal.

He explained that he had just bought a new jet to add to the fleet of airplanes that he leased. Our beautiful young captain was ferrying it back to Lusaka from the United States and had merely made a small detour to pick us up in Johannesburg. He went on to assure us that her flying credentials were in good order, which may very well have been true, although I was quite sure the FAA would not have approved her methods of flying. However, that was Africa, and following FAA rules was optional. I later came to understand the ubiquitous nature of that attitude throughout many parts of the world: it is not considered a mistake to violate the rules; the mistake is in being caught.

Flying in Africa demanded that one adopt a fatalistic attitude; otherwise, it would be impossible to board many domestic flights into remote areas. Visiting a job site might require traveling in a small, single-engine plane piloted by a captain who was obviously recovering from a hangover, or who ignored the normal warm-up routine, or flew slightly above the treetops to follow a road or the coastline for navigation because the gauges did not work, or left the cockpit door open for ventilation. Although there were many challenges to traveling in Africa and the Middle East, boredom was not one of them.

The economies were being developed and the natural resources in the region were rapidly being extracted and utilized; it was necessary to stay close to the activity. During my three years working for Caterpillar Overseas, I visited almost every country in Africa and the Middle East at least once, and often several times, in support of the dealers' operations. Although I found it interesting and educational to experience the many different cultures and peoples of whatever country I was in at that time, it was always a greater pleasure to board the Swissair flight back to Geneva and retreat, with my family, to the natural beauty and clean air of the Swiss Alps.

Living in Geneva during the late 1970s provided a unique opportunity to enjoy the Alps. Our entire family enjoyed the mountains in both summer and winter, and took advantage of every opportunity to get out from under the clouds that hung low over Geneva for much of the year. A short one-hour drive, up winding mountain roads, usually brought us into glorious sunshine and blue skies. From there we could look down on the fluffy white clouds that lay below us like an immense blanket. In the summer, we hiked the many trails and visited the quaint villages; in the winter, we skied. It was paradise.

A BOILING CALDRON

Over the years, I had heard much about Zermatt (the quintessential Swiss village) and the Matterhorn, and I was anxious to explore the area firsthand. One warm summer weekend, we took the train eastwards, along the shores of Lake Geneva, through the resort town of Montreaux, and up the Rhone Valley to the small town of Visp. There we boarded the train that snaked its way further up the valley on a narrow-gage cog railway. The scenery and character of the valley changed from lowlands to steep gorges that overlooked the river, with Alpine villages nestled on mountain slopes. The train climbed slowly, with endless determination, through several tunnels and then finally to Zermatt.

As we stepped out on the main street, the Matterhorn suddenly appeared in full solitary splendor—a giant of a mountain. It was breathtakingly beautiful, remote, dominating, and aloof. I stared at it for several minutes, taking in its beauty and allure. For centuries, the Matterhorn has held a fascination and a mystery that attracts admiration and enthusiasm. During those first few moments, seeing it with my own eyes, I understood why that was. It was looking right back at me, with a silent power that beckoned me to stand atop of it. Its invitation could not be refused.

The next day we wandered around, exploring and absorbing the quaint surroundings of Zermatt, and I visited the Swiss Alpine Mountain Guide Office[23] to inquire about possibilities for climbing. Each guide took only one climber who must be insured for personal accidents, third-party risks, and rescue transportation by Air Zermatt's special high-altitude helicopters. The guides were very careful to determine whether the client had the ability, and the stamina, to do the climb. Summit day would involve 8 to 10 hours at a relatively high altitude, and it was important to be in top physical condition and have some rock climbing experience, including practice with crampons. Of course, ambition and determination were as important as physical conditioning.

About 50 years ago, after much research and investigation, the scientific community arrived at a consensus that the crust of the Earth is made up of several tectonic plates, which are continuously moving around in different directions and at different speeds, like leaves on the surface of a pond.[24] About 90 million

---

23   Every qualified Swiss Mountain Guide is required to complete a strict period of training followed by a set of final exams under the supervision of two experts. The lengthy and thorough training of a qualified Swiss Mountain Guide is the climber's best assurance of a safe and successful climb. Look for a fully qualified guide certified by the International Federation of Mountain Guide Associations (IFMGA): http://www.ivbv.info/. See also the collection of articles, *Zermatt: A Guide to Zermatt and its Culture*, compiled by Robert Guntern, Germeindepresident Zermatt (1995).

24   Bill Bryson, *A Short History of Nearly Everything* (2003); that is an incredibly interesting, entertaining, and well-written book about our world, the universe, and us. Mr. Bryson takes us from the Big Bang to the rise of civilization, seeking answers to where we came from and where we might be going.

years ago, the African and European plates collided, and the Alps were born. To geologists, the visible geological scars and lines of fusion near Zermatt clearly display the effects of that collision. In 1986, a study of the geological depth structure of the Alps revealed that the African plate slid over the European plate during a process of about 60 million years. The two plates converged and rose to create the mountains in the region of Zermatt. The Matterhorn (4,478 meters) is part of the African plate. Over time—lots of it—glacial and water erosion slowly caused the rock to disintegrate, and, voilà, the Matterhorn was born! Although nearly at an end, the pressure of that collision remains, and the Matterhorn continues to rise, at the rate of about one millimeter a year, along with the other 38 peaks in Switzerland that are over 4,000 meters, 29 of which are immediate neighbors to the Matterhorn.[25]

In 1786, Mont Blanc, the highest mountain in the Alps, was climbed. During those early years, the primary goal of climbing was to reach the summit, and proper ethics of climbing required "fair means"—that is, climbing without the use of guides or technical aids. Today, that method of climbing is called "free solo." Soon after the Mont Blanc summit was reached, several other peaks in the Alps were conquered. Thus began the "Golden Age of Mountaineering."

Later, rock climbing emerged as a sport, separate and distinct from mountaineering. Rock climbers aim at conquering difficult pitches, whereas mountaineers seek to reach the summit and conquer the mountain. Soon rock climbers began to use a variety of technical aids—pitons, bolts, belays, rope, climbing nuts, and carabineers (safety snaps). The development and use of those climbing aids provoked the debate about the ethics of rock climbing and mountaineering, one that has continued for over a hundred years.[26] The debate centered on what should be acceptable in terms of "fair means," margin of safety, use of aids, and altering the environment. Traditional climbers argued in favor of the purist form of the sport and refused to use the technical aids that were becoming popular. Unfortunately, several fell to their death while climbing unprotected—there is no escaping the consequences of mistakes on the mountain.

Some traditional climbers began to concede that technical devices were okay for protection, but not okay as an aid to ascend, and the ethical debate raged on. Today, rock climbing is considered bolt-protected face climbing, and the main goal is to get up the face of the rock with safety and enjoyment. Methods that

---

25 Guntern, *Zermatt*, was particularly informative and greatly helped with my research of the area. For more information, numerous other references about Zermatt and the Matterhorn are readily available from libraries and the Internet.
26 Matt Perkins, "Rock Climbing Ethics: A Historical Perspective," *Northwest Mountaineering Journal* (2005), http://www. mountaineers.org/nwmj/05/051_Ethics.html.

A BOILING CALDRON

formerly were considered unthinkable are now commonplace, such as rappel-placed bolting before the first ascent, hanging off the face on gear while rehearsing a movement or establishing a route, and chipping the rock to establish a handhold. Today, most new climbers learn the necessary technical skills in the artificial environment of an indoor climbing wall, and, unfortunately, the traditional skills of route finding and coping with dangerous environments are often not part of their training.

The debate on the ethics of how much of the climbing environment should be artificially altered will continue; however, it is the climbing that is important, not necessarily the methods. To each his own, I say, as long as the methods used are enjoyable and fall within the individual climber's comfort zone of acceptable risk. After all, nothing requires more individual responsibility and accountability than climbing mountains. Make your own choice to either "free solo" or bolt yourself to the face of the mountain—and enjoy! Nature is not going to object.[27]

The Matterhorn is more striking than any of its neighboring peaks, because it stands alone, detached from the surrounding chain of mountains. Its isolation means that there is no protection from the winds, and by late afternoon the combination of the warm south side and the cold north face can form an innocent-looking cloud cap, in which there is a microclimate with swirling mists, electrical storms, and violent blizzards, while the surrounding areas may be basking in warm sunshine; such extremes can be present even in summer. For that reason, it is strongly recommended that climbers get a very early start and be off the mountain by early afternoon.

Although the Matterhorn is not the most difficult 4,000-meter peak in the region, by August of 1865, it was one of only two Alpine peaks that had not yet been conquered. Edward Whymper, a lithographic artist and illustrator from England, had arrived in Zermatt in 1862 to capture the Alps on canvas for the edification of the British public; instead, he was captured by the Alps. After six unsuccessful attempts, on July 14, 1865, he and a group of guides and fellow climbers set out for the summit once again along the Hörnli Ridge—seven climbers in all. Everything went well, and at 1:40 p.m., Whymper reached the

---

27 The latest, purest form of climbing, called Deep Water Soloing (DWS), started recently in Mallorca. This sport is climbing without any ropes or protective equipment on sheer vertical faces—where foot placements barely allow room for all your toes—over bodies of water deep enough to blunt the force of a fall. If you become too tired, you simply fall off into the water, although the subsequent need to swim, the jagged rocks, and the sharks can take away some of the fun. With DWS, the only way down is to jump. Tonsai on the Phang Nga Peninsula in Thailand is a popular DWS site: *Asian Wall Street Journal*, April 13–15, 2007, W18.

summit and boisterously planted the British flag on the top.

Unfortunately, in one disastrous moment during the descent, a member of the party slipped, threatening to pull all seven climbers 1,500 meters down the north face. Only the breaking of the rope saved Whymper and his two guides, but the other four plunged to their deaths. Much controversy surrounded the accident, which cast a dark shadow over the entire idea of risking lives to achieve glory by conquering mountains. Whymper left the Alps and later continued climbing in the Andes and the Canadian Rockies, forever haunted by the accident.[28]

> *The ablest pens have failed, and I think will always fail, to give a true idea of the grandeur of the Alps. The minutest descriptions of the greatest writers do nothing more than convey impressions that are entirely erroneous—the reader conjures up visions, it may be magnificent ones but they are infinitely inferior to the reality.*
> —EDWARD WHYMPER, SCRAMBLES AMONGST THE ALPS

The Matterhorn can be a dangerous mountain for those not experienced and/or well prepared. Most climbing accidents can be traced back to either poor preparation for the ascent or exercising poor judgment while on the mountain. Having the right equipment (and knowing how to use it) is most important—climbing shoes, helmet, crampons, *piolet* (ice axe), ropes, safety equipment, and proper clothing. Fortunately, many books and much advice are readily available to anyone who wishes to learn about such things. Good preparation includes, among other factors, knowledge and experience with route finding (an acquired skill), teamwork with your climbing partner, awareness of weather conditions, personal climbing skills, physical limits, and energy reserves. Falling rocks pose a danger, but that risk can be mitigated by choosing the right route, being familiar with who and what's above you, and wearing a helmet, of course. Moreover, it is important to allow as much time for the descent as for the ascent, and to realize that energy reserves are considerably less on the descent—often making it the most dangerous part of the climb.

In my case, I clearly was not ready, and so preparations began in earnest. I devoured books about mountaineering, worked at getting physically fit, and "scrambled in the Alps" at every opportunity. Getting fit is the simple part—not easy, but simple—you just have to do it. Fitness for climbing includes both

---

28 There are many references readily available on the Internet that describes the first ascent of the Matterhorn. For firsthand descriptions, see Edward Whymper's own books: *Scrambles Amongst the Alps* (1871) and *The Ascent of the Matterhorn* (1880). It is noteworthy that the north face of the Matterhorn was not conquered until August 1, 1931, by two young men from Germany, Franz and Toni Schmid.

cardiovascular fitness and muscular strength, especially upper body strength. I chose running to build my cardio endurance and slowly, steadily, worked my way up to about 20 to 25 miles a week at a pace of about eight miles per hour for 50 to 60 minutes. My squash matches took on new meaning; I played more frequently to develop flexibility, fitness, timing, and total body strength. In addition, I focused on building strength in my hands, arms, and shoulders. One way to do that, of course, was to climb, and I was fortunate to be working with Dave Lees, a proficient young climber with the patience to teach me much of what he knew under actual climbing conditions. My friend Al and I went with him to the local Salève Mountains, near Geneva, at every opportunity. Eventually, we were coping with reasonably steep rock faces and scaling ice pitches on the glaciers in Chamonix.

Climbing the Salève with Dave Lees and Al Wickert. Dave was an accomplished climber who was willing to teach us what he knew under actual climbing conditions.

Climbing is like most other sports in terms of preparation, except that with climbing, poor preparation brings much greater risk. I soon discovered that it also required intense mental focus and concentration, in combination with carefully applied physical strength and agility—all working together in complete

A BOILING CALDRON

harmony. In that sense, climbing is unique. Unlike most other activities, it provokes an intensely passionate feeling of being alive and living life to the fullest. My senses came alive in a way I had not thought possible—my toes and feet developed an enhanced sense of touch, much like my fingers; my legs and foot muscles developed the ability to instinctively sense the security of the rock as they took my weight; my eyes learned to pick out the fine details of potential handholds and foot placements above, and, suddenly, a natural route up the face would come into view. My nose and ears learned to sense the air, the wind, and the humidity, and provided me with an early warning of weather changes. There is no substitute for experience.

Finally, after about 18 months of preparation, I was accepted into the Swiss Alpine Club, and decided that it was time to do the climb. I had already completed arrangements with the Zermatt Mountain Guide Office. It was a fine day in August of 1978 when I took my family to Zermatt, to be near me during the adventure. I met the guide, Richard Andenmotten, to discuss the schedule and what to expect during the climb. Richard was a very experienced climber who had been to the top of Zermatt over 400 times. He suggested that I take a couple days to relax, explore, and savor that remarkable village.

Then, to assess my abilities, Richard led me up several routes on the Riffelhorn Mountain. Although much shorter, those routes had degrees of difficulty similar to what would be encountered on the Matterhorn. Near the end of the day, we peered over the edge of a sheer rock face about 1,000 meters above the floor of the valley. He instructed me to climb over the edge, down about 30 meters, and traverse horizontally for about 50 meters. Obviously, Richard wanted to evaluate my tendency to acrophobia—fear of heights. Many of us have a healthy fear of heights, but if it becomes an irrational obsession, a debilitating panic can set in—a serious problem when climbing mountains. Fortunately, I remained calm, but I did not spend much time looking down! During that traverse, the weather suddenly changed and our hair literally stood on end. In addition, Saint Elmo's fire[29] was visible from the top of a steel stake that Richard was using as a belay to secure the safety rope to which I was attached. It was a warning of possible imminent lightning, and Richard became very concerned. I completed the traverse as quickly as possible and we hastily retreated off the

---

29 St. Elmo's fire is an electroluminescent coronal discharge caused by the ionization of the air during thunderstorms inside of a strong electric field. It is usually a strong indication of imminent lightning, although some believe it discharges the electrical potential and reduces the likelihood of a lightning strike. Physically, Saint Elmo's fire is a bright pink-purple glow, appearing like fire in some circumstances, often in double or triple jets, from tall, sharply pointed structures. Saint Elmo's fire is named after Erasmus of Formiae (also called St. Elmo), the patron saint of sailors, some of whom hold its appearance to be auspicious: http://en.wikipedia.org/wiki/St._Elmo's_Fire

top of the Riffelhorn.

The guide, Richard Andenmotten, on the top of Riffelhorn Mountain with the Matterhorn in the background.

Then, just two days before the scheduled Matterhorn climb, I was instructed to hike from the village of Zermatt to the Rothorn Hut (3,198 meters) and back to Zermatt. That was a demanding nine-hour hike to well above the tree line, with a steep change in elevation of 1,590 vertical meters. The last few kilometers required trudging through about 20 centimeters (8") of new snow without much of a trail to follow. Obviously, that was meant to be a test of my physical endurance, and I was very thankful for having done all that cardio training. Richard gave me a passing grade and declared that I was ready to go.

After a day of rest and mental preparation, we took the cable car to the Schwarzsee ski station. The appointed day had arrived with glorious sunshine and clear skies. I enjoyed a leisurely lunch with my family on the outdoor patio under the warm sun while the Matterhorn loomed over us. From that close vantage point, the east face looked smooth and flat, and the Hörnli ridge seemed very sharp and steep—intimidating! However, when viewed from on the mountain, the east face is actually covered with many large boulders and rocks of all sizes. And, close up, the Hörnli ridge is wide enough to climb, and not too steep. That is the easiest and most accessible route—the route that Edward Whymper took on his first successful ascent. The Hörnli Ridge is considered a scramble rather than a rock climb and is graded a 2 to 5 (Moderately Easy to Very Difficult), primarily because of the airy exposure and the steepness of the mixed rock and snow conditions above the Shoulder, which is the most difficult section, consisting of steep rock and ice several meters high.[30]

After lunch, I said good-bye to my family and struck out on an easy two-hour hike to the Hörnli Hut (3,260 meters). That was the starting point, and the hut was full of climbers from many different countries, all hoping to reach the summit. The Hörnli Hut is set up with bunk beds in the style of a dormitory, similar to a traditional mountain hut. Only blankets and pillows were provided. By about 9 p.m. everyone was in bed. I managed to get some sleep, but it was an anxious and restless night, coping with the tension and apprehension. By 3:30 a.m., most climbers were awake, dressed, and fussing with their climbing gear. I managed a quick and hearty breakfast, threw on a small pack, attached the headlight, and followed Richard out the door. He seemed anxious to get going, so we roped up and set out for the summit. I later learned that the guided climbers get to go first, and the Swiss guides ranked the highest. The regular climbers generally come last; however, a few had got up very early to get ahead of everybody.

One of the biggest problems when climbing the Matterhorn is finding the route. It is a confusing obstacle course, even in daylight. At night, one can easily become disoriented, and much time and energy can be lost searching for the quickest and safest route. Fortunately, Richard knew the way like the back of his hand, so my tasks were to focus on finding good handholds and foot placements, and maintain a reasonable and steady pace.

The rock was dry most of the way up, but in some places quite loose. Occasionally, someone shouted, "Achtung!" and we held our breath and hugged the face until it seemed clear—there was not much natural protection. Periodically, we heard a minor rumble as small boulders gained momentum, dislodging other rocks and debris as they charged their way down the exposed face to eventually perish on the glacier at the foot of either the east or north face—a visual reminder of what might happen to us if we became careless, or were unlucky. Falling rocks, dislodged by careless climbers, represented one of the greatest dangers, and I was relieved when the morning light began to improve visibility.

A few hundred meters below the Solvay Hut, we made a short stop to take a drink and attach the crampons to our boots, in preparation for the snow and

---

30 Rock climbers, mountaineers, and other climbing disciplines give a grade to a route that concisely describes the difficulty and danger of climbing it. Several factors contribute to the difficulty of a climb, including the technical difficulty of the moves, the required strength and stamina, the level of commitment, and the difficulty of protecting the climber. The French alpine system uses six overall difficulty grades (1 to 6, with 6 being the most difficult), taking into consideration the length, difficulty, exposure, and commitment-level (that is, how hard it may be to retreat).

icy conditions ahead. My guide checked the straps to ensure that they were secure, and we set out again. The crampons gave a good feeling of security as they dug into the slope, but required a bit of getting used to. Near the Solvay Hut, we had to traverse a narrow path across the packed snow on a very steep and treacherous section. A few climbers going down passed us going up on that section, which required great care and attention. One climber had to stand still, close to the wall above the path, while the other party carefully stepped around him and continued. We negotiated that section safely and made our way to the Solvay Hut.[31]

The village of Zermatt with the Matterhorn in the background. The dots indicate the route up the Hörnli ridge.

As we arrived at the hut, it became clear that a climber was in trouble. He was crouched down, in a fetal position, obviously distressed, visibly shaking, and unable to move. A couple of other climbers were trying to comfort him. A brief conversation revealed that, while traversing the treacherous snow path earlier, his fiancée had slipped when adjusting her stance and fell to her death several hundred meters below. Later, the helicopter came in and took him off the mountain, and recovered his fiancée's body far below. They were the typical inexperienced tourists, out for a quick scamper to the top of the Matterhorn,

---

31 B. P. Truffler, *The History of the Matterhorn* (2005); The Solvay Hut is named after Ernest Solvay, a Belgian industrialist who, in 1915, provided generous funds to build a hut on the Hörnli Ridge, only 475 meters below the summit. In 1966, a new smaller one was erected at the same site to replace the original one that was demolished. The new hut provides emergency shelter for six climbers, and is intended only for emergencies, although climbers sometimes use it as a shelter for the night. Plainly, a building at 4,000 meters, on the side of the Matterhorn, is both demanding and costly to maintain.

A BOILING CALDRON

with no guide, rope, proper boots, or crampons. The Matterhorn has more than its fair share of tragedies, mainly because many would-be climbers are led to believe that it does not require much preparation. Some have been known to attempt the climb wearing only light clothing and a pair of runners.

Although my guide was respectful toward me the entire time, he showed some disdain for the climbers traveling without guides, especially those unprepared for the mountain and its dangers. Guides ferry climbers up and down the mountain during the busy summer months, and I expect it would be exhausting, boring, and unpleasant work at times, especially with climbers who become uncomfortable and do not enjoy the climb. Unfortunately, when that attitude is expressed to regular solo climbers, it creates a backlash that leaves them with a poor opinion of commercial mountaineering and professional guides whom, as one fellow said to me later, "drag you up and down the mountain at such a speed that you barely remember the experience." I was exceedingly thankful to be with an expert who knew the route. We remained roped up the entire time and I was confident that, if I slipped, he could prevent me from falling.

Since there was nothing we could do for the climber who had lost his fiancée, we continued our climb with a new sense of caution and respect for the mountain. About 30 minutes beyond the Solvay Hut, the route shifted more to the north face and became nearly vertical and very exposed. Any tendency to experience acrophobia would surely have become evident there. Progress slowed as we scrambled over rock outcroppings, or circled around them, watching for loose stones and searching for that perfect handhold. The most difficult section was an area called the Shoulder (4,200 meters)—a section of steep rock and ice several meters high. We reached it at a time when my energy reserves were lagging, the air was getting thinner, and the high-altitude winds were becoming noticeable. I suddenly became intensely focused on each handhold and foot placement, and avoided looking down—the exposure was alarming, and even a small stumble could have resulted in a free fall for several hundred meters. Fixed ropes helped with the ascent and provided safety, and, fortunately, we did not meet anyone who had reached the summit and was descending, or anyone wanting to pass us on the way up; otherwise, our progress would have been slowed significantly. The steep wall sections near the Shoulder are too narrow to accommodate two lanes of traffic and bottlenecks can occur. During the 1990s, as more and more climbers attacked the mountain, bottlenecks reportedly became quite common.

It was becoming noticeably more difficult to get oxygen and I tried to concentrate on breathing regularly in rhythm to my footsteps—breath out during exertions, breath in between exertions—poetry in motion! About 30 minutes before the top we had to do a zigzag traverse across a steep snow and ice field, making good use of the crampons as we kicked the front points securely into the surface, step by step. By then, the persistent wind had become quite chilly and, even though the sun was showing its face over the horizon, it felt like the coldest time of the day.

Finally, after approximately four hours of climbing from the Hörnli Hut, we reached the summit at about 8 a.m. on August 28, 1978. We surveyed the panorama—first the tiny village of Zermatt, then the Bernese Alps, the Monte Rosa, and the surrounding peaks. The Italian Alps stretched off in a multicolored sea, and my guide pointed out the French Alps with Mont Blanc—the highest peak in the Alps—in the distance. Words cannot adequately describe the view at sunrise—it was glorious tranquility and adventure. The views of the Alps, on both sides of the ridge, were spectacular. At that moment, I felt the Matterhorn was embracing me, happy that I had made a successful ascent. Richard and I celebrated our success with a drink, a small energy snack, and a toast to each other for having reached the summit.

The descent was uneventful, but my strength and energy reserves were certainly depleted. I took the lead going down so that Richard could belay me if there were any slips or missteps. One should always try to face down the mountain during the descent for the sake of better visibility and sure-footedness; but it takes practice, since the natural tendency is to "back climb," to turn around and face the mountain and go down backwards. Of course, when on a near-vertical face back climbing is essential. We rappelled down a few pitches on the steeper sections near the top, since it was safer, quicker, and required less energy.

Shortly after noon, we arrived back at the Hörnli Hut. Richard presented me with the coveted Matterhorn Summit pin that indicated a successful climb, and I thanked him for his professionalism and leadership. The climb was over. After a well-deserved rest and hot lunch, it was with considerable satisfaction that I struck out on a leisurely stroll down the trail toward Schwarzsee. My family was waiting there and we shared hugs and a small celebration before heading back down on the cable car to Zermatt.

Before returning home to Geneva, we took another walk around the Matterhorn cemetery with greater reverence and a newfound respect and introspection about life, death, risk, and reward. I was glad to be healthy enough to be truly living, grateful to be able to enjoy the natural environment of which we are all part, and thankful that we lacked nothing important. I know why people are drawn to climb mountains, why some are even drawn to attempt the seemingly impossible challenges that nature presents. It is a feeling like no other—an intense sensation of being truly alive as an integral and important part of nature and the universe. Each year I try to spend some time skiing, and every encounter with the mountains brings back that intensely passionate feeling of being alive, of joyous living that began with the Matterhorn.

Relaxing with my family at Schwarzsee after the climb.

On that August day in 1978, there were about 25 climbers on the mountain. Today, it has been written, the Matterhorn is the most climbed mountain in the world—it is not uncommon to have over 200 climbers on the mountain each day during high season—a formidable social event. Since my climb in 1978, fixed ropes have been installed nearly from top to bottom of the Hörnli ridge. That has made the climb an overcrowded tourist attraction, and the guidebooks recommend getting an early start to avoid the long queue just below the summit, even though it can accommodate about 40 people at a time! I expect the legendary Swiss guide Ulrich Inderbinnen would be turning in his grave because of that commercial development.[32]

Despite attempts to tame it, the mountain continues to transform itself and remind us of its independence. On August 18, 2003, the historic ridge that gave Whymper such a difficult time collapsed after an unusually hot summer. The erosion, which has gone on for millions of years, continues. The mountain is

---

32 In June 2004, the Zermatt region lost a legend. Mr. Ulrich Inderbinnen, a well-known and much respected guide, passed away at the age of 103. He made a remarkable achievement by climbing the Matterhorn for the 370th time at the age of 90 to celebrate the 125th anniversary of the first ascent by Edward Whymper. It is said that he never owned a telephone, and to hire his services one had to search through the village of Zermatt asking for his whereabouts. He used to say that he never got bored with climbing the Matterhorn. The only inconvenience was that the people climbing with him were too slow for his taste! A remarkable man. See http://www.hiking-in-switzerland.com/Mountain-Switzerland.html.

alive.

Author on the summit of the Matterhorn
August 28, 1978.

8

EAST IS EAST

CATERPILLAR FAR EAST LTD.
HONG KONG
(1979 — 1982)

> *Oh East is East and West is West,*
> *and never the twain shall meet,*
> *Til Earth and Sky stand presently*
> *at God's great Judgment Seat,*
> *But there is neither East nor West,*
> *Border, nor Breed, nor Birth,*
> *When two strong men stand face to face,*
> *tho' they come from the ends of the earth!*
>
> —Rudyard Kipling, from
> The Ballad of East and West

At 10 minutes past midnight, on September 9, 1976, Mao Tse-tung died, ending his 27-year rule—an era of unimaginable terror and destruction in China.[33] Earlier, Deng Xiaoping had made his most famous remark in defense of his support for greater productivity, after the famine of the Great Leap Forward: "It doesn't matter whether it's a yellow cat or a black cat, as long as it catches mice." Deng Xiaoping figured that promoting prosperity was the best way to keep the Communist Party in power. In December of 1978, the Third Plenum of the National People's Congress confirmed the need for economic modernization; the goal was to be a fully modernized country by the year 2000. It was clear to Deng Xiaoping that it would not happen without access to for-

---

33 Jung Chang and Jon Halliday, *Mao: The Unknown Story* (2005), a groundbreaking biography of Mao Tse-tung, based on decades of research and interviews with virtually everyone inside and outside of China who had any dealings with him.

eign technology, foreign expertise, and foreign capital. Therefore, reform had to include a new "open door" policy, to draw capital from the west. Foreign firms were offered the opportunity to enter into joint ventures, and special economic zones were opened up that provided preferential tax treatment—four were established along the coast of China in 1979. Thus began the economic stampede that took place in China during the next several decades.[34] Much later, in 1992, Deng Xiaoping made his famous southern tour of China and further reinforced the "Deng Xiaoping Theory of Reform" with his comment, "Poverty is not socialism. To be rich is glorious."

Early in 1979, I was asked by Caterpillar to relocate once again—this time to Hong Kong, the headquarters for Caterpillar Far East Limited (CFEL). In 1967, the division had been established to handle the administration and marketing activities in the Far East. The following year, a parts distribution facility was added in Singapore to support the growing population of Caterpillar machines. It was a time of many large construction projects, including thousands of miles of new highways, new and larger airports, and projects related to mining, energy, and water resources in many parts of the world.

During the 1960s, Caterpillar's employment had increased by 50 percent, and worldwide manufacturing space doubled. The dealers shared in that rapid growth and the overseas dealers especially demanded more support from Caterpillar. In 1970, Caterpillar's sales outside of the United States exceeded 50 percent of the total. Japanese competition—most notably Komatsu, and most notably in Asia—was becoming the biggest foreign competitive threat. It was important that our dealers develop capabilities to counter the threat; that was CFEL's primary responsibility in Asia. It was an exciting time to be there.

Economic expansion is always limited by the amount of available energy. Traditionally, coal had accounted for over 70 percent of total energy consumed by China, but the Chinese Communist Party (CCP) determined that oil was an essential commodity for export in order to finance their modernization. Crude oil reserves were in the northeast, especially near Daqing, in Heilongjiang province, and in the northwest near Urumchi, in Xinjiang province.

Caterpillar had been selling products in China since 1975 and, by 1979, they were in even greater demand to help develop the oil reserves. When the Chinese bought our products, they also demanded the transfer of technology. Therefore, my first assignment was to spend two weeks in Beijing giving a technical training seminar to a group of petroleum engineers. I was assisted by a great colleague, Jan Evans.

Chinese escorts met us at the airport in Beijing and helped us deal with the

---

34 W. Scott Morton and Charles M. Lewis, *China: Its History and Culture*, 4th ed. (2005).

formalities and board the bus to the hotel. Beijing was a gray, overcast, and dusty place. The people glanced at us briefly with much suspicion and apprehension. They did not smile and appeared quite glum, and there was a pervasive climate of fear and depression. People eschewed attention and tried to be as invisible as possible. They did not speak unless it was necessary, for fear of standing out from the crowd. There is a saying that "the nail that sticks up is the one that gets hammered down;" the average citizen tried to avoid being that nail—it was a matter of survival. Everyone wore the same blue Mao suits, buttoned up to the neck, with the little matching cap—they have been called the "army of the blue ants." We found it nearly impossible to tell the men from the women unless they were in close proximity to us. The exception to this general behavior was the children, of course, because they were like all children—they looked at us with intense curiosity and smiled widely at our strange appearance. As we smiled back, the parents quickly glanced at us and herded their children away. Young soldiers in poorly fitting uniforms randomly walked the streets or stood out in front of important-looking buildings, holding rifles that were surely of WWI vintage. They clearly were not members of a highly disciplined, fearsome fighting force.

Thousands and thousands of bicycles jammed the streets. A few cars and trucks from the '40s and '50s slowly worked their way along the pavement; drivers leaned on their horns in a vain attempt to displace the bicycles, pedestrians, and carts overloaded with a wide variety of goods. All the confusion created a cacophony of noise, but I soon noticed that there were almost no sounds of people talking, laughing, or communicating, as one would normally expect.

The Beijing Hotel was the only place in the city where Western businessmen could stay. The place was neat and tidy, and reasonably clean, and the furnishings were still in quite good condition. It appeared as if nothing in the hotel had changed in the last forty or fifty years, which reminded me of a setting for an old movie. The rooms were not large, but were comfortable enough, with very high ceilings, a cooling fan that worked, and a large window overlooking the street out front. A couple of Chinese women attended each floor to provided service. They hovered around and attentively looked for an opportunity to earn a small gratuity.

The Beijing Hotel was to be our home for the next two weeks. We settled in and then went down to the lobby to look around and have a beer; there was a bar and a restaurant in the corner. The lobby was busy but not crowded, and the clientele were Western businessmen and overseas Chinese. They were certainly not locals, as was evident from their dress. The Tsingtao beer, which originated from the coastal town of the same name, was as good as we had been led to believe. Apparently, the brewery, built by the Germans many years before, had been protected during the chaos and destruction of the Great Leap Forward and of the Cultural Revolution. Some things are always considered sacred.

We could only spend our U.S. dollars at the Friendship Store, since hard currency was officially banned. The punishment for giving or accepting hard currency was severe, especially for the local Chinese, and foreign visitors could be expelled from the country. We had been warned not to lock our suitcases when leaving our rooms, because they would likely be searched from time to time. That prompted me to lay a trap to confirm whether it was happening, by positioning items very specifically so I would know if they had been moved. Sure enough, the suitcases were opened and searched every day that I was there. It was also generally accepted, although not confirmed, that the rooms were bugged and every conversation monitored, and perhaps recorded. We were conscious of that and paid close attention to the topics of our conversations. The rotary dial phone worked well, and we could call home whenever we liked by asking the hotel operator to connect us to the number in Hong Kong. We assumed that those conversations were monitored. There was a vintage radio that worked, and one station had good music, but there was no information that gave us a clue about what was happening outside of Beijing.

Within a day or so, we relaxed and found our accommodations quite comfortable. The food was almost exclusively Chinese style, and after trying to order some "eggs over easy with bacon" for breakfast one day, we reverted to the Chinese fare. I found it amusing that the Western magazines we had brought with us disappeared from the rooms the day before we were scheduled to leave.

At 8 a.m. Monday morning, we arrived at the hotel conference room and set up our training materials for the seminar. After waiting for about an hour, the students arrived, dressed mostly in typical blue Mao suits. They were different from the locals we had seen on the street—although shy, their eyes were brighter, they were not afraid to hold eye contact, and they smiled and made us feel at ease right away. Our students were clearly some of the few remaining members of the educated class that had survived the Cultural Revolution. One member of the group, obviously the leader, made introductions and explained through a translator how the next two weeks were going to unfold. Classes would start at about 9 a.m. and finish at about 3 p.m., with an hour for lunch, five days a week. It soon became obvious that the leader was a member of the Chinese Communist Party (CCP), assigned to "supervise" the group and make sure they followed the rules. Individual civil liberties in China were very much restricted in the late 1970s.

EAST IS EAST

Chinese customers attending the Technical Seminar in Beijing—1978; Jan Evans is standing in the middle, and the author is standing third from right.

The petroleum engineers had traveled considerable distances to attend our seminar, which required special permission from the CCP officials. In 1979, a Chinese citizen could not travel out of his own region without express permission. At the beginning of the first day, I observed the leader handing out little yellow slips to all the students. Must be coupons for lunch in the hotel, I thought, but it turned out that the yellow slips gave the students official permission to enter the hotel for the next day's classes; local Chinese citizens were not allowed to freely enter the Beijing Hotel. I then understood the reason for all the soldiers guarding the entrance.

Jan and I took turns covering the material. I presented the technical stuff and Jan reviewed the material related to application, performance, and operation of the equipment. It progressed quite well, although working through a translator certainly slowed down the delivery and pace of the presentation; however, he did not hesitate too much and seemed to be doing a good job. It was impossible to know for sure. After the first couple of days, the students began asking questions that had nothing much to do with the material we presented. Rather, they wanted to know about design details, most of which, I knew, was proprietary information: "How did you heat-treat that casting?" "Why did you decide to weld that joint instead of bolt it?" "What is the cylinder pressure under full-load?" "How did you control the injector so that the fuel entered the combustion chamber at the right time?" Those questions had nothing to do with the operation and use of the Caterpillar equipment that they had just acquired, and it dawned on me that our students might not be our customers, as expected. Later we found out that some were, but most of them were part of a design team working on the development of the local Chinese oil field machinery, and were picking our brains for technical information that might help them solve their own engineering problems. I dealt with the situation by explaining the simplest concepts in excruciating detail, drawing upon my engineering training and experience in the research labs—and faking it when necessary. It's quite surprising how much time one can spend explaining the intricate design details and the manufacturing processes involved in making simple parts. Certainly, no proprietary engineering information was revealed, and they learned nothing from us that was not fully explained in any freshman textbook on basic mechanics, but they seemed pleased.

At the end of the second day, I said to Jan, "We have two more weeks of this… with more free time than work time. What are we going to do?"
"Well, why don't we explore the city?" Jan ventured.
"Great idea."
It seemed obvious that the best mode of transportation was the bicycle, so that is how we found ourselves at the Friendship Store, inquiring about renting bicycles. The concept of rental had certainly not yet found its way to the Friendship Store, because the fellow behind the counter had no knowledge of the word, even though his command of English was remarkably good.
"Okay," I said, "do you sell bicycles?"
"Yes, we do," he said, as he led us to a whole rack of shiny new bikes.
"Do you sell any used bicycles?"
"Not to foreigners."
"Do you buy used bicycles?"
"Yes, of course."
"Okay, how much for a new bicycle?"
Eventually, we bought two new bicycles for the equivalent of about $100 each, with the promise that we could sell them back in two weeks for a "reasonable" price, if they were in good shape. We happily rode off down the street toward Tiananmen Square, as the locals watched in astonishment. Visiting foreign businessmen riding bicycles were not a common sight in Beijing—we may have been the first.
During the next two weeks, we rode up and down the main streets and hutongs, taking pictures of the surroundings. The children would come out and stare as we smiled and took their picture; we were probably the first "round-eyed" humans they had ever seen. We rode into the Forbidden City[35] with no restrictions and wandered through the many rooms and vast gardens. One weekend we struck out on a longer excursion and visited other famous histori-

---

35 The Forbidden City was the Chinese Imperial Palace from mid-Ming Dynasty to the end of the Ching Dynasty. It is located near the center of the city of Beijing.

cal places in Beijing. We were never stopped by the authorities and requested to go a particular way, or told we should not be in certain areas; and we freely took pictures of anything and everything. The major challenge was finding our way back to the hotel after a few hours of exploring, and not being able to read the Chinese map or ask directions. We felt completely safe and secure, although I am confident we were watched the entire time. That treatment seemed typical of most travelers, which was a surprise considering the tight restrictions placed on the local population.

At the end of our seminar, we returned to the Friendship Store and sold our "used bicycles" for $85—two weeks of use for $15—perhaps the best bargain I've ever enjoyed. Jan and I have since recalled the incident many times with great amusement and pleasant memories.

The seminar went well, the students were pleased, and we made some new Chinese friends who invited us to visit the job site. Several weeks later, I accepted that invitation and boarded a regularly scheduled flight from Beijing to Urumchi in the province of Xinjiang, on a Soviet Ilyushin jet that had seen many years of service. I sincerely hoped the engines were maintained better than the visible part of the craft. As we approached the runway in Urumchi, the pilot suddenly engaged the thrust reversers when we were still about a hundred feet off the ground—the plane fell like a rock, bounced a couple of times, and finally skidded to a stop—surely, our pilot had been used to landing on small aircraft carriers! I felt frightened for a moment, but most passengers acted as if the situation was quite normal.

During my entire career, I have never seen a place as remote and primitive as Xinjiang province in the far northwest corner of China, close to the Russian border. Near the job site, the Uyghur people lived in small homes made from earth and mud, and scratched a meager living out of what appeared to be nothing more than a bit of grass and scrub. The Chinese have since gone on to develop the petroleum resources in the region, and it is satisfying to know we made an early contribution. I hope the Uygur people in Xinjiang Province benefited.

In 2007, when I visited China once again, Shanghai and Beijing were modern and thriving cities that rivaled Hong Kong and other major cities of the world. Despite the progress, much of the country was still quite primitive, although by then, Urumchi had modern hotels and other amenities.

The business in China occupied much of my time in Asia, but Indonesia and Malaysia were active market areas too, and the dealers there required significant time and attention. Both were growing rapidly and facing many challenges finding people, expanding facilities, and improving service capabilities. The logging industry was booming and the Caterpillar track-type tractor was the preferred machine for dragging the logs out of the dense jungle. Visiting our customers in remote areas of the world was one of the enjoyable personal benefits of my nomadic career, and the logging camps in the remote areas of Borneo were a good example. Those trips usually entailed a long flight from Jakarta to an airstrip in the jungle, most of a day in a jeep bouncing along on rough logging roads to the river, and then three or four hours in a small boat up the river through the jungle to the camp. Accommodations were sparse, and the mosquitoes looked like they were on steroids, but it was not uncommon to be served fine wine and excellent food prepared by well-trained chefs. Eating well was one of the few pleasures of living in the logging camps of Borneo, and it was important to keep the workers well fed and as comfortable as possible, since they often stayed there for many weeks at a time.

Asia offered a wide variety of societies and culture, but none quite like Nepal. I was first intrigued by the country when I went there in early 1980 to visit a customer building a road through the mountainous terrain near Kathmandu. Nepal seemed a country of extremes—from beautiful mountain peaks towering above us, to dusty earth and yak dung beneath our feet, and golden Buddha statues intermingled with poverty, desperation, and third-world living conditions. Nepal is a land-locked Himalayan country about the size of England, bordered by Tibet to the north and India to the south, east, and west. The Mountain Region is part of the Himalayan mountain range that separates the Indian subcontinent from the Tibetan plateau. Although the people of the Himalaya region are different in many ways, they all seem to share the common quality of gentleness. They are quick with a smile and live a simple life influenced by tradition and in harmony with their beautiful land.

The modern theory of plate tectonics attributes the formation of that mountain range to a collision of the Indo-Australian continental plate with the Eurasian plate, about 70 million years ago. The Indo-Australian plate continues to move under the Tibetan plateau at a speed estimated to be about 67 millimeters a year, which pushes the Himalayan range upwards about 4–5 millimeters a year—geologically, a very active area.

The name "Himalaya" is from a local language, and means "the abode of snow." "Himal" is the Nepalese word for "snow-covered mountain." It is the highest region in the world and contains eight of the world's ten highest mountains. Mount Everest is the highest peak in the region at 8,848 meters (29,028 ft), and sits on the border between Nepal and Tibet. The Nepalese call it "Sagarmatha," meaning "Mother of the Universe." The Tibetans call it "Chomolungma," which means "Mother Goddess of the Earth."

To appreciate the enormous scale of the Himalayan peaks, one should consider that Aconcagua's peak, in the South American Andes, at 6,962 meters, is the highest outside the Himalaya region, while the Himalayan system has over 100 peaks exceeding 7,200 meters. Several attempts have been made to get an accurate measurement of the height of Everest; the official accepted altitude is 8,848 meters (29,028 ft) to the top of the snowcap. That is the height above sea level, of course. However, when measured from its base, it is only 5,200 meters (18,400 ft) above the Tibetan Plateau.[36]

Nepal has a very diverse landscape and climate, ranging from warm and humid in the south, to cold and mountainous in the north. Hilly and mountainous terrain has made it very difficult and expensive to build roads and other infrastructure projects. In the 21st century, poverty is still acute, and about half the working-age population is underemployed. There is a severe shortage of skilled labor and the per capita income is less than $300 per year. The country has experienced a turbulent and unstable political history and that pattern continues into the 21st century.

Kathmandu is the capital city and the largest in Nepal. The intense mysticism and culture of the region was overpowering as I roamed around the city in 1980—Mani stones, prayer flags, and prayer wheels inscribed with Buddhist prayers in Tibetan script, daily worship in temples to appease the gods, and even a living Goddess incarnate as a young girl. While wandering around Kathmandu, I caught a glimpse of the living Goddess peeking out the window of her residence. The black shadowing around her eyes made her easily recognizable. The *National Geographic*[37] website describes the tradition as follows:

> Tradition holds that Durga (goddess of destruction and blood sacrifices) is incarnate in a young girl from a caste of silver and goldsmiths. High priests choose the girl based on several physical characteristics, such as "neck like a conch shell" and "eyes like a cow." Then, to prove she is the Kumari Devi—the incarnation of Durga—the girl must pass a series of horrifying tests…Once selected, the girl moves into the Kumari Bahal, the residence of the Kumari Devi, with her family. She leaves only for ceremonial occasions a few times each year and remains the Kumari until she experiences a serious loss of blood or her first period.

---

36   The tallest mountain as measured from its base is Mauna Kea in Hawaii at 10,200 meters (6.3 miles), although it is only 4,205 meters (13,796 ft) above sea level. By the same measurement of base to summit, Denali (also known as Mount McKinley), in Alaska, is also taller than Everest, although its height above sea level is only 6,194 meters (20,320 ft).

37   www.nationalgeographic.com/nomad/nepal .

EAST IS EAST

Out of curiosity, I stopped by the offices of a couple of trekking agencies and picked up some literature on doing a trek, although at that time I did not have any definite plans to make it happen. But, before long, that would change as the peaks of Nepal captured my imagination.

✥

9

NAMASTE[38]

NEPAL
(1980)

I have climbed my mountain, but I must still live my life.

— Tenzing Norgay[39]

After returning home to Hong Kong, I reviewed the literature in more detail and became interested in the possibility of trekking Nepal. Over the next few weeks, I discussed the idea with Curt Caughey and Ed Wilcox, a couple of friends also working in Hong Kong. They expressed serious interest, which motivated me to investigate the details and put a plan together. The most appealing alternative was a trek to a peak called Kala Patthar that overlooked the base camp of Mount Everest and provided a close-up view of the highest mountain in the world. Departing from Kathmandu, we would fly to the small village of Lukla at 2,860 meters (9,383 ft) and then take the route that would lead us to Namche Bazaar, Tengboche, Dingboche, Gorak Shep, and, finally, to Kala Patthar at 5,643 meters (18,514 ft). Although the trek itself did not seem particularly difficult, the "extremely high" altitude might be a challenge. High altitude is defined as:

High = 2,438–3,658 meters (8,000–12,000 ft)
Very High = 3,658–5,487 meters (12,000–18,000 ft)
Extremely High = 5,500+ meters (18,000+ ft)

The literature said that our trek would require a minimum of three weeks or

---

38   *Namaste* is a Nepali greeting that conveys respect for one's soul.
39   On 29 May 1953, a New Zealand mountaineer, Sir Edmund Hillary, and the Sherpa mountaineer, Tenzing Norgay, became the first climbers known to have reached the summit of Mount Everest. They were part of the ninth British expedition to Everest. Neither has ever revealed who reached the summit first, but Sir Edmund Hillary is given the benefit of the doubt.

so, including time for acclimatization on the way up. That presented a problem, since we could only allow 12 days for the entire journey, including travel time to and from Nepal. How could we manage to avoid the risk of Acute Mountain Sickness[40] (AMS) without allowing time for acclimatization? While reading a book on trekking in Nepal, I happened across the name of a diuretic (Diamox) that was sometimes used as a prophylactic for altitude sickness.[41] The local doctor in Hong Kong empathized with our situation and said the drug was available; however, he added that it was very powerful and quite dangerous because of the detrimental effect on the kidneys. He seriously cautioned us not to take it any longer than necessary. We took note and bought the drug, just in case.

Soon thereafter, I contacted the Caterpillar dealer in Nepal, who recommended a reputable trekking agency in Kathmandu.[42] We discussed detailed preparations over the phone and scheduled 10 days in late November when the weather is normally quite good. The trek was approximately 100 miles long from the village of Lukla to Kala Patthar; that distance meant we would have to move fast for about 10 to 12 hours each day; there would be very little time for sightseeing or acclimatization. In addition, much of the distance would be through numerous steep hills and valleys, so that the total change in elevation would be significantly greater than simply the difference of 9,130 feet between Lukla and Kala Patthar.

For that reason, the trekking agency suggested that we hire porters to carry all our stuff—food, drinks, tents, cooking utensils, sleeping bags, ground sheets, and blankets; we would carry only a light daypack with a jacket, camera, water, and some snack food. We agreed. In 1980, there were few teahouses, hotels, or hostels along the way for accommodations, and we prepared to sleep in tents and cook outdoors on an open fire every day. Nowadays, there is a string of reasonably comfortable accommodations, all the way from Lukla to Gorak Shep—the "launching pad" for the ascent of Kala Patthar.

On November 21, 1980, we flew from Hong Kong to Kathmandu and spent one night in a local hotel. Early the next morning, our guide, Jangbu, met us and took us to the local airport to board a flight to Lukla. The STOL (short take-

---

40 The illness caused by high altitude is called Acute Mountain Sickness (AMS). It can occur due to elevation, rate of ascent, and the susceptibility of the individual. It is important to note that susceptibility is not related to any specific factor, such as age, sex, or physical condition. When symptoms become severe, the illness is called High Altitude Pulmonary Edema (HAPE) or High Altitude Cerebral Edema (HACE), which occurs when fluid leaks through the capillary walls into either the lungs or the brain due to lack of oxygen. At that point, the illness is life threatening, and the victim must go to a lower altitude immediately. At 12,000 ft, there are 40 percent fewer oxygen molecules per breath than at sea level, so the breathing rate must increase to give the body the oxygen it needs.

41 Stephen Bezruchka, *A Guide to Trekking in Nepal*, 3rd ed. (1976).

42 Annapurna Mountaineering & Trekking PVT Ltd., Box 795, Durbarmarg, Kathmandu, Nepal.

off and landing) aircraft carried about eight people. There was a bit of fog that morning, and shortly after we were airborne, the pilot got word that there was too much fog at Lukla to land safely, so we turned back. We were disappointed because we were losing a whole day, and our time was already tight. However, Jangbu said that "the clouds in Nepal have rocks in them," and that it was not wise to fly around in the fog. We did not argue.

Fortunately, the next morning was clear and we were able to depart. The flight to Lukla was only about 45 minutes, over steep valleys and sharp peaks. Depending on whose opinion you would like to accept, you sit either on the right or on the left side of the plane to get the best view—it does not really matter. Suddenly, the roar of the engine dropped as we approached the short landing strip at Lukla—a flat area perched on the shoulder of a cliff. The gravel runway sloped upward about 10 degrees, which helped to slow the plane as it approached the sheer rock face at the far end, next to the small Quonset hut that was the terminal. The flight was successful, and we arrived in clear skies and bright sunshine, although the plane wreckage along the sides of the runway was a little disconcerting.

Lukla at 2,860 meters (9,383 ft) is where most people visiting the Himalaya start their journey up the valley. In Nepalese, "Lukla" means "place with many goats and sheep," and small herds of those animals were around when we arrived. We were already a day behind schedule, so we quickly unloaded our gear and gathered around our support team of Sherpa[43] porters and cooks—17 in all, ranging from young girls to old men. They already had a ground sheet spread out with our lunch ready so we could eat before heading up the trail. Seventeen sherpas for three hikers seemed a bit excessive, but Jangbu explained that all were needed because we would be moving fast and so could not carry much of anything—understood. We felt good about being able to support the local economy and help alleviate the high unemployment. The head cook, Kaji, supervised all the logistical duties and activities during the trek.

It was already noon of day one when we arrived at Lukla, so instead of looking around the village we hastily headed off toward Phakding, where we planned to spend the night. The sherpas had already sped off carrying packs as big and heavy as themselves and were already out of sight. The trail took us

---

43 The Sherpa are an ethnic group from the most mountainous region of Nepal, high in the Himalayas. In Tibetan, *shar* means East, and *pa* is a suffix meaning "people": hence the word *sharpa* or *Sherpa*. Sherpas migrated from eastern Tibet to Nepal within the last 500 years. A female sherpa is known as a "sherpani." The term *sherpa* (the preferred spelling with a lower-case first letter) is also used to refer to local people, typically men, employed as porters or guides for mountaineering expeditions in the Himalayas. They are highly regarded as elite mountaineers and experts in their local terrain, as well as having good physical endurance and resilience to high altitude conditions. However, a sherpa is not necessarily a member of the Sherpa ethnic group.

up and down the terrain—more down than up—and we lost about 600 feet of altitude on the walk to Phakding. Nevertheless, it was a relatively easy walk on a wide and foot-friendly trail, and we were in good spirits as we chatted with each other and Jangbu.

Phakding is bisected by the raging Dudh Kosi River ("Milk River"), which looked like it might be good for white-water rafting. We crossed on a rickety, old suspension bridge (just wide enough for a yak) that swayed as we carefully stepped on each wooden cross member. The water was a milky blue-white color from glacial silt and dissolved minerals. While on the bridge, we had our first glimpse of the ubiquitous prayer flags. Each one had a prayer written on it, and the idea was that each time the flag flapped in the breeze, the prayers were sent heavenward. The same prayers were carved into the Mani stones. Jangbu told us it is customary, in order to show respect, to walk to the left of the Mani stones, prayer walls, and poles scattered along the trail from time to time.

Sherpa guide, Jangbu, (middle) with friends along the trail.

It was dusk when we arrived in Phakding; the sherpas already had a roaring fire going and dinner preparations were well along. Our first meal was typical of the food served during the entire trek. There was very little variety, but it was tasty—mainly potatoes, vegetables, rice, and lentils, all boiled in a sauce with some meat and a little curry. The Nepalese call the dish *dal bhat*, and we enjoyed every bite.

After dinner, the porters erected individual tents for each of us and prepared our sleeping bags for the night. There was very little for us to do except relax, take in the surrounding views, and enjoy the hospitality.

Early the next morning, I heard a shuffling outside the tent, followed by a pleasant "Good morning." Outside, a sherpa crouched with a cup of sweet milky tea. That would be our much-appreciated wake-up call for the duration of the trek. Breakfast consisted of eggs, biscuits, soup, porridge, and some plain pancakes. We all ate with gusto, packed the gear, and followed Jangbu up the trail toward the town of Namche Bazaar. The trail crossed a bridge over the Dudh Kosi River and ascended about 2,500 vertical feet, on a grueling switchback clinging to the side of the steep valley—the largest elevation gain during a single day of the entire trek. It was late in the afternoon when a small, plain-looking house came into view, and then a few more as we climbed higher. The Sherpa had already set up camp in an opening not far from the center of town, and offered us a welcome drink as we arrived.

Sherpa porters on the trail; they often carry loads equal to their own weight.

With a noticeable shortening of our breath, the effect of the altitude was becoming evident. Fortunately, no one was showing signs of AMS (Acute Mountain Sickness)—we had each taken a Diamox as a precaution, since there was no time to stop for acclimatization. Typically, a couple of days would be spent in Namche Bazaar for that purpose, but we could only spend one night there before heading off to Tengboche. However, we explored the village as much as we could that evening, despite the exertion from the climb up from Phakding.

A typical street scene in downtown Namche Bazaar.

Namche Bazaar (3,440 meters/11,286 ft) is a large, U-shaped village perched on the edge of a deep gorge. Almost everyone trekking in the Khumbu region stops there—it is the gateway to the high Himalaya and all trekking permits have to be checked at the police checkpoint in Namche. For many years, it has been a market town where Tibetan traders from the north do business with Nepalese traders from the south. The village has many shops, and a market selling everything imaginable, including meat, vegetables, assorted crafts, baskets, new and used clothing, trekking gear, and a wide variety of trinkets. Today, there is a cybercafé with an Internet connection, but in 1980, the Internet was yet to be invented. In contrast, yak dung is still used as fuel for cooking and heating, as it was then.

After a hearty breakfast, we checked our packs and headed toward Tengboche. At first, the trail was a gentle uphill grade along the side of a steep downward slope that ended at a stream that ran through the village. A steep descent through a rhododendron forest brought us to a swing bridge over a waterfall on the Dodh Koshi River. Throughout the day, it was up a ridge and down the other side, repeatedly. Occasionally, we met a few porters and yaks as they headed down, but for the most part, we were alone on the trail. As we climbed higher, the foggy patches near Tengboche indicated we had reached cloud level. The famous Buddhist Monastery at Tengboche suddenly came into view, as well as our campsite, which the Sherpa had already established. We had gained about 425 meters of altitude and the high mountains came into better view.

After a short rest, I walked to the Tengboche monastery, respectfully removed my boots, and entered just inside the front archway. I did not feel as if I belonged so did not venture further in. For years, all the great Everest expeditions have visited the monastery to light candles and ask the gods for good health and a safe climb. Eight years after we were there, on January 19, 1989, an electrical fault caused the monastery to catch fire and burn to the ground. Many artifacts were lost, but a few trekkers helped save some books and paintings. It has since been completely rebuilt with money donated from all around the world.

The next morning, as I poked my head out of the tent to accept the morning tea, I was surprised to see a light dusting of snow covering everything in sight. The clouds had broken and the scenery was stunning—it is reported that Tengboche is one of the most beautiful places on Earth, and I could see why many thought so. The shining peak of Ama Dablam was visible behind the monastery, and the tip of Everest glowed in the sunlight above the Lhotse ridge. Today would be a long 8–10-hour day, because the plan was to get all the way to Dingboche. It was already our fourth day on the trail and we only had six more to get up to Kala Patthar, and return to Kathmandu.

We got an early start and enjoyed the distraction of each new towering peak that came into view as we slowly moved up the valley. Beyond Tengboche, the trees thinned out, and the terrain mainly consisted of rocks and boulders, with a bit of tough grass and tundra vegetation. Jangbu had arranged for us to have lunch at the home of a local Nepalese family, which was an interesting and welcome break from the routine of eating lunch on the trail.

*Lunch at a Nepalese family home.
Left to right, Ed Wilcox and Curt Caughey sitting on the bench sipping tea.*

The woman of the house served us some watery stew and, of course, the traditional local milk-tea. Her two small children sat quietly on the dirt floor, looking at us shyly with inquiring eyes, while the house and everyone's lungs filled with smoke from the yak dung burning in the open fireplace. We left with a much better appreciation of primitive Nepalese life in the Himalaya.

After a few more hours of walking, and a short mid-afternoon break, we arrived at Dingboche, a desolate town with no trees but with very impressive mountain views. It was there that I noticed we had fewer porters in the group. Jangbu explained that as we consumed the food and liquids, the porters could be left behind one by one as the load was reduced.

By then our end-of-day activities were becoming routine—hydrate, relax, eat, relax, explore (if there was something new to see), hydrate, discuss the day, discuss tomorrow, hydrate, and go to bed. The beautiful sunset in Dingboche broke the routine; the sky was clear and the sun created a kaleidoscope of colors that changed from shades of orange to red and then to deep purple as it slowly disappeared behind one of the many ridges.

The porters had picked a campsite near the "Himalaya Hotel," a long, narrow stone structure that one would never identify as a hotel without the sign being visible. Inquiring about availability, Jangbu was told they were full for the night, but could always squeeze in three more paying guests. Jangbu and the porters would sleep in tents outside with several other trekkers. The altitude at

Dingboche was 4,410 meters (14,470 ft)—about the same altitude as the top of the Matterhorn—and the temperature was near freezing at night, so we looked forward to indoor accommodations for a change.

After dinner, as we prepared to settle down for the night, it became apparent that the "bed" was a long wooden bench that was to be shared with several other trekkers, stacked side-by-side like cordwood. Despite our protesting, the proprietor insisted on putting his daughter, who appeared to be about 9 ½ months pregnant, outside in a tent for the night to make room for paying guests; he assured us that she was a strong girl and would be okay.

It was not a peaceful night. Despite the snoring all around me, I had just managed to doze off when there was great commotion in the tents outside as the daughter gave birth to a baby girl. Fortunately, she had help from both her mother and a local midwife.

An eventful night at the "Himalaya Hotel,"
–24 November 1980–

Then, a few minutes after the situation had settled down, a young Sherpa came through the door and climbed into a sleeping bag already occupied by a local girl quietly sleeping next to Curt. We appreciated his attempts to be quiet as he squeezed himself in—the Sherpa into the sleeping bag, that is. However, the moaning and thrashing about that occurred shortly thereafter convinced me that about nine months down the road there would likely be another birth in the community. There was not a lot of sleep to be had that night. The next morning, we paid the proprietor and then headed up the trail to Gorak Shep. Jangbu assured us the young mother and her new daughter were doing fine. The young lovers that had been thrashing about the night before were still dead to the world, buried in that sleeping bag. We all felt a bit envious.

The plan for day five was to get to Gorak Shep, the highest and last campsite on the trip. As we walked north from Dingboche, a stunning view of Ama Dablam appeared—no wonder it is called the Matterhorn of the Himalaya. We passed a field of rock cairns, erected as memorials to climbers who had been lost on the mountains, and entered a trail that followed the lateral moraine of the Khumbu Glacier, a monstrous chunk of ice. All around, the hills were bleak, with nothing but rocks and gravel. Fortunately, the bleakness was offset by white peaks that were incomparable to anything I had ever seen. Late in the afternoon, as we came up over the last ridge of the glacier, we saw the campsite of Gorak Shep and, behind, the peak of Kala Patthar—called the "Black Rock," because it appears as a big black lump against the stunning whiteness of Pumori (7,161 meters/23,494 ft) in the background.

Gorak Shep is a frozen lakebed covered with dirt and sand at 5,164 meters (16,942 ft). It is the last acclimatization stop for most Everest expeditions. From there, it is a short walk to the Everest Base Camp (5,380 meters/17,600 ft) and from there onward, the climbing becomes much more challenging, up what the Dalai Lama has called "the steps to heaven." For us, the altitude was now taking its toll. We had to concentrate on our breathing and take slow, deliberate steps. That night we slept fitfully. Despite the Diamox, Curt was beginning to show mild symptoms of AMS, so it was good that by tomorrow we would be heading back down. The plans were to ascend Kala Patthar first thing in the morning, before Curt's symptoms worsened, and then descend as far as possible, to Dingboche, we hoped.

The next morning, November 26, 1980, was day six of our climb. It was bright, clear, and cold. We got an early start and headed up the trail to the peak of Kala Patthar, taking deep breaths and short, deliberate steps. The oxygen concentration there was less than half of that at sea level, so the going was slow. The trail took a dip through an ancient lakebed and then followed a series of switchbacks as it traversed the eastern side of the mountain, where it became quite steep until it reached the ridge of the summit. A few more minutes of scrambling over large rocks and boulders brought us to the top, at 5,643 meters (18,513 ft).

The view was a contrast of bleakness and desolation, and the stunning beauty of the enormous peaks surrounding us on all sides. The base camp was below us, about a mile away, and the triangular flank of Mount Everest rose up from the Khumbu Glacier. We sat down to rest, look around, and take some photos of the awesome view. Curt's symptoms were not improving, so, after one last look around, we headed back down the trail to Gorak Shep, where we put on our daypacks and began the return trip to Lukla, about five days away.

NAMASTE

American Thanksgiving happened to occur during our return trip to Lukla, and as we happily scampered down the trail, we complained to Jangbu about not being able to celebrate that important holiday with a turkey and all the trimmings. By then, we had established a close comradeship with him and felt comfortable fussing about it. Lo and behold, when we sat down for dinner that evening, we were served a roasted "turkey" with potatoes and vegetables. We eventually discovered that, at some point during the day, Jangbu had managed to acquire a live rooster from a local resident. That was a very special event for us, and much appreciated, especially knowing the difficulty that must have been encountered in surreptitiously acquiring what we suspected might have been a family treasure. Certainly, it was a Thanksgiving dinner to remember.

When asked about his conquest of mountains, George Leigh Mallory[44] said, "Have we vanquished an enemy? None but ourselves." Compared to going to the top of Everest—almost two more vertical miles above where we had stood—our climb to 5,643 meters (18,513 ft.) was next to nothing. Nevertheless, we returned home with great feelings of accomplishment and satisfaction. Certainly, we had vanquished ourselves in reaching the top of Kala Patthar—and for us that was more than nothing. We had accomplished our objective.

On Everest, the area above 8,000 meters (26,250 ft) is called the death zone. At that altitude, temperatures dip to extremely low levels, and any exposed skin can quickly become frozen. The cold temperatures also freeze the snow, which increases the risk of death by slipping and falling. In addition, the high winds are a potential danger. The atmospheric pressure at the top of Everest is only about one-third of the pressure at sea level, which means there is only about one-third as much available oxygen. Most climbers use bottled oxygen to make the ascent. By the end of 2006, there were 3,050 ascents to the summit of Everest by 2,062 individuals, of whom 203 died. The conditions on the mountain are so difficult that most of the corpses have been left where they fell. Some are easily visible from the standard climbing route.

As I write this in 2008, independent trekking is not allowed; each trekker must have a guide and porter at the very least, and arrange the trek through a rec-

---

44 George Herbert Leigh Mallory (1886–1924) was an English mountaineer who took part in the first three British expeditions to Mount Everest in the early 1920s. On the third expedition, in June of 1924, Mallory and his climbing partner, Andrew Irvine, both disappeared somewhere high on the northeast ridge during the final stage of their attempt to make the first ascent of the world's highest mountain. The pair's last known sighting was only a few hundred meters from the summit. Mallory's ultimate fate was unknown for 75 years, until his body was finally discovered in 1999. Whether or not they summitted before they died remains a subject of speculation and continuing research.

ognized agency. Those measures help ensure the safety of the climbers and, in addition, help support the local economy of Nepal. The trails in the Himalaya are usually quite steep, rocky, wet, and slippery—or dry and dusty—and often narrow with a considerable drop within a pace or two of the main path. Many different environmental and climatic conditions add to the challenges. It is prudent to check a couple of good trekking books and make careful note of the travel tips provided; they change from time to time. Do not forget to bring iodine to treat all water before drinking, and be sure to choose a reputable trekking agency.

To be fully appreciated, Nepal has to be experienced—from the mountain vistas to the ubiquitous mystical culture of the region. With a little preparation and good planning, a trek to Kala Patthar is, for most, a realistic goal. If I can do it, so can you; it is not necessary to be an accomplished mountaineer.

NAMASTE

Resting on the summit of Kala Patthar at 18,513 ft, with the peak of Mount Everest in the background. The peak of Everest is about two vertical miles above where we sat. Left to right: the author, guide Jangbu, Curt Caughey, and Ed Wilcox.

–November 26, 1980–

10

INTRAPRENEURIALISM

CATERPILLAR TRACTOR CO.
PEORIA, ILLINOIS, USA
(1982 — 1986)

Good management rests on a reconciliation of centralization and decentralization, or decentralization with coordinated control. From decentralization, we get initiative, responsibility, development of personnel, decisions close to the facts, flexibility—in short, all the qualities necessary for an organization to adapt to new conditions. From coordination, we get efficiencies and economies.

—Alfred P. Sloan Jr., My Years with General Motors

THE entire world experienced a recession in the early 1980s, and all markets and industries suffered badly. Construction and energy projects declined; mining operations were closed and international competition became fierce. Developing countries experienced extreme levels of debt; during the first six months of 1982, the prime rate exceeded 16 percent and the yen-dollar exchange rate exceeded 200. Japanese manufacturers—Komatsu and Hitachi—had a cost advantage as high as 40 percent over Caterpillar in some product categories, partly because of currency imbalance. To aggravate that already difficult situation, a labor strike took place at Caterpillar, which lasted seven months. Sales fell from $9.2 billion in 1981, to $5.4 billion in 1983, and in 1982, the company lost money for the first time in its history. Management had no experience dealing with such a situation—it was the first seriously challenging time for everyone. Caterpillar had no choice but to launch a program that would slash 20 percent from operating costs and over $500 million from capital expenditures. In 1980, Caterpillar announced its first significant layoff in over 20 years—average employment fell from 89,266 in 1979, to 58,402 in 1983, a reduction of over 35 percent. By 1984, six plants had been closed—the first closures in half a century. There were perceptions in the industry that Caterpillar had become arrogant and aloof, and appeared to be taking their leadership position for granted—always a dangerous sign. Some industry pundits speculated that Caterpillar was just another arrogant producer from the "rust belt" that would fade away like International Harvester, Allis Chalmers, and Euclid.

In 1982, during the middle of that upheaval, I was asked to take another assignment as the head of a division at the Caterpillar headquarters in Peoria, Illinois. It was a difficult decision for us as a family, since we were quite settled in Hong Kong and certainly enjoyed Asia. Besides, I had been on the job just long enough to establish a good working relationship with the dealers and become effective. However, I was fully aware of the challenges facing the company; it was not the time to be uncooperative. If management thought I could make a greater contribution in head office, so be it.

Compared to other regions where I had worked, I found Asia to be the most enjoyable. Its people set that region apart from all the rest. It was my experience that, generally, the ethnic Chinese tended to be smarter, more diligent, harder working, friendlier, and more attentive to their health and well-being than most. We were sad to leave Asia, not knowing that 18 years later I would have the opportunity to return—during, as it turned out, another exciting time to be there.

Upon arriving in Peoria in 1982, I was thrust into the middle of the 20 percent cost reduction program that was already underway. The company was losing money and struggling to recover, and all managers needed to downsize their organizations. That was perhaps the most difficult task that I have ever been asked to undertake in business—and there was no consolation in knowing that all other managers were required to do the same thing. Capable, loyal employees were told there were no longer jobs for them. Upon hearing the news, most either hung their heads and fought back tears or displayed various degrees of anger. Many had children in college and some were single parents trying to support infants. I struggled to put on a stoic, businesslike face while trying to be empathetic; it was impossible not to share their pain.

Real estate prices in the Peoria area were falling precipitously, and good employees walked away from their homes of many years because they no longer had a job and could not borrow enough money to sell their houses—they owed the banks more money than their homes were worth. Several families dropped their keys off at the bank, rented a trailer and headed elsewhere, looking for work. Worldwide, over 25,000 Caterpillar employees lost their jobs. The difficult task of letting people go, although it did not take long, was traumatic. Everyone was suffering and the best antidote for me was to get back to work,

INTRAPRENEURIALISM

doing what I was being paid to do.

The Service Operations Division was responsible for supporting the worldwide marketing organizations with service support for the products, including facility design, specialized service and diagnostic tooling, oil analysis equipment and programs, and service vehicles. In addition, the Division assisted with the development of the Service Information System (SIS) for dealers and the marketing programs designed to demonstrate the value of Caterpillar dealers' service capabilities. Lastly, the Division played a major role in the NPI process as the new products reached the end of the development cycle and entered production. Several support elements had to be in place with the dealers, before the new products were delivered to customers.

My position had worldwide responsibilities and provided me with the opportunity to become familiar with many more dealers and market areas. For the first time, I had the opportunity to work with dealers in South America. They were not yet up to North American standards and it was necessary to go further "back to the basics" than I ever imagined would be necessary. I became much more familiar with the many internal processes associated with handling the dealers' needs related to facilities, tools and equipment, human resources development, and warranty administration. Those experiences broadened my perspective and understanding of the whole business and proved to be immensely valuable during future years as I took on greater management responsibilities.

During that period, Donald Fites, a senior Caterpillar executive, worked hard to "break the mold" and develop a new culture designed to elicit ideas from employees and convert the organization from a centralized hierarchy to a decentralized intrapreneurial organization.[45] He was looking for ideas to start new entrepreneurial ventures within the larger organization that would not only convert cost centers to profit centers, and increase revenue and reduce costs, but also to spark entrepreneurial behavior that would change attitudes and jolt the organization out of the non-responsive state of apathy, comfort, and arrogance into which it had fallen.

A few months after I took over the Service Operations Division, it struck me that we were developing specialized tools and equipment to help dealers service the products, but there had been no serious attempt to market and promote them. It seemed to me that we could use the broad array of service tools and equipment to develop a legitimate and independent intrapreneurial business unit. After all, we already had a design team, a supply chain to manufacture and package the products, a logistics network in place, and a large number of customers all around the world. I took that idea to Bill Springer, a key member

---

45 Intrapreneurialism refers to entrepreneurial behavior practiced within a large organization.

of my team; he also became excited about it and provided invaluable assistance in making it happen.

With excitement and anticipation, we set about developing a comprehensive business plan to convince top management to approve the idea. We surveyed dealers to get the "Voice of the Customer"—how could we improve the tool development function and be more effective in providing dealers with a wide variety of tools, equipment, and supplies for their service operations? The answers were not surprising—dealers wanted better value, lower prices, better product support, and a good availability of a broader range of products than just specialized proprietary tools that no one else offered. Dealers suggested they could sell generic tools to a wide variety of businesses in the heavy equipment industry, as well as to their own customers. General-purpose tools and equipment for servicing heavy machinery were not readily available in many remote areas in the world, so the Caterpillar dealer could enjoy incremental external sales. The idea represented a legitimate intrapreneurial opportunity.

The business plan was accepted, and a letter signed by the then-Caterpillar Chairman, George Schaefer, dated September 6, 1985, announced the formation of the new venture called "Caterpillar Service Technology Group" (CSTG). I became the general manager of the group, charged with the task of making the venture happen. Another new internal venture was announced at the same time, to develop and market custom products for low-volume, specialized applications. George Schaefer's announcement defined how these ventures were to operate within the corporation:

> Although these ventures will operate as divisions of Caterpillar Tractor Co., they will be managed as separate and independent profit centers responsible for their own business planning, product development, pricing, sourcing and personnel. The managers of each venture will report to a multifunctional board of directors comprised of various Caterpillar officers and managers. These boards will in turn be responsible to the Executive Office.

Early on there was some residual doubt about whether CSTG could really become a truly autonomous group, but it did; it was certainly "breaking the mold" at Caterpillar in 1985. Our first Mission Statement summarized our vision:

> To be a constructive force in advancing and improving the technology of service in all industries that use products manufactured by Caterpillar. To serve as a catalyst and a mechanism for developing, collecting and sharing knowledge, products and information on how to attain that goal.

Donald Fites was an active champion of the decentralized intrapreneurial organization, comprised of independent business units that were more responsive to the needs of the marketplace. He became the chairman of the board of directors of CSTG. The "business unit concept" meant that revenue and costs would be tracked separately so that a meaningful profit and loss statement could drive business decisions for the unit. CSTG developed its own supplier relations, handled its own pricing and promotions, and even designed and managed its own compensation programs, including incentives—unheard of at the time within Caterpillar. We broke new ground by managing CSTG to generate incremental revenue by doing more effectively what the company was already doing—truly a leap of intrapreneurialism. The venture added new products, including shop supplies, general-purpose tools, and major service equipment, such as dynamometers, track presses, service truck bodies, and hydraulic test centers. The goal was to satisfy the total tooling and service supply needs of Caterpillar dealers and customers, and to be a low-cost and convenient one-stop shop for all service needs.

Donald Fites played a major role in leading Caterpillar through the difficulties of the early 1980s, taking care of the daily operations as well as preparing the organization for the future. He restructured the marketing functions to get employees closer to customers and dealers—a change that was long overdue. He managed a structural change from a centralized hierarchy to a decentralized intrapreneurial organization that became more responsive to the marketplace. Authority was delegated further down in the organization.

It took great courage and fortitude to implement those changes because they flew directly in the face of Caterpillar's traditional culture that centralized the vast majority of decisions in General Office (headquarters), even though the decision makers were often not close to the dealers and customers where the actual business took place. Many thought that Caterpillar's traditional culture was too entrenched to allow the changes to occur, not believing that the sacred cows could be slaughtered. However, from my early vantage point, it was a welcome change and stirred many employees out of a depressing funk caused by financial losses, layoffs, and plant closures. It soon brought new life and excitement to the organization.

During the difficult period of the early 1980s, I was able to observe how different executives behaved as they managed and led their teams. Some seemed unable to escape the drudgery of day-to-day trivia; they always looked busy, energetic, and active, but careful examination revealed that they were usually "fighting fires" and "killing alligators" in a haphazard manner without due consideration, instead of preventing fires or draining the swamp. They usually lacked courage in dealing with difficult personnel situations, tolerating them far too long. They never managed to escape the dark shadows of the trees in order to rise up and look down on the forest in the clear light of day.

In contrast, others seemed to handle difficult challenges effortlessly, with dispassionate thinking, a clear sense of purpose, and a laser-like focus on achieving results, never losing sight of the overall goal. They stayed close to the trees when necessary, but never lost sight of the forest. This has been termed the "helicopter effect," and over the years, I came to judge it an important attribute of a manager and an essential attribute of a successful leader. My experience has shown that it is not a skill to be learned; it is an innate talent to be developed and honed through training and experience. One either has it or does not. Of course, a manager without the talent can be successful, provided he/she is coached by a leader who has it. However, if neither has the talent, the organization will struggle and likely fail.

INTRAPRENEURIALISM

The story of the Caterpillar Service Technology Group—its history, its values, and the people who made it happen. CSTG was one of the company's first internal business ventures to be managed as a separate and independent profit center responsible for its own business planning, product development, pricing, sourcing, and personnel.

INTRAPRENEURIALISM

The summer of 1986 arrived. During my 20 years with Caterpillar, I had traveled much of the world and had been actively involved in many interesting situations and events that few people get to experience, all of which led to a greatly expanded knowledge and understanding of both life and international business. All the while, I had enjoyed working with many first-class people in the worldwide Caterpillar family, and frequent changes in responsibilities and challenges had prevented any possibility of boredom or restlessness creeping in. Nevertheless, on August 8, 1986, I wrote a letter to Donald Fites announcing my decision to resign from Caterpillar Inc.[46]

My nomadic lifestyle had put a severe strain on my family as we moved from Canada to the United States, to Europe, to Hong Kong, and back to the United States, continually adapting to new cultures, customs, food, languages, schools, communities, and living conditions. In addition, dealing with the pressures of my changing work situations created additional anxieties and frustrations. Eventually, it all contributed to the deterioration of my first marriage, deterioration that seemed to creep in very gradually as we lived our exciting, but hectic day-to-day lives, neglecting our relationship, and in denial of what was happening to our marriage. As the song says, "breaking up is hard to do"— especially when ending a 23-year relationship, most of which was good. We attempted to "fix" it with counseling and then decided that moving closer to family and familiar surroundings in Canada might help—that was my primary reason for leaving Caterpillar. However, the move was only a distraction; outside influences seldom heal a struggling relationship, and Betty and I separated in 1987 and divorced in 1989.

No doubt, the midlife crisis that had taken a stranglehold on me was a contributing factor. The literature describes a midlife crisis as a period of dramatic self-doubt that many middle-aged men (and some women, too) go through when they realize their life is half over and they have not yet accomplished what they set out to do—and I was a textbook example. There were other triggers as well, all of which created a desire to make significant changes to my career, marriage, and other aspects of day-to-day life. It is difficult to judge the degree to which my midlife crisis contributed to the breakdown of our marriage. It seems to me that, overall, the relationship simply died of neglect when the bad significantly outweighed the good. It might have been saved with early preventative maintenance, before the scale was too heavily weighted on the negative side, but that is mere speculation. The main thing was to learn from the experience and

---

46 In 1986, Caterpillar Tractor Co. changed its name to Caterpillar Inc.

be more attentive to the ongoing maintenance of future relationships.

In our so-called "age of enlightenment," we should all aspire to a high level of satisfaction from a personal relationship, and a relationship does not have to last forever to be a success. Certainly, suffering in silence for the sake of endurance and longevity cannot qualify as success. In contrast, a separation or divorce does not necessarily mean the relationship deserves a failing grade. Although my relationship with Betty ended, there was definite lasting value obtained. She gave me the love of three children; she taught me a lot about people and interpersonal skills; and she brought me out of my introverted self. I am certain that my life is better than it otherwise would have been had we not married. During our 23 years together—most of which were happy—it seemed our personalities merged to a degree, and after we split up, I know that the positive aspects of that merger stayed with me. It was a valuable experience. My second marriage, with Hélène, has also resulted in a merging of our personalities, from which we both benefit at times. I consider it a sign of a good relationship.

During the years between my two marriages, I was engaged, at different times, to two other women. Those relationships seemed to start out well, but they soon fell into a state of conflict and disagreement. Fortunately, they ended before a marriage took place. My relationships with Betty and Hélène were certainly not in that category; they met the test of good love—productive, secure, well adjusted, and consistent. I am confident that my emotional intelligence developed significantly during that traumatic phase of my life.

Loving another person inevitably brings joy and frustration, and a whole industry has been built up to help people either find or deal with personal relationships. There are good relationships and there are bad ones, and I have experienced both. My definition of a good relationship is very simple: it makes you feel good most of the time. And naturally, a bad relationship makes you feel bad most of the time—absurdly simple. In my experience, most people tend to think relationships are far more complicated than necessary, which only makes them more difficult to maintain and evolve.

Although it may seem an overly simplistic dichotomy to some, as I see it, a good relationship is based on good love, and a bad relationship is based on bad love. Bad love produces mood swings, depression, stress, anxiety, suspicion, and insecurity. And most importantly, bad love entails sacrifice, and some mistakenly believe that sacrifice is a virtue.

Good love, on the other hand, requires no sacrifice of yourself to your partner and no sacrifice of your partner to you. What you do for his/her happiness is important and beneficial to your own—that is not sacrifice; it benefits both parties. Good love is not unconditional; it must be earned and is therefore, conditional; it is too precious to be shared indiscriminately. Good love is a spiritual exchange for mutual benefit. Good love requires that you offer a positive value to your partner; it is the selfish pleasure of feeling worthy of someone's love, and being with someone worthy of yours. Good love may not always produce transient thrills—palpitations, flushes, and exciting allure—but it should produce a feeling that everything is right with the world. Good love makes you feel productive, secure, well adjusted, consistent, and appreciated.

Using those simple definitions, a couple can easily determine if they are in a good or bad relationship—and surprisingly, many are not sure, or being sure, prefer to stay in denial. Some believe that any love is good love, or at least better than none at all, even if it causes grief and disappointment—an abusive relationship, for example. I have watched a few people go from one bad relationship to another—each time hoping that, with "tender loving care," healing will occur and a glorious future will one day arrive—it is what I call the "wounded puppy syndrome." Often people gravitate toward bad love because it distracts them from psychological problems or simply from the need to get on with their lives. Strive for good love.

In August 1986, we relocated to Oakville, Ontario, Canada, and I joined Canadian Kenworth as Vice President of Sales and Marketing. If the previous 20 years at Caterpillar can be described as a pleasant ride with good friends on a merry-go-round, then the next several years outside of the Caterpillar "family" can be described as a frantic ride on an out-of-control roller coaster, with many devious, conspiratorial, and insecure colleagues who had marginal concern for integrity, teamwork, and good business judgment. Fortunately, I also met several great colleagues and made good friends who were exceptions to that general characterization, and I am exceedingly grateful for their support, cooperation, and friendship. Over the next several years, I leaned heavily on my experiences at Caterpillar to guide me in fighting off the attacks and surviving. When I eventually came out into the sunshine on the other side and returned to the Caterpillar world 12 years later, I was much further up the learning curve, with a vastly broadened understanding of life in the corporate jungle.

11

ANOTHER LIFE

(1976 — 1991)

If you want to run, then run a mile. If you want to experience another life, run a marathon.

—Emil Zatopek, Olympic Champion [47]

Mountaineering was not the only challenge that I imposed on myself during my time away from work. While living in Switzerland in the 1970s, long-distance running gradually became a part of my normal routine. My sole initial intent was to get fit so I could enjoy the mountains with friends on weekend outings, and climb the Matterhorn before leaving Switzerland. That required good cardiovascular fitness, and, although distance running struck me as being rather boring, it seemed like the best and most efficient way to prepare.

The thought of my completing a marathon had never approached the realm of possibility. However, as my fitness level improved, and my running distances became longer and more comfortable, I began to contemplate attempting a 10K,

---

[47] Emil Zátopek (1922-2000) was one of the greatest runners of the 20th Century. He achieved legendary status when he won the 5,000-meter, the 10,000-meter, and the marathon at the 1952 Olympic Games in Helsinki. "The Locomotive" or the "Bouncing Czech," as he came to be known, dominated long distance running from 1948 until 1954 when he won a remarkable 38 consecutive 10,000-meter races, including 11 in 1949 alone. He set 18 world records over various distances, including every record from 5K to 30K, and won four Olympic gold medals and one silver. He was the first to run a 10K under 29 minutes and the first to run 20K in one hour. In 1952 at the Helsinki Olympics, despite a doctor's warning that he should not compete due to a gland infection two months before, he won the 5,000 meter, the 10,000 meter, and the marathon, all in a span of eight days. He set a new Olympic record in all three events, and he had never run a marathon before! http://www.runningpast.com/emil_zatopek.htm.

or half-marathon. After considerable encouragement from a fellow runner, we both entered a half-marathon in support of a local charity event. Surprisingly, I managed to run continuously and finish, standing, in 1 hour and 52 minutes. That gave me confidence, and I soon began to sign up for other half-marathons. It must be emphasized that speed was not important; my only objectives were to complete the distance at a full run, enjoy the experience, and avoid injury.

After the dry, cool breezes of Geneva, running in the heat and humidity of Hong Kong presented a new challenge. In addition, it was mainly up and down hills on picturesque trails through tropical vegetation that covered much of the island. Nevertheless, there was a very large and avid group of runners in Hong Kong, and I was soon part of that group. Running became enjoyable as an end in itself; climbing mountains was no longer the motivation. I had simply become addicted to long-distance running and actually found it relaxing—a great stress reliever. My best ideas and clearest thinking often occurred while settled into the steady pace of a long run—I can't explain why.

The marathon originated from the Greek legend of Pheidippides, a soldier, who allegedly ran from the plain of Marathon to Athens, to announce that the Persians had been defeated at the Battle of Marathon, in 490 B.C. The details are sketchy, but legend has it that, after completing the run and delivering his message, he promptly dropped dead. Many years later, the organizers of the first modern Olympics, in 1896, promoted a race to commemorate the Marathon run and to popularize long-distance running. The first marathon was won by Spiridon Louis in 2 hours, 58 minutes, and 50 seconds. The length of that race was 24.85 miles, but the length was not considered too important, since all participants ran the same distance. At the 1908 Olympics in London, the race started at Windsor Castle. The distance was set at 26 miles, but 385 yards were added so that, from her viewing box, the Queen could watch the runners cross the finish line. Eventually, in 1921, the International Amateur Athletic Federation (IAAF) adopted the distance of 42.195 km, or 26.22 miles, which became the official marathon distance.[48]

Graduating from half-marathons to a full marathon was not an easy task. Nevertheless, my addiction drove me to complete six marathons in all: Hong Kong (1980 and 1981), Honolulu (1983), Chicago (1984), Calgary (1989), and Vancouver (1991). My fastest time was in Chicago, at 3 hours and 35 minutes, but Honolulu was the most exciting event. Crowds cheered us on and bands played the entire length of the route. At one point, I was suddenly startled as a spectator jumped right in front of me. I judged her to have been about 65 to 70 years old, and about 300 pounds. Besides that, she was in her birthday suit and

---

48 Sandy Treadwell, *The World of Marathons* (1987).

obviously still celebrating from the night before. I seem to recall her asking me about the possibility of taking a short break.

Long-distance runners[49] share certain idiosyncrasies; some would say they share weird personalities. Most have a fetish for fitness, some to an extreme degree. They tend to be pensive, introspective, reserved, shy, and antisocial—or at least, discriminating and selective with whom they socialize. Some of them counter these tendencies by acting overly gregarious at times, but that is not their natural inclination. Based on my own observations, I would add one more characteristic to the list—long-distance runners also tend to be rather lonely people. Whether male or female, young or old, married or divorced, most of the runners I met were in bad, or deteriorating, relationships. I was no exception, and for me, long-distance running was very therapeutic. However, once they overcame their loneliness, they generally, and rather suddenly, stopped running long distances. Forrest Gump (remember the movie?) was a classic long-distance runner and exhibited these characteristics to a tee. Many studies have shown that exercise is an excellent treatment for depression, reducing depressive symptoms by as much as 50 percent, which is about the same effect as taking medication.[50]

Expert opinions vary on how to train for a marathon. In the 1980s, the standard recommended training plan included three phases—the buildup, the stabilization, and the taper. During the buildup phase, it was recommended that average weekly mileage increase gradually to 65 to 70 over a period of 16 weeks. That was to be followed by about 8 weeks of stabilization during which the body adapted to the stress of training. During the two weeks before the event, weekly mileage gradually tapered off to about 25. That allowed the body to store reserves for the major effort demanded by the marathon.

I generally followed that plan, usually running 5 to 6 times a week, but my weekly mileage never exceeded 30—35. I alternated a hard workout with an easy one, and about every 2 weeks, I would do a long run of 12 to 15 miles. That program was enough for me, but everyone seemed to have a slightly different individual program that worked best for them.

It is necessary to stay rested because overtraining can result in diminished endurance and speed, and provoke injury. I learned to listen to my body and took an extra day or two off if I felt overly tired. Training causes muscle tissue damage and time must be allowed for the tissue to heal stronger than it was before—and build strength. Marathoning has a strong psychological component,

---

49 A long-distance runner can be defined as one who consistently runs 20 miles a week or more, year-round. This requires considerably more time, effort, and commitment than the average jogger who may do 10 miles a week or less.
50 *Harvard Health Letter*, April 2008, 2.

so mental toughness is imperative to maintain discipline, during training and while running the marathon. I encourage anyone wishing to attempt a marathon to become knowledgeable about proper preparations—before, during, and after the race.

The halfway point of a marathon is generally considered to be at about mile 20. That is because the glycogen, which is stored in the body for energy, is normally depleted after that distance, so that the body must then begin to burn stored fat.[51] Since fat does not burn efficiently, fatigue increases noticeably—it is called "hitting the wall." The most common mistake that marathon runners make is starting out too fast, which means fading too quickly and then being unable to maintain a steady pace and complete the distance.

Almost all long-distance runners complete at least one marathon, and many complete several. A few are truly addicted; they refuse to listen to their bodies and so continue to run until, literally, their bodies break down, forcing them to quit. Subsequently, they often become partially disabled, which initiates significant withdrawal symptoms, including depression. I experienced my very first running injury in the Vancouver marathon—a minor tear in the meniscus of my left knee—during cold, wet, and windy conditions. Fortunately, it was only a minor and temporary disability, but my body was talking to me, and it was time to listen. That was my last long-distance run—I did not want to risk another injury that might prevent me from enjoying other higher priority activities, such as squash, skiing, and snowboarding. Fortunately, my withdrawal symptoms were minor and I quickly became adjusted to a modest amount of exercise and activity.

Like most, I was a middle-of-the pack marathoner who never aspired to win any races. My goal, at first, was simply to get fit. Then running became both enjoyable and therapeutic—an end unto itself. If you are looking for a personal goal that offers many tangible and intangible benefits, run a marathon. You will be proud that you did, and I promise that you will then go on to accomplish other goals you had thought were beyond your abilities.

---

51 Glycogen is a form of glucose that functions as the primary short-term energy storage in our cells. It is commonly referred to as animal starch and is made primarily by the liver and the muscles.

ANOTHER LIFE

Running the first of two marathons in Hong Kong. Eventually completed six marathons: Hong Kong (1980 and 1981), Honolulu (1983), Chicago (1984), Calgary (1989), and Vancouver (1991)

12

TRUCKING ALONG

CANADIAN KENWORTH LTD.
MISSISSAUGA, ONTARIO, CANADA
(1986 — 1989)

There is only one honest impulse at the bottom of envy, and that is the impulse to punish the man with a superior capacity for happiness.
—H. L. Mencken

Kenworth was founded in Portland, Oregon, in 1910, by George and Edward Gerlinger, and became known for its custom-made trucks with the extra power needed by the truckers in the west. That tradition of custom design continues to this day. Engines, drive trains, suspension systems, frame rails, and the cross members can be custom-ordered to produce the most cost-effective configuration for a customer's specific application. In 1945, Kenworth was purchased by PACCAR Inc.[52] PACCAR continued to operate Kenworth as a separate company, which began to grow rapidly. By 1950, Kenworth trucks were operating in 27 locations outside the United States, and the product line consisted of over 30 models. In 1954, Canadian Kenworth was established to manufacture and market heavy-duty vehicles in Canada. In 1955, Kenworth became an integral part of the PACCAR organization and began production in Burnaby, B.C. By the early 1970s, Kenworth was also producing in Ste. Thérèse, Québec, just north of Montréal.

When I joined Canadian Kenworth in 1986, PACCAR had 15 factories in

---

[52] PACCAR Inc. is a multinational technology company that manufactures premium commercial vehicles sold around the world under the Kenworth, Peterbilt, and DAF nameplates. The company traces its corporate roots back to 1905, when William Pigott Sr. founded Seattle Car Manufacturing Co., to produce logging equipment at its plant in West Seattle, USA. It has established an excellent reputation for durable, reliable, and high quality products. http://www.paccar.com/.

5 countries, and its products were in use around the world. In Canada, the truck market was quite strong and the plant in Ste. Thérèse was operating at near capacity, with product being sold in both Canada and the United States. Kenworth had sales offices scattered across Canada to support the dealers assigned to each region; the distribution system was very similar to that used by Caterpillar, except that the dealers were much smaller in terms of sales, assets, and people. The sales and marketing team was well qualified and knowledgeable about the products, their applications, and the industry itself. I felt quite comfortable working with that team of professionals.

Everything about Kenworth was new for me—a new organization, new people, new products, and a new dealer organization. I fell into my traditional leadership role as the "coach" and explained the fundamentals of my management style to the team. The responsibilities of the coach are to select the team members, provide support in the form of sales tools, training, and motivation, and to create a working environment that is conducive to high productivity. Another important responsibility of the coach is to develop a "game plan"—a strategy for execution. It is important to understand that the coach is responsible for the success of the team, but he never "scores"; he can only create the system and environment that allows the players to score. In order to win, all players must work together as a close-knit team, perform their individual responsibilities, and execute the plan. Attitude and desire are extremely important; as Vince Lombardi said, a team must have a desire to win and a belief that it can win. It is not whether you win or lose that counts, it's whether you win. My management style seemed well accepted by the team, and we set out with confidence to grow the business.

After a few weeks on the job, I discovered my boss, Jerry,[53] and I shared a personality conflict and would have difficulty establishing a good working relationship. That was not the first time I had encountered such a conflict, but this time it was more intense. It was also unexpected—there had been no evidence of a problem during the interview process. Clearly, our management styles conflicted—his was primarily autocratic; mine was participatory. I was as stubborn as he was and neither could flex to the other's style, which no doubt exacerbated the situation. Jerry's background had been primarily in manufacturing, and perhaps in an adversarial environment typical of a unionized American manufacturing organization, his style may have been notably successful—no doubt it had been or, surely, he would not have been promoted to the head of Canadian Kenworth. However, as far as I was concerned, a command and control management style was not appropriate when the employees were some of

---

53 A pseudonym

the brightest people on the planet. In my experience, knowledge-workers never responded well to autocratic leadership, nor did they perform well in a culture of fear and intimidation. Our personality conflict was obvious to the entire organization; it hurt productivity and performance, and became exacerbated as the months wore on. Ironically, despite our difficulties, Jerry was a fun person and easy to be with in social settings. We enjoyed many pleasant dinners and private social events with customers, sharing "war stories" about our experiences and situations. However, on the job, it was an entirely different story. Jerry came as close to a "Jekyll and Hyde" personality as anyone with whom I have ever been associated.

Despite the difficult working environment, I had a team to coach and was determined to win in the marketplace against competition. I soon discovered that many of the Kenworth dealers had an unusually strong distrust of the company, and a few dealers carried alternate or competitive products for "protection" against the perceived risk of a sudden and surprise cancellation of the Sales and Service Agreement. I made it clear to the team that we had to rebuild trust with our dealers—mutual trust in our respective organizations. Within a few months, improved communications with dealers resulted in better understanding and cooperation, and the team was able to make remarkable progress. Dealers began to show a higher degree of confidence and commitment to the business—it was all about attitude. Progress was particularly evident in dealer development programs, especially in the two major market areas, Toronto and Montreal.

The sales team became focused on selling value and benefits, rather than trying to compete on price. Clear and consistent goals, strategies, and Key Performance Indicators (KPI) were tracked and monitored to keep the team focused on customers. It never failed to amaze me how paying close attention to customers could improve a business—and improve it quickly. A Fleet Sales Program was introduced that uncovered new sales opportunities, and market share grew significantly during 1986 and 1987—a 24 percent improvement in eight months. Simultaneously, margins improved and incremental profits were significant. This was not a typical turnaround situation, but there was certainly opportunity to improve.

Over the years, I became involved with a wide variety of packaged sales training programs designed to teach the soft skills of selling and getting the order. In my experience, most of these programs do little good, and cost a lot. Early in my career, transactional analysis (TA) was presented as the panacea to improve customer communications. Within a few years, a new methodology came along: videotaped role-playing and psychology to help us understand personality types—thinker, feeler, intuiter, sensor, or whatever (I am a thinker). I have experienced them all, and agree with those who believe this training has little effect on sales or customer satisfaction. Nevertheless, although our sales team was already quite good, we conducted several soft-skills training sessions, and I crossed my fingers and hoped the team would learn something that improved their ability to sell—I could never be sure whether they did.

Being a good sales representative is not easy, but it is simple. The best sales representatives are those who (a) have a plan, (b) establish rapport, (c) clearly point out the benefits to the buyer (a feature may or may not be a benefit), (d) explain how the benefits will solve the customer's problem, and then (e) ask for the order. The best way to learn the ropes is by going out in the field with someone who is good at it. The worst mistake would be to visit a customer, looking like a vagrant, with no useful information in hand, and nothing but a cigarette pack to take notes on—it happens more often than one would imagine. The second worst mistake is failing to ask for the order when the customer is ready to buy! The best training programs are those that take the sales rep through the actual selling process with real customers, follow up to make sure they are practicing what they were taught, and finally guarantee results.

In April 1987, I was asked to take responsibility for the manufacturing plant at Ste. Thérèse as Vice-President of Operations. Specific responsibilities included the cost reduction program, the PACCAR Integrated Quality System implementation (TQM), field service operations, and warranty administration. In addition, it had been discovered that unscrupulous practices had been going on at the plant, and the only way to clean up the mess was to make several management changes. That became my first task. The new assignment was my first experience in leading a high-production manufacturing operation, with about 1,000 unionized employees. It would be a baptism of fire. Fortunately, when faced with daunting circumstances, my determination to succeed and win usually became particularly strong.

 I began to spend two to three weeks a month at the Ste. Thérèse plant, getting to know the people and the operations there, and helping to solve problems. A high-production custom manufacturing operation has many systems and processes in place to manage operations: material flow from suppliers, bills of material, product specifications (almost every truck coming down the line was different than the one in front or behind), orders for fabricated components, surplus and obsolete inventory, and quality systems. It may strike the reader as surprising that one of the most challenging tasks was the painting rather than the manufacturing process. When customers paid $120,000 for a new truck, they expected a perfect paint job. To achieve that perfection required a "clean room," correct air pressure balance, and precise spraying equipment and application, followed by a careful drying process. Often we had to apply special paint designs with one-of-a-kind logos and pinstripes, which required skilled artisanship. It was easy to make a small mistake that would require us to start over—an expensive and time-consuming task that disrupted the flow throughout the plant and delayed delivery. Caterpillar never had to meet those exacting customized paint requirements—their customers were not as emotionally attached to their products, as were most truckers, especially owner-operators. Plant management was pleased to give me a crash course in all those processes and systems, and I rapidly climbed up a new learning curve.

The required management changes were made, and the new team came together and performed remarkably well. Unscrupulous behavior always poisons an organization and is detrimental to productivity, quality, morale, and general performance. The "bad apples" have to be dealt with expeditiously; otherwise, many people assume that unscrupulous behavior is acceptable, and the rot grows. I acted quickly to remove the poison, and the Ste. Thérèse organization became revitalized and eager to get back on a winning track. It was a pleasure to work with the new team—and a pleasure to be away from the constant conflict and the environment of fear and intimidation at the head office in Mississauga.

A major capital expenditure project, to double the capacity of the Ste. Thérèse plant, began in 1987. It had to occur without disrupting current production schedules, even though the construction would take place within the existing plant operations. It was a great lesson in professional project management, and I am pleased to say that the team's performance was excellent overall. The new management team was in place, the capital projects were on track, and the plant operations were improving according to plan.

Despite the progress in achieving record results, my conflict with Jerry continued. By late 1988, the situation was becoming intolerable—for both of us—so on December 1, 1988, I resigned from Canadian Kenworth and accepted a position as Senior Vice President and Chief Operating Officer of Canadian Foremost Ltd., in Calgary, Alberta. Despite the stress at Kenworth, the decision to resign was not spontaneous—much thought and deliberation went into it. In addition, aside from allowing me to escape a bad situation, the position at Foremost held authentic worldwide general management responsibilities for all functions of a public company (listed on the Toronto Stock Exchange), and I knew it would be a new learning experience. Canadian Foremost was a smaller company, which would require hands-on involvement in all areas of the business. Ironically, Jerry was relocated back to the United States shortly after I left.

After leaving Ste. Thérèse, I was surprised to receive the following memo from the Ste. Thérèse management team:

> To: M. E. Marwood
>
> We would all like to thank you for the assistance, leadership and guidance you gave us over the past nine months. The professionalism of your approach at systematically solving problems and tackling new projects to improve the efficiency of the plant, reduce cost of the truck or improve quality, was very well received. It is hoped that process can continue so that some day in the future we will work together as a professional team of managers in a manner you would be proud of.
>
> We hope that some of the pride you demonstrated in our product, our work and our outcome as a major truck assembly plant will rub off on all of us so that we may continue to improve on a continuous basis.
>
> It is too bad you could not continue in your position at the plant but we assume that your sales and administrative skills were needed more desperately elsewhere.
>
> Good luck in your new assignment and don't hesitate to request from us any assistance we can give you.
>
> Signed [by the nine department managers at Ste Thérèse.]

That memo made it all worthwhile. A leader is only as successful as the people he has on his team, and I was very fortunate to have a winning team at Ste. Thérèse. One month after I left operations, the team went on to achieve an all-time record for the best quality index of any PACCAR plant at the time. By the end of 1988, the plant had achieved record production numbers and record profit contribution for the organization. Those results speak for themselves, and for the team that achieved them.

> *One is apt to think of people's affection as a fixed quantity, instead of a sort of moving sea with the tide always going out or coming in but still fundamentally there: and I believe that difficulty in making allowance for the tide is the reason for half the broken friendships.*
>
> —Freya Stark

13

A TURNAROUND

CANADIAN FOREMOST LTD.
CALGARY, ALBERTA, CANADA
(1989 — 1992)

And the word is Capitalism. We are too mealy mouthed. We fear the word Capitalism is unpopular. So we talk about the free enterprise system and run for cover in the folds of the flag and talk about the American Way of Life.

—Eric A. Johnston

THE industrial off-road vehicle industry began in western Canada in 1952, when the geophysical oil exploration companies were confronted with the muskeg swamps of northern Alberta. That was the year W. Bruce Nodwell, the founder of Canadian Foremost Ltd., developed the first specialized vehicle to move men and equipment through difficult terrain. A decade later, those machines had established a reputation as being the best for doing the job, particularly in soft unstable conditions. The early designs were tracked machines that traveled over soft ground, carrying very heavy loads. Later, in the 1970s, all-terrain wheeled vehicles were developed to reach out to other markets. By 1990, Foremost's product line consisted of approximately 20 different models with carrying capacities ranging from 5 to 70 tons. Production volumes were relatively low because most units were individually designed to suit the customer's specific needs. Usually, those needs were to accommodate a wide variety of extreme climatic conditions—tropical, arctic, or desert. Therefore, production methods needed to be flexible to accommodate the unique demands of custom-built, handcrafted products. A significant number of Foremost's units used Caterpillar engines.

Initially, the primary markets included northern Canada and Alaska; how-

A TURNAROUND

ever, during the 1980s, the reputation of the products had generated significant interest from international markets and, by 1990, about 75 percent of sales were to foreign customers in South America, the Middle East, Africa, China, and the USSR. In March 1986, Foremost signed a commercial agreement with the USSR State Committee for Science and Technology, the Soviet Ministry of Gas, and the Soviet Ministry of Oil and Gas Construction, to develop a large all-terrain tracked carrier to haul large pipeline construction equipment, and oil and gas equipment, over the arctic tundra of northern Siberia. The carrier, called the "Yamal," was the largest of its kind in the world. The product was successfully demonstrated to Soviet dignitaries in March of 1988. The success of the project resulted in the formation of a joint venture with the Soviets, called Foremost Progress.

In March 1988, Foremost diversified its activities with the acquisition of Drill Systems International Ltd., a company that manufactured and sold specialized drill rigs that were used in mineral exploration, water wells, and environmental sampling. They used a unique "reverse circulation" technology, which provided more rapid and cost-effective geological sampling than the traditional core drilling method. Drill Systems International served many of the same customers in the same industry as Foremost, which added synergy to the relationship.

When I joined Foremost in 1989, it was a victim of the worldwide recession, particularly the drastic slowdown in the oil and gas industry. Customers had deferred capital spending for exploration as they adopted a "wait and see" attitude. Foremost was also suffering from the cost of supporting the previous year's acquisition of Drill Systems International. During my interview, I was made aware of that situation, but upon arriving at Foremost, I discovered the company to be in much worse condition than expected: It was losing money, carrying a lot of debt, and hemorrhaging cash—a formula for disaster. This was very disconcerting and I began to wonder if I had made a mistake taking on the responsibility. Certainly, I wished I had investigated the situation more thoroughly.

Clearly, a turnaround was necessary to staunch the flow of cash, turn the corner toward profitability, and put the business back on a path to sustained recovery. A turnaround is the reversal of performance from decline and failure to recovery and success. The first stage was to execute a crash program to stop the decline (called the consolidation stage), followed by actions to strengthen operations, lower the break-even point, and become profitable (called the growth stage). Simple, across-the-board cost cutting is a defensive tactic that can hurt long-term sustained recovery, and therefore, it was necessary to focus on areas that do not harm core business operations.

It was not particularly important how Foremost had arrived in that state of

A TURNAROUND

crisis, but there were many contributing factors: the markets had softened significantly, overhead costs had swollen, debt was growing, the organization was overgrown for its level of revenue, and there was anxiety, as well as inaction, in the upper echelons. The problems were obvious. If professional turnaround consultants had been brought in, they would have looked at the various business segments, identified what was profitable and what was not, and then would have advised, "fix it, sell it, or shoot it." The desired outcome was to get the six key business elements—purpose, strategy, operations, organization, resources, and environment—strengthened and working in harmony.

Almost all employees knew that immediate action had to be taken in order to turn the business around; however, Jack Nodwell, the son of the founder and CEO, was too emotionally close to the employees and the business to make the necessary hard decisions. After all, it was their "family," and they had been together for years. It became obvious that my job as an outsider with no emotional baggage was to do what had to be done. It was up to me to take charge of the planning and execution necessary to stabilize the business and then nurse it back to health. The problems were obvious and the situation was urgent—we did not have a lot of time to make it happen. I had never been involved in an urgent turnaround before and had to learn fast—really fast. In 1989, the tried-and-true Odiorne problem-solving methodology was the only one that I knew well enough to trust.

My first order of business was to develop a written turnaround plan of action that was acceptable to the Board of Directors. It consisted of four elements: 1) develop commitment to the need for change and instill a sense of urgency, 2) define and execute clear objectives and shared expectations, 3) develop and implement a communications plan, and 4) establish a sound financial and management reporting system. The plan was approved and its execution begun. It started with an all-employee meeting to develop a Mission Statement that clearly identified the kind of business we were in, the kind of organization we wanted to be, and the strategic direction for the future. We hired a professional facilitator to conduct the strategic planning exercise with every single employee participating. A camel has been described as a horse designed by a committee, and that is how I would describe our Mission Statement. The facilitator was more concerned with including everyone's random comments than with identifying a coherent direction for the business. Nevertheless, at that stage of the process, even though it was not perfect, it was a starting point—besides, we all knew what had to be done.

During the strategic planning exercise, we identified what was working and what was not, and we gathered ideas from the employees. The workers in the trenches always know what the problems are and often know how to fix them.

A TURNAROUND

Some hard decisions had to be made and I needed both their input and their support. Objectives and work plans were developed; every employee was told what was happening and the direction in which management planned to take the business. That was the only way in which employees could support the hard decisions. Most employees became committed to the plan and joined the turnaround team, eager to make it successful. In a turnaround situation, it is not possible to over-communicate—employees, shareholders, and the public all had to be kept fully informed.

During 1989, the company took several turnaround actions, including: selling an under-performing business unit that was consuming free cash flow; slashing costs associated with the Russian joint venture; and restructuring, consolidating, and integrating the vehicle operations with the Drill Systems operations. All operational processes underwent in-depth study—with regard to engineering, product development, materials management, accounting, sales, and marketing functions. The idea was to identify opportunities for further cost reductions without cutting into essential capabilities. In addition, production facilities were consolidated to eliminate duplicate functions, and product support activities for the various business units were combined for additional synergy. At one point, we had a few firm customer orders but did not have enough cash to buy the raw materials needed to build the product—talk about frustration! Fortunately, the customer helped us through our dilemma by advancing the necessary funds.

In April 1990, I became President, Chief Operating Officer, and a member of the Board of Directors. Although cash flow had improved, profitability was still negative and more cost cutting needed to be done. Therefore, a new business plan for 1990 was developed to further restructure the business, reduce costs, and establish a lower break-even point. Throughout the transition period, it was critical to work closely with the banks to maintain their trust and confidence that the plan was both realistic and achievable—and that the turnaround was working.

By 1991, it was obvious that the plan was working and significant improvements were evident—overhead costs were down by over 35 percent, inventory levels had dropped by over 38 percent, cash flow had turned positive, and the company had reached the break-even point. In summary, recovery actions had included a restructuring of management and operations, reorienting the product/market focus, improving staff productivity, and aggressively lowering costs in all areas. The organization became revitalized and was on a path toward achieving sustainable growth.

Just as we were turning the corner toward sustained profitability, a group of outside investors expressed interest in making a significant equity investment

A TURNAROUND

in the business and taking control. We had been in casual negotiations with them for several months and I supported the transaction in principle, because it would give the company greater ability to expand into the energy services business. Negotiations seemed to be going well and a tentative closing date was scheduled for several weeks away. I needed a break from the stress and intensity of performing the turnaround and decided it was a good time to schedule some vacation. Little did I suspect that our friendly negotiations were going to turn negative.

A Board meeting was called suddenly, and deliberately, during my absence. The purpose was to expedite the closing of the transaction, obviously, without my approval. The new shareholders were to be appointed to the Board and given broad authority to unilaterally amend my employment contract and to take "dramatic action" in managing operations without further approval of the Board. Clearly, my fiduciary duties and responsibilities as an officer and voting member of the Board were being usurped and abrogated. I was being forced out. No wonder they did not want me at that Board meeting.

In takeover situations, these events are not uncommon and I understood that my role was to be assumed by the new shareholders—I was no longer needed to provide leadership. Therefore, March 26, 1992, was my last day with Canadian Foremost, and I left with significant regret and disappointment that the situation was not handled with much more professionalism and integrity, especially after I had successfully led the development and implementation of a winning turnaround plan for the business. Foremost issued the following news release on March 24, 1992:

> Canadian Foremost Ltd.
>
> News Release
>
> Calgary, Alta. —March 24, 1992—Canadian Foremost Ltd. of Calgary, is pleased to announce the appointment of Mr. Murray Edwards and Mr. Jim Grenon to the Board of Directors. Mr. W. Bruce Nodwell, who has served the Board since 1971, and who developed tracked vehicles as early as 1952, has retired from the Board.
>
> Mr. Maurice E. Marwood has resigned as President of the Company and Mr. J.H. (Jack) Nodwell will resume responsibility for the overall direction and management with the assistance of the new Board. The Directors would like to take that opportunity to thank Mr. Marwood for the leadership he has provided as President.
>
> With the previously announced Bronco acquisition and an investment of $150,000, a total of 476,960 Class A non-voting and 399,085 Class B voting shares have been issued to Mr. Grenon's holding company, Grencorp Management Inc., Mr. Murray Edwards

A TURNAROUND

and Mr. Ronald Mathison. The purchase price was $1.39 for Class A shares and $163 for Class B shares. Grencorp Management Inc., Mr. Edwards, and Mr. Mathison have acquired their investment as part of a merchant banking venture with the firm Peter's & Co. Capital Limited.

The Company currently has 2,298,656 Class A non-voting and 1,923,347 Class B voting shares issued and outstanding. Foremost is a public company listed on the Toronto Stock Exchange under the symbol CFY.A and CFT.B.

FOR FURTHER INFORMATION, PLEASE CONTACT

Jack Nodwell,

Chairman & CEO

Unfortunately, that was not the end of it. Subsequent events occurred that continued to "rub salt in the wound," but recalling them would serve no useful purpose. Suffice it to say that I periodically reflect back on my Foremost experience as a low point in my career; nevertheless, it was a valuable firsthand learning experience about how greed and the desire for power can override concern for integrity. My only regret was not being able to continue working with that team of dedicated and loyal employees who had made our turnaround a success—the success that, ironically enough, attracted the outside investors. I have often wondered whether the events that unfolded were part of a hidden agenda that dated back to when I was initially hired—the timing of the takeover was suspicious.

It is interesting to observe how different people react to an employment termination. One colleague at Foremost, who met the same fate as I, decided to go off into the woods for three months to vegetate—saying he needed a break for some introspection. That was not for me. I immediately embarked on a journey to find another position, following the traditional approach of contacting numerous recruiters and working my established network of business contacts, knowing that most positions are filled without involving recruiting agencies. For me, the process of searching was enough of a break; in fact, it was a dramatic break from the previous few months experience at Foremost. I successfully spent the first half of 1992 searching for another career assignment, and on June 17, 1992, I became Vice-President and General Manager of Robbins & Myers Canada Ltd., in Brampton, Ontario, Canada.

A TURNAROUND

The "Magnum," one of Canadian Foremost's largest off-road vehicles designed for carrying heavy loads over soft ground.

A TURNAROUND

About a year earlier, while still working in Calgary, I had met Hélène Stein; we were married on July 4, 1992, and relocated from Calgary, Alberta, to Brampton, Ontario. Hélène had two sons from a previous marriage—Lawrence and Andrew; the younger son, Andrew, moved to Brampton with us and Lawrence went to live with his father in Windsor, Ontario. This was a difficult adjustment period, mainly for Andrew as he struggled to adjust to a new school and deal with a new stepfather—one he would rather not have had around. However, we accommodated each other and eventually became quite close.

Married Hélène in Calgary, July 4, 1992. Back row: Lawrence and Dale; Front row: Andrew, the author, Hélène, and Pamela.

14

MIXING IT UP

ROBBINS & MYERS CANADA LTD.
BRAMPTON, ONTARIO, CANADA
(1992 — 1995)

It is very difficult to make predictions, especially about the future.
—Niels Bohr

The businessman who says that business affairs and human rights are separate subjects simply hasn't thought very deeply about the system of which he is a part. The free market—call it capitalism, if you desire—is built around freedom of participation by sellers...freedom of choice by buyers...freedom for individuals to choose their own way of life in terms of goods and services they elect to buy...and determination by the free buyer (not the government) as to what succeeds and fails in the marketplace.[54]

—Lee L. Morgan, former Chairman of the
Board of Caterpillar Tractor Co.

Robbins & Myers Inc.[55] began in 1878 as a gray iron foundry in Springfield, Ohio. Its primary business involved supplying high-quality castings for agricultural machinery and bicycles. Later, the product line expanded to include a variety of motor powered fans. In 1929, the company began manufacturing its own line of hoists, cranes, and winches for use in assembly line operations; in 1936, it entered the industrial pump market and became the first North American licensee of the progressing cavity pump design, invented by

---

54 Lee L. Morgan, text from an address, Lecture-Arts Series, Bradley University, Peoria, Illinois, April 5, 1978.
55 http://www.robbinsmyers.com/index.php.

the French scientist René Moineau.[56] Early Robbins & Myers progressing cavity pumps served general industrial markets, where they rapidly became known for their ability to handle the most difficult pumping applications. Over the years, after several acquisitions and divestitures, the company became focused on providing products and services for the management of the movement, properties, and transformation of fluids.

In early 1992, Robbins & Myers purchased the assets of Prochem Mixing Equipment Ltd. of Brampton, Ontario. Prochem manufactured high-efficiency agitators and mixers for use in waste treatment, oil and gas, pulp and paper, food, pharmaceutical, and chemical process industries. Several of the products were custom-made, including one with an 18-foot diameter impeller. The products continued to be marketed under the Prochem name, although the company had by then been renamed Robbins & Myers Canada and given the worldwide mandate to design, manufacture, and sell the Prochem line, as well as sell and market the line of Robbins & Myers pump products in Canada. The acquisition of Prochem and the broadened mandate of Robbins & Myers Canada created the need to establish new leadership for the business. That was my challenge: a post-acquisition integration of the Prochem organization and business operations into the structure and culture of Robbins & Myers Ltd.

Once again, I established myself as the "coach" and set about building a winning team. I spent significant time visiting key customers and dealers to establish effective relationships and to reassure them that the changes would be to their benefit. A three-year Strategic Plan was developed in order to set the direction for the long-range growth of the business. Fortunately, it was not a crisis and the changes could be implemented methodically to minimize disruption and ensure a smooth integration. The employees of Prochem, and the Robbins & Myers management team at the head office in Ohio, were all very professional, and I was completely comfortable working with them.

Leading a post-acquisition integration was certainly different from the turnaround challenge at Foremost; however, several situations were comparable and required a similar approach. For example, Prochem had been a privately held company with a strong, entrepreneurial and autocratic leadership, whereas Robbins & Myers followed professional management methods with a participative style of leadership, similar to my own. The employees at Prochem were obviously concerned about how those fundamental differences would be sorted

---

56 In 1930, René Moineau invented the Progressing Cavity Pump (PCP). In a progressing cavity pump, a rotor turns inside a stator, producing a steady flow based on drive speed. Progressing cavity pumps are ideal for pumping viscous, particulate, abrasive or fragile products. Changing the geometry of the rotor governs the pump's output. Therefore, a PCP can be designed to deliver precise and continuous flow of even the most difficult materials, which makes it possible to match a PCP with virtually any customer application.

out. Duplicate resources were rationalized and certain redundant positions were carefully eliminated while retaining the important technical and management resources. Practices were well entrenched at Prochem, but few policies and procedures were consistent with those of Robbins & Myers. In particular, Robbins & Myers had well-defined disciplines related to design and product development; getting those disciplines accepted was difficult because the engineers saw no reason to change what had been working for many years. Similarly, changing sales administration practices to improve the quality and professionalism of the proposals to customers met resistance.

In January 1993, Robbins & Myers Canada signed a distribution agreement with Peacock Inc. to sell and service Prochem mixers in the provinces of Ontario and Québec. Peacock Inc. had already been marketing Moyno pumps for the previous year.[57] Later the same year, Robbins & Myers acquired JWI Inc. of Holland, Michigan, which manufactured and sold a line of small portable mixers for use in the food and chemical processing industries and in the wastewater treatment industry. Those products perfectly complemented the larger industrial mixers manufactured by Robbins & Myers Canada. I was involved in the due diligence process and the negotiations leading up to the JWI Inc. acquisition—another interesting learning experience for me. The JWI Inc. manufacturing operations were moved from Holland, Michigan, to Brampton, Ontario, in September 1993.

We also undertook a major project to install a new Enterprise Resource Management System (ERM) that affected the entire organization. Starting at square one, we found it necessary to develop compatible part numbers, bills of materials, routings, and all the accounting components of the system. It was an agonizing process but had to be done in order to effect the integration of the new business units.

New human resource policies and procedures had to be written to harmonize performance evaluations, job classifications, and salary ranges with those of the Robbins & Myers organization. In addition, it was necessary to comply with the Canadian Employment Equity and Pay Equity legislation. Dealing with all of those key issues was disruptive to the organization, but, again, essential to the process.

Then, in late 1993, Robbins & Myers made a decision to become ISO9001 certified. That fad had not totally disappeared and a few of our larger customers wanted their key suppliers to be certified. The documentation required for certification was onerous and the pressures of day-to-day business delayed its

---

57 Peacock, Inc was a distributor of high performance engineered industrial, instrumentation and process control products, world-class pumps and engineering services. Effective January 2005 Peacock, Inc. changed its name to Weir Canada, Inc., a business unit of Weir Services Division.

completion. In an internal newsletter, the Manager of Quality Assurance for Robbins & Myers Ltd. made the following comment:

> First and foremost, it will benefit our customers by insuring they receive the highest quality products in terms of design, materials, workmanship and testing. It also differentiates Robbins & Myers' products from our competitors and enhances the *perceived image* of our products in the marketplace. Finally, it assures that we can meet or exceed the quality specifications of customers throughout the world. [Emphasis added]

The key words of that statement were "perceived image," because as long as we were working toward certification, we received the same treatment by customers as if we were certified. The final audit was scheduled for September 1994, but it never quite happened and there was no discernable effect on our sales results.

In May of 1994, Robbins & Myers completed more acquisitions, including Chemineer, Pfaudler, and Edlon. Chemineer manufactured mixing and agitation equipment for the process industries in direct competition to the mixing products manufactured by Robbins & Myers Canada. Pfaudler manufactured glass-line steel storage and reactor vessels for the chemical processing and pharmaceutical industries. Edlon designed and fabricated coated fluoropolymer equipment for both the process and electronic industries. Those acquisitions further expanded Robbins & Myers' focus on fluid management and created synergies in technology, products, and international marketing.

Chemineer happened to have a business unit in Canada and I expected to lead another post-acquisition integration. However, it was not to be. Chemineer's industrial mixer business in the United States was larger than the Prochem mixer business in Canada, so the management in Dayton, Ohio, decided to move the Canadian operations to Ohio and integrate them into Chemineer.

No doubt, it was the correct decision; unfortunately, it made my position redundant. Robbins & Myers wanted me to stay until the transition was completed, and structured a retention incentive and severance package for me that was accepted on January 13, 1995. My last day at Robbins & Myers Canada was March 15, 1995—the end of another short-term assignment, the third one in a row since leaving Caterpillar. Fortunately, the President of the Fluids Handling Group, Alan Cockrell, handled my situation in a very professional manner and maintained the company's integrity right up to the end.

I immediately set out in search of another opportunity, and soon joined with Crane Canada Ltd. as President and a member of the Board of Directors. The company was a subsidiary of Crane Co., a diversified manufacturer of highly engineered products, headquartered in Stamford, Connecticut.

The opportunity presented a dilemma because Crane was primarily a consumer products company, manufacturing and selling a range of indoor plumbing fixtures made of enameled steel, pottery, and fiberglass—a business well outside my scope of experience. However, they were looking for professional management and leadership skills rather than product or industry knowledge, and so I underwent comprehensive interviews in both Canada and the U.S. After reasonable study and deliberation, I accepted the assignment. In March of 1995, immediately after the conclusion of the transition at Robbins & Myers, I relocated to Montréal and joined Crane Canada Ltd.

MIXING IT UP

The young and capable management team at Robbins & Myers Canada, Ltd. completed a successful post-acquisition integration of Prochem Ltd.

15

A SILK PURSE FROM A SOW'S EAR?

CRANE CANADA LTD.
MONTRÉAL, QUÉBEC, CANADA
(1995 — 1998)

Resolution:

I am resolved to conduct my business in the strictest honesty and fairness; to avoid all deception and trickery; to deal fairly with both customers and competitors; to be liberal and just to employees; and to put my whole mind upon the business.

—Richard Teller Crane

Richard Teller Crane moved to Chicago from New Jersey in 1855. On July 4 of the same year he issued the above resolution and formed R. T. Crane & Bro. with his brother Charles. The company manufactured and sold brass goods and plumbing supplies, and it supplied pipe and steam-heating equipment for large buildings throughout the city. Later the firm expanded and eventually manufactured engines and steam pumps. By 1890, it changed its name to Crane Co. By then the company had sales offices in Omaha, Kansas City, Los Angeles, and Philadelphia. During the 1920s, Crane was the world's leading manufacturer of valves and fittings. In 1959 Thomas M. Evans acquired Crane and proceeded to turn it into a global conglomerate that made aerospace equipment as well as plumbing supplies.

Indoor plumbing was becoming popular in the early 1900s, and Crane Co. capitalized on that trend by introducing matching fixtures—toilet, tub, and lavatory—with distinctive colors and harmonious designs. Through careful advertising, promotion, and creative design, Crane successfully glamorized affordable bathroom fixtures for the average North American consumer.

Crane entered Canada in 1906 with a modest plumbing and heating whole-

A SILK PURSE FROM A SOW'S EAR?

sale business in Winnipeg. By the time I joined the organization in 1995, the business had expanded to include plants in Stratford and Trenton, Ontario, and St. Jean, Québec. A complete product line was available to satisfy discriminating tastes—enameled steelware, pottery, and modular fiberglass and acrylic products.

My assignment at Crane turned out to be another very turbulent experience. The head office in Stamford expected us to make a "silk purse from a sow's ear." The main problem was the high-cost structure of the plant in St. Jean, Québec. There had been no significant capital improvements for several years and the manufacturing methods were not much different from when the plant was originally built in 1931. Methods and processes were severely antiquated, especially compared to the modern state-of-the-art plants against which we were competing. In addition, Crane was recovering from a lingering product problem that represented a significant liability associated with a class action lawsuit and the settlement of insurance claims. Fortunately, the other two manufacturing plants in Trenton and Stratford, Ontario, were modern and much more productive and cost-effective than the St. Jean plant.

In 1995, when I joined Crane as President, the company was selling almost exclusively to the wholesalers, which, in turn, sold to the retailers and contractors. Fearing a backlash from the wholesalers, the previous management had made no serious attempt to sell direct to the big-box retail stores—RONA, Home Hardware, Canadian Tire, and The Home Depot—even though the strong and growing DIY (Do-It-Yourself) segment shopped at those stores.

We needed volume to lower the per-unit costs of production, so I decided to "kill the sacred cow" by cutting out the wholesalers as intermediaries, and selling directly to the retailers. Fortunately, the big-box stores eagerly accepted our products, and sales exceeded expectations. There was no significant backlash from the wholesalers, because Crane had a good reputation, and therefore, both the wholesale and retail outlets wanted to sell the products. It is often surprising how a perceived problem, which turns out to be nothing more than a ghost, can prevent an organization from doing the right thing.

Selling to the wholesale distributors involved a system of rebates that struck me as a bit odd. It worked this way: The manufacturer, in effect, invoiced the wholesalers for more than the wholesaler would eventually have to pay for the product. The "overcharge" was held in reserve by the manufacturer until it was paid as a rebate (refund) at the end of the year. As I saw it, we sat on a big chunk of our customers' cash during the year—money that we owed them but did not remit until the rebate was paid at the end of the year.

Why was that practice deemed necessary? Remarkably, the salespeople working for the wholesalers knew the cost-of-goods-sold and were allowed to discount away most of the profit. Therefore, the funds (rebate) that we held back until the end of the year represented a significant portion of the wholesalers' profits for that year. That did not make much sense to me. If the wholesalers had carefully managed their selling prices and margins—in other words, their salespeople—they could have enjoyed that rebate money as working capital throughout the year.

At an industry association meeting one day, I suggested that instead of paying an annual rebate, we could pay it semiannually. My idea was enthusiastically accepted. Then I suggested, why not pay it monthly? That idea met with hesitation because they could see where I was going with my logic. Finally, I asked why not just include it on the face of every invoice so that margins could be higher on every transaction. That provoked strong objections because it required that they modify their entire selling process. I had to retreat, go along with the rest of the industry and play the annual rebate game.

Had that concept been proposed to the previous organizations at which I had worked, it would have been met with hysterical laughter—why would you want to let your suppliers sit on your cash that could be earning interest in your bank account instead of theirs? However, to eliminate the rebate system, one would have to manage prices, margins, and the selling process very carefully. The amount of the rebate was usually a function of the volume of business during the year (like a volume discount); thus, some considered it to be an incentive to buy more. However, a rush to buy more at the end of the year to get a higher rebate only meant that they bought less the following year, since managing inventory turnover was obviously important.

In 1986, Bill Smith, at Motorola, studied six decades of quality improvement methodologies to find a way to reduce variations in manufacturing process outputs. He was inspired by previous luminaries and developed a new structured, data-driven, problem-solving methodology he called Six-Sigma.[58] Six-Sigma asserts that business processes can be Defined, Measured, Analyzed, Improved, and Controlled (DMAIC). Those five phases logically defined problems, implemented solutions based on underlying causes, and utilized the best practices for holding the gains and making sure that the solutions stayed in place.[59] The methodology was designed to eliminate waste in business operations and prevent defects in any process. It employed tools of breakthrough statistics, quan-

---

58   Numerous books and references on Six-Sigma are available on the Internet and in book form. For example: http://www.isixsigma.com/.
59   It was intriguing to me, and somewhat ironic, that except for the statistical tools that Six-Sigma applied to analyze the data, the DMAIC methodology was almost identical to George Odiorne's six problem-solving steps that I was taught shortly after joining Caterpillar 30 years before.

titative benchmarking, process diagnostics, and control techniques—standard methods used by Certified Quality Engineers. While developing Six-Sigma, Bill Smith followed the Crosby principle, which stated that preventing defects was preferable to inspecting for quality and correcting defects, and that quality should be measured in monetary terms.[60] However, unlike Crosby, Smith did not expect zero defects—just almost zero. To achieve the Six-Sigma quality standards, only 3.4 defects per million opportunities are allowed (DPMO). Although that goal is virtually unachievable, gains are realized through the process of working toward it.

Crane Co. decided to implement Six-Sigma throughout the organization, and in 1996, I was trained as a Six-Sigma Deployment Champion during an intensive course spread over 14 consecutive 12-hour days. To complete the course successfully, managers had to demonstrate their knowledge by applying several of the Six-Sigma statistical techniques to sample data used in the case studies. That training convinced me that Six-Sigma could be a powerful methodology when applied correctly.

At Crane, we immediately launched several Six-Sigma projects in an attempt to lower manufacturing costs and improve productivity. Those projects resulted in some token changes to the equipment, processes, and management structure. Some cost savings were realized, but not enough to overcome the underlying problem. The basic disease was still thriving—a labor-intensive, antiquated manufacturing process with a high-cost structure—and it was not going to be cured without major capital investment.

In the early 1990s, Stern Stewart & Co.[61] had launched a new management tool they called Economic Value Added (EVA™). EVA was promoted as a way to "translate the theories of modern finance and economics into practical solutions." In calculating business performance, EVA only recognized the earnings that exceeded the cost of the capital required to generate those earnings. In 1996, Crane Co. introduced EVA™ to measure the performance of its various business units and to determine the performance bonus for the business unit managers.

Indeed, it is true that in order to create wealth, profit must exceed the cost of

---

60 Philip B. Crosby, *Quality is Free* (1980), introduced the "Zero Defects" quality standard. The main principles of Crosby's program were that preventing defects is preferable to inspecting for quality and then correcting those defects, and that quality should be measured in monetary terms—the Price of Nonconformance (PONC). Quality was achieved when the product met the customer's needs—"fitness for use." In other words, an inexpensive watch could be a quality product if it met the customer's expectations; it did not have to be a Rolex.

61 http://www.sternstewart.com/ny/.

A SILK PURSE FROM A SOW'S EAR?

capital. It seemed like a good performance indicator, but I soon discovered that EVA™ discouraged capital investments precisely at the time they were needed by Crane Canada to reduce costs and become competitive. In fact, adopting EVA™ encouraged avoidance of new investments—precisely an antigrowth strategy. EVA™ encouraged managers to reduce assets (that is, milk the business) so that results would look better in the short term and our bonuses would be bigger! Unfortunately, we implemented EVA™ to the detriment of shareholder value and the long-term viability of the business. EVA™ is not a panacea. There are better metrics to measure business performance.[62]

We were squeezed between the pressure to achieve impossible returns for the shareholders and the pressure of not having the tools and capabilities in place to make it happen. We developed a variety of alternative scenarios but none looked very attractive given the internal problems, the excess capacity in the industry, the political uncertainty, and an anemic economy. Although results were modestly improving, they were still mediocre with little chance of getting much better.

I do not have the gene for keeping quiet, for "going with the flow," or for standing on the sidelines—I need to be in control, to take action, and to show progress. Therefore, at each quarterly review meeting, I pushed for a longer-term solution. That became an irritation to top management in Stamford and created strained relations. The HR professionals would describe the situation as "a difference of opinion regarding the strategic direction for the business."

During previous years, the parent company, Crane Co., had made several lukewarm attempts to find a buyer for the business; but nothing happened. The price may have been too high, given the serious structural problems—any buyer could see them immediately. Management in Stamford fully understood the situation but continued for years to procrastinate instead of making the decision to either divest or invest. However, procrastination is a decision not to take action where action is needed, and these problem were not going away by themselves; in fact, they became more serious every time a competitor invested in a new high-technology, state-of-the-art manufacturing operation anywhere in the world. Mr. Evans, the CEO, was not one to be indecisive and I strongly suspect he was reluctant to divest of the business that had been most closely associated with the Crane name from the very beginning. You mention "Crane" anywhere in North America and most people immediately think of high-quality, glamorous bathroom fixtures. It had to be a tough decision.

It soon became evident from the industry grapevine that top management in Stamford was surreptitiously orchestrating my departure—which made me

---

62   Carl W. Stern and Michael S. Deimler, eds., *On Strategy*, 2nd ed. (2006), 240.

A SILK PURSE FROM A SOW'S EAR?

wonder about the significance of the resolution made by Richard Teller Crane when he first started the company in 1855. Fortunately, the professionalism of Hill Clark, the President of Crane Co., and Richard Phillips, the Director of Human Resources, salvaged the situation, and in October 1997, I accepted a reasonable severance agreement and left the company at the end of the year. It was the right decision. I left with the knowledge that several improvements had been implemented that increased the value to the shareholders and a potential buyer, despite the inherent structural problems that still existed.

A few years later, the inevitable happened and the company was sold to Crane in the United States and is now called Crane Plumbing Corporation, a wholly owned subsidiary of Crane Plumbing Limited USA.[63] It is no longer part of Crane Co., the original company. Divesting of the business was the right thing to do, and should have been done many years earlier. Crane Plumbing Corporation continued to operate two facilities—a pottery in Trenton, Ontario, and a steel and acrylic manufacturing operation in Stratford, Ontario. The St. Jean plant was closed, of course.

※

Company founders look upon retirement as something between euthanasia and castration.

—Leon A. Danco

The severance agreement with Crane included outplacement services, so I had a nice office in downtown Montréal to use during my search process. One day in December of 1997, shortly after the Crane assignment ended, I took a break to enjoy a coffee in a small café on Rue Sherbrooke in Montréal. The temperature was around minus 10°F. The wind was gusting around the corner of the building at about 30 mph and the windchill felt like minus 40°F. Having been in the rat race for 32 years, I was contemplating retirement—recently the idea had been lurking in my brain more frequently than I wanted to admit. The dictionary gives a variety of definitions for retirement:

1. To leave a job/career voluntarily, at or near the usual age for doing so;
2. To leave a place, position or way of life and go to a place of less activity;
3. To stop engaging in daily activities and go to bed.

That particular day, the third definition seemed quite appealing; however, I had a fear of being destitute, remember, and the fear periodically emerged and drove me on. Besides, what would I do if I retired? Surely, I was not yet beyond

---

63 http://www.CranePlumbing.com .

A SILK PURSE FROM A SOW'S EAR?

the point of making a useful contribution. Certainly, matching wits with a fish, playing shuffleboard on a cruise ship, or trying to hit a little white ball into a hole had no appeal.

There are already over 70,000 centenarians in the United States; the number doubled during the 1980s and again during the 1990s. In 1999, the U.S. Census Bureau estimated that by 2050 there would be over 800,000 centenarians.[64] My mother and her brother lived to be over 90, so I could live for another 25 or 30 years. I wondered how much money it would take. Did we have enough? Enough is a relative concept, of course, because it simply depends on the lifestyle to which you have become accustomed, or would like to become accustomed. Numerous websites offer Retirement Planners to help us get a feel for what it is going to take, but they always want us to make assumptions, and if we make the ones that truly represent our aspirations, most of us would have to keep working forever.[65] The cessation of paid work is not accompanied by a cessation of expenses.[66] Each year *Fortune* magazine publishes a special investors' issue with a headline that reads, "Retire Rich: Take Control of your Future." This, of course, is simply to sell more magazines to the baby boomers because I have never discovered much advice beyond "save more, invest more and spend less." Now there's a novel idea.

I have occasionally made presentations to young, aspiring business people at universities or business events, and describe life as a three-legged stool. The three legs represent work, play, and love. What else really matters?[67] Life is supported and kept strong by the three legs under the stool. If one of the legs is weak or missing, the entire stool is in danger of collapsing. If we do not like our work, that leg of the stool will be weak and our well-being, happiness, and enjoyment of life will suffer. Similarly, if we do not make time for spiritual values, hobbies, or recreational pursuits, or if our relationships are dysfunctional, our life will become unstable and wobbly. It is important to maintain a balance between life's three critical success factors.

---

64 "Living to 100: What's the Secret?" *Harvard Health Publications*, January 2008.
65 Alicia H. Munnell and Steven A Sass, *Working Longer: The Solution to the Retirement Income Challenge* (2007); the authors provide a wealth of evidence about retirement decisions, and suggest that the future prospects for many retirees are miserable if they rely only on pensions and savings.
66 Cato the Elder, *De Algri Cultura*, (Second Century B.C.)
67 Some will say spirituality matters, and of course, it does; however, spirituality is an integral part of each of these three critical success factors. See Chapter 24.

A SILK PURSE FROM A SOW'S EAR?

Life is a simple three-legged stool.

Contrary to what psychologist and the sociologists would like you to believe, life is not complicated—it is a simple three-legged stool. Of course, although it may be simple, it is not easy; it takes much hard work and careful maintenance to keep all three legs strong so that your life can be steady, firm, and able to withstand the many challenges and misfortunes that come along from time to time. Doing work that you enjoy is a crucial part of life. What you do is not important—so long as it is productive—but enjoying it to a ripe old age is very important.

I may have been more fortunate than most because I can honestly say my work has, for the most part, been enjoyable. Of course, we all have a bad day occasionally, and that is true whether or not we are working. My rule is one bad day per week, no more—20 percent of the time, on average. That means 80 percent of my working life has to be enjoyable. With the right attitude, even when things are not going well, work can be fun if progress is evident, or will soon become evident. Several years ago, it struck me that since we spend at least half our waking life working it should be enjoyable most of the time. If it isn't, then stop doing it and find something that is fun—life is too short to spend half of it doing something you do not enjoy.

The *Economist* had a good article on the subject of work, called "Gerontocapitalism."[68] The columnist suggested that retirement rots the brain; my own casual observations have confirmed that to be so—do your own private survey. I would much rather be playing the game than standing on the sidelines. Kirk Kerkorian sets the example, still a corporate raider at 88 years old. Carl Icahn, at 69, is a youngster by comparison and still very much in the corporate

---

68 *Economist*, December 24, 2005, 14.

A SILK PURSE FROM A SOW'S EAR?

game. Then there is Rupert Murdoch, who bought the *Wall Street Journal* at 76, and Sumner Redstone still at the helm of Viacom at 82—it is reported that he equates retiring to dying. And don't forget that Pope Benedict XVI got the job when he was 78; his challengers in their 60s were considered too young. Ronald Reagan was first elected President at 69 and he served two terms. My hero is Ray Kroc who got the idea of fast food, started the McDonald's restaurant chain when he was 52, and spent the next 30 years building it up. Of course, these men work for themselves so no one can force them to retire. Maybe it is the fun of playing the game. Certainly, it is not a fear of being destitute.

In 1881, Otto von Bismarck originally fixed the official retirement age in Germany at 70; in 1916, it was reduced to 65 because presumably that was the longest most people could be expected to live. Angela Merkel, the current chancellor, plans to raise it to 67 in 2035. In 1925, the retirement age in Britain was set at 65, and the Pensions Commission has proposed that it keep rising in line with life expectancy. In the United States, the "official old age" of 65—cynically referred to as "statutory senility"—began with the passage of the Social Security Act of 1935. It was a means of removing older workers to make room for younger ones during the great Depression—a substitute for death.

Being old in North America can relegate you to being a nonperson.[69] Often, these nonpersons are dispassionately removed from the labor force at an arbitrary age—65 at Caterpillar. They are stereotyped as being physically used up and/or mentally deficient, as if their skills had suddenly evaporated. They suffer the ultimate in job discrimination. It is often jokingly referred to as being past the "use by" date.

Sometime during the early 1970s, Caterpillar conducted a seminar intended to help managers coach those who were approaching retirement. I distinctly remember being shocked when the Human Resources department told us that they had discovered an alarming statistic: the average life expectancy of a Caterpillar employee after retirement was approximately six months. Lives ended quickly after forcible expulsion from the "family" because of mandatory retirement. The counselors taught us how to coach each imminent retiree through the difficult transition period. For decades, as the company was growing, compensation and benefits were good, and it was great place to work; turnover was low. A paternalistic "cradle-to-the-grave" company culture contributed to the situation. It may be better now; the *Peoria Journal Star* recently reported in a news story that, according to Caterpillar, 94 retirees are over 95 years old, and 13 of those are over 100.[70]

It is up to each of us individually to understand and to accept that early

---

69 Richard Mowsesian, *Golden Goals, Rusted Realities: Work and Aging in America* (1987).
70 http://pjstar.com/stories/042708/TRI_BGEQCQ3G.027.php .

retirement is a deviation, and that maintaining the skills and expertise to remain employable is a priority. Unfortunately, some eagerly wait the day they can escape the drudgery of a job they do not enjoy. Work should be a source of life's satisfactions rather than a drudgery from which to escape. It is at the very core of our existence; it is part of our identity and our sense of self-worth. Retirement, on the other hand, is a fabricated artifact of our society and should not be mandated by either government or company policy. Change careers, go back to school, do volunteer work, mentor the young, write a book, explore the universe—but don't retire. Traditional retirement is a conspiracy of the young against the old. Do not be a victim of the conspiracy. Retirement scares Stanley Bing too:[71]

> "It's going to be great!" you tell yourself. "Wake up at noon every day like I did when I was a teenager! Have a bagel! Play 36 holes of golf! Couple of drinks at the 19th green! Wake up and do it again the next day! That's what I call living!" Right. Have you thought about what 25 years of that would be like? Get this: A life of incessant recreation and indolence is enough to drive any business entity like you or me mad after 3.5 years.

Stanley Bing goes on to lay out the details of a strategic retirement plan. Recently, he came up with an even better solution—to retire on the job.[72] He describes the various techniques to implement that alternative. Come to think of it, I have known several individuals who have developed that skill to perfection.

In traditional Chinese culture, "old" signifies respect and middle age extends until about 80. Traditionally, the most important birthday in the Chinese culture occurs at the age of 60. That is the age when both the animal and the element symbol of the Chinese lunar calendar are the same as the year of birth. The children are expected to arrange and pay for a grand celebration to show respect and to express thanks for what their parents have done for them. Perhaps it comes as no surprise that the older I get, the more I appreciate Chinese culture.

Although I briefly contemplated the idea, retirement was not for me. Therefore, after a few days of skiing and snowboarding at Tremblant, and a few extra games of squash at the Montréal Badminton and Squash Club, I continued on my journey, seeking another work assignment—the fourth time in 12 years. I was 57 and becoming quite convinced that I could not hold a job. If there is power in positive thinking, now was the time to test the theory.

Before I could make any progress on that task, Mother Nature conspired to

---

71 Stanley Bing, "Secrets to a Happy Retirement," *Fortune*, June 26, 2006
72 Stanley Bing, *Executricks, or How to Retire While You're Still Working*, (2008)

create a serious situation—the North American ice storm of 1998. It was one to remember. On January 4, 1998, a low-pressure system over the Great Lakes, moist air from the Gulf of Mexico, an air mass near the Bay of Fundy, a high-pressure area over Labrador, and another near Bermuda all acted together with the wrath of God to create widespread havoc.[73] Freezing rain and drizzle fell over eastern Ontario, extensive areas in southern Québec, northern New York, and northern New England, including parts of Vermont, New Hampshire, and Maine. Heavy rain fell on southern Ontario and western New York, as well as much of the Appalachian region from Tennessee northward, creating severe flooding, while further east, the Canadian Maritimes received heavy snow. The storm lasted over 80 hours, from January 5 to 10, 1998, and after the freezing rain had finally stopped, a steep drop in temperature made the situation worse.

About 1,000 steel pylons (reportedly, the most solid in the world) and 35,000 wooden utility poles, all supporting the electrical grid collapsed in a chain reaction under the weight of the ice. More than 4 million citizens were without electricity, mostly in southern Québec, western New Brunswick, and eastern Ontario. Many people died of hypothermia, or from carbon monoxide poisoning due to using generators or other heat sources as they desperately tried to remain warm. The lack of electrical power also greatly affected the farmers as they could no longer provide water or adequate ventilation to their barns full of livestock. Many animals died. All power to the island of Montréal was cut off for several days, which prevented the city's water stations from operating. Even after power was restored, large areas of Montréal were closed due to chunks of ice falling from rooftops and endangering pedestrians and motorists. The bridges and tunnels linking Montréal with the south shore were also closed for fear of ice chunks falling from the superstructures. With the roads blocked by fallen trees and broken power lines, and with the roads coated with a heavy layer of ice, emergency vehicles could hardly move.

Emergency rescue teams were brought in from places such as Prince Edward Island and Nova Scotia, along with teams from the United States. The Canadian Forces helped restore power to affected homes in eastern Ontario and western Québec; it was the largest operational deployment of Canadian military personnel since the Korean War. They helped provincial and municipal workers clear roads, rescue people, evacuate the sick, shelter and feed about 100,000 people, and ensure that farmers had the generators and fuel required to keep their operations going. Military engineers and technicians and hydro and telephone crews worked around the clock repairing and replacing downed transmission towers and utility poles.

---

73 http://en.wikipedia.org/wiki/North_American_ice_storm_of_1998.

A SILK PURSE FROM A SOW'S EAR?

The weight of ice brought down millions of trees, and 5,000 damaged trees in Montréal's Mount Royal Park had to be cut down. Québec's maple syrup industry and orchard regions were devastated. Three weeks after the end of the ice storm, there were still about 700,000 people without electricity. Estimates of material damages approximated $4–6 billion for all the areas affected. Further south, flooding from the same storm system caused millions of dollars in additional damage.

For three days, Hélène and I huddled under blankets around our fireplace, trying to keep our bodies warm and our spirits up, listening to the news on our battery-powered radio. We were far more fortunate than most. Living close to Montréal on Ile des Soeurs meant that we got our power back quite quickly. Meanwhile, we did not have to go to any of the emergency shelters, but chose instead to tough it out with a few of our neighbors.

The disaster brought out the best and the worst in people. Many willingly lent a helping hand to those in need. Others brought in container-loads of small generators and fuel and sold them for cash at onerous prices right out of the back of the containers—gouging those suffering the greatest hardship.

It was sometime during the third day, as we were running out of firewood, that Hélène and I looked at each other and fantasized about a vacation to the warmth of the Caribbean. I had no work obligations—we could go now! However, common sense prevailed and we decided the time was not right—but the fantasy remained in our minds. In fact, Hélène later told me she fantasized about what it must be like to live in a paradise of year-round sunny, warm weather; white sandy beaches; and crystal-clear waters.

Some believe that powerful thoughts can produce powerful results. Maybe they can, because a few days later I stumbled across an advertisement in the *Globe and Mail* about an opportunity to work in the Bahamas as President and Chief Operating Officer of the Caterpillar dealership. It was a serendipitous discovery and definitely meant for us—another tipping point.

The normal period of courtship ensued and by March of 1998 Hélène and I had arranged to relocate to the Bahamas—sunny warm weather, white sandy beaches, and crystal waters. Hélène would have her paradise and I would once again be back in the Caterpillar family, working on the dealer side of the business. It was truly, a win-win situation. Any residual thoughts about retiring had evaporated. Life can be unexpectedly splendid.

16

ISLANDS IN THE STREAM

ATLANTIC EQUIPMENT & POWER LTD.
NASSAU, BAHAMAS
(1998 — 2003)

> *One of the most rewarding things about being associated with Caterpillar is that we provide true value to the industries we serve and the communities we live in. We really help make things better. At the end of our time on Earth, I think everyone will look back and wonder, "Did I make the world a better place?" As Dealer and Caterpillar people, we will be able to hold our heads up high and say, "Yes, we did. We made things better for our employees, our customers and our communities."*
>
> —Jeff Whiteman, Caterpillar Dealer Principal

THE distribution of Caterpillar products is fundamentally a simple business—not easy, but simple. The dealer buys products from Caterpillar, then sells them to customers and provides after-sales service support. The dealer does not have the difficult task of designing and manufacturing highly sophisticated, state-of-the-art products in high volume for worldwide consumption—that's Caterpillar's job. Although selling and servicing is conceptually simple, success or failure depends on proper execution—and that is not easy. Customers buy Caterpillar products primarily because they have a problem that needs solving. It is the dealer's responsibility to help them find the most productive and cost-effective solution. That requires professional and consultive selling skills and capabilities in place to implement solutions.

Successful dealers establish themselves as "Total Solution Providers"—and that's where it gets difficult. A Solution Provider must invest in up-to-date facilities, tools, and equipment; they must have a sales force trained to focus on the customer and solve problems, and skilled technicians who know how to diagnose and efficiently fix technical problems. It has proven to be a formula for success; it gave Caterpillar a distinct competitive advantage and helped justify a premium price. Perhaps the most important reason for the success of Caterpillar has been the strong, independent dealer organization the company established soon after it was formed. Of course, Caterpillar's products were good, but competitors' products were often adequate and offered good value for some applications. However, seldom could the competition match Caterpillar's worldwide dealer organization and its attendant support capabilities. Donald V. Fites said, "Our single greatest advantage over competition was, and still is, our system of distribution and product support."[74] It became my challenge to make the business model succeed in the Bahamas.

The Islands of the Bahamas[75] are mountain plateaus that emerged as a result of volcanic action hundreds of thousands of years ago. As the islands grew, they hosted countless generations of coral, which today comprise the islands' limestone base. The Arawak Indians (also known as "Lucayans") were the peace-loving indigenous inhabitants of the Bahamas when Columbus arrived in 1492. They had wandered up from South America through the Caribbean and arrived in the Bahamas (the Lucayos) around the ninth century AD. Subsequently, the missionaries and other Europeans attempted to convert the Arawak Indians to Christianity with marginal success and then proceeded to kill them off to the last man during the following years.[76]

The geography of the islands attracted many well-known pirates, including Blackbeard, Henry Morgan, and Anne Bonney, who lured unsuspecting ships into the treacherous, shallow waters, and then plundered their cargo. The pirates dominated the Bahamian waters for about 50 years until Woodes Rogers, an English privateer, drove them out. Britain first claimed the islands in 1670, and, in 1674, English settlers from Bermuda arrived, searching for religious freedom. At that time, the islands were uninhabited and the settlers formed the first British colony on what is now the island of Eleuthera, and began a prosperous agricultural economy. Britain soon recognized the Bahamas as a colony and, in 1718, Woodes Rogers became the first governor.

Both Britain's war with Spain, and the American Revolution, brought periods

---

74 Fites, "Make Your Dealers Your Partners," *Harvard Business Review*, March 1996. At the time, Donald V. Fites was the Chairman and CEO of Caterpillar in Peoria, Illinois.
75 The Spanish bestowed the phrase "Baja Mar" on the islands, which means "shallow sea."
76 James A. Michener, *Caribbean* (1989), a historical novel, accurately depicts the history of the region from the time of the native Arawak tribes until about 1990.

of prosperity to the islands through privateering: government sanctioned piracy. Following Britain's defeat in the American Revolutionary War, southern loyalists relocated entire plantations to the islands, along with their slaves, and grew cotton under the protection of the British. During the American Civil War, Bahamians became wealthy running Confederate cotton through the Union blockade to English mills and shipping military equipment to Confederate rebels. Eventually the Loyalists' slaves were freed and the Bahamas became a favorite holiday destination for the wealthy. Most Bahamians today are descendents of the slaves brought by the settlers from Bermuda, and the southern Loyalists from America—none are indigenous.

The Bahamas gained independence from Britain in 1973, although the British monarch still had formal executive powers, vested in the Governor-General. In practice, the Governor-General acted upon the advice of a Cabinet of Ministers appointed from the House of Assembly.

The Commonwealth of the Bahamas consists of about 700 islands, 29 of which were inhabited. The total population was less than 300,000, and over two-thirds resided on New Providence Island, where Nassau, the country's capital city is located. Although the Bahamas is relatively wealthy compared to other countries in the Caribbean, its economy depended primarily on two main industries: tourism (60 percent of GDP), and financial services (15 percent of GDP).

In the early 1800s, the Bahamian island of Inagua became a center for the production of sea salt. Large flat areas were easily flooded with seawater and the hot sun shone almost all the time; therefore, the water evaporated quickly. The sea salt collected in the saltpans and was then harvested using Caterpillar products. During my time in the Bahamas, Morton Salt employed about 70 percent of the people on the island and produced about a million tons of salt per year for export.

Atlantic Equipment and Power Limited was first established on Inagua in 1935 to support the local salt industry. Twenty years later, it was appointed the Caterpillar dealer for the Bahamas, and also for the Turks, and Caicos Islands in the West Indies. The Crothers family purchased the business in 1977, and the Cayman Islands were added to their territory in 1981. Atlantic was a typical dealership, selling and servicing the broad range of products manufactured by Caterpillar. About 40 percent of the business was related to power generation, and Atlantic was recognized as the leader in the application and installation of standby and prime power for hotels, offices, and electric utilities throughout the territory. The other 60 percent of revenue was from the sale of construction machinery and product support services.

ISLANDS IN THE STREAM

The Bahamas was a tax haven and offered a unique business climate. There were no taxes on capital gains, corporate earnings, personal income, sales, inheritance, or dividends. That tax freedom was available to all resident corporations, partnerships, individuals, and trusts. In addition, there were no restrictions on the free repatriation of profits. Because there were no taxes, the government revenues came primarily from relatively high duties levied on most imports. For example, the majority of the products imported by Atlantic were subject to duties of about 42 percent, according to value.[77]

For those so inclined, that situation created a significant incentive to evade duties by smuggling—a ubiquitous practice that everyone politely preferred not to talk about. Many Bahamians shopped in the United States at prices significantly lower than domestic Bahamian prices and then used an interesting variety of creative methods of importation to avoid the high Bahamian duties. The high duty situation was also an incentive for Atlantic's customers to buy parts from Caterpillar dealers in the United States instead of from us. Caterpillar discouraged dealers in the United States from selling to Bahamians, but ignoring the rules was usually not a problem for most dealers—only being caught, which seldom happened.

The tax-free situation in the Bahamas provoked many discussions about the "unfairness" of the system. Many believed that since we did not pay tax, we received a "subsidy" that we did not deserve. In fact, you receive a subsidy when the government takes positive action to confiscate someone else's property and give it to you—property that does not belong to you. In contrast, you enjoy a "tax break" when the government *takes no action* and allows you to keep the wealth, profits, and property that you already own, and have earned by right. We should all stand up for capitalism and free enterprise, and proudly defend our right to our own wealth and property. We must vigorously oppose the claim that tax breaks are subsidies. Profits belong to the producers, and government or society in general does not have the right to claim it at whim through taxation.

❧❧❧

When I arrived in the spring of 2004, Atlantic was doing okay, but its growth had slowed. The challenge was to revitalize the business and launch it on a path of continuous growth and improvement. The geographical territory was small, and the business was correspondingly small in comparison to most other Caterpillar dealers. The employees were quite experienced with many having been in the business for over 15 years.

---

77 Certain specific government customers served by Atlantic were exempt, or partially exempt, from the duties on products imported for their own use.

ISLANDS IN THE STREAM

In 2004, Atlantic represented over 30 diversified product lines in addition to Caterpillar. One key manager described Atlantic Equipment and Power as a "general store" with everything for everybody, "jack of all trades, and master of none." I knew from experience that a Caterpillar dealer cannot function successfully as a "general store;" I did not accept our employees being modestly knowledgeable about many things and not fully versed on anything. It was important for the entire organization to devote its energy to the Caterpillar business and forget about the many other ancillary products that were distracting attention from the main task. It was important to become "masters" at selling the Caterpillar products and servicing Caterpillar customers.

Therefore, I once again established myself as the "coach" and, together with the management team, went through a traditional planning exercise to develop a new strategic direction for the business. A new Mission Statement was developed, along with a statement of Common Values and Corporate Objectives.

We placed priority on becoming well acquainted with customers and demonstrating by our actions that we wanted to earn their business. The new approach immediately resulted in increased revenue from both prime products and parts. Significant investments were made in tools, equipment, vehicles, and training. Those improvements, along with management changes and closer supervision of the day-to-day work in service operations resulted in significant turnarounds in quality, efficiency, and productivity—and, of course, in profitability.

During my five years in the Bahamas, we continually provided training to advance the knowledge and understanding of our Bahamian employees, and to prepare them for a better future. Unfortunately, despite the training, there was not much evidence of learning—and it was learning that we needed. Consequently, I commissioned an independent organization to test the literacy of some employees. The experts discovered—much to my chagrin—that many of our young, intelligent staff (males, especially) could not learn because they could not read and write effectively. Therefore, we decided to bring in experienced Philippine technicians to help upgrade the technical capabilities of the service department and to provide on-the-job training for the Bahamian technicians.

Shortly thereafter, another experience indicated the extent of the literacy problem in the Bahamas. Administrators from a nearby high school asked if I would support the school with a contribution that would allow them to buy books for a remedial reading program, and a few copies of the popular software program "Fixed on Phonics" for the same purpose. Further inquiry revealed that the books and material they needed would normally be used in grades 2 and 3, but instead, would be used to teach students in grades 11 and 12 to read.

Private funding was necessary because the Ministry of Education would not approve the purchase of grade school reading material for high school students. As is typical of many government ministries, they figured that if they refused to acknowledge the problem they could pretend it did not exist. Ironically, the officially published literacy rate was quite high as judged by the number of high school certificates awarded. Unfortunately, neither teaching nor graduation certificates necessarily indicate that learning has taken place.

It was reasonable to conclude that the high rates of functional illiteracy in the Bahamas contributed to the high rates of crime. Fox Hill Prison in Nassau seemed to be full of strong, intelligent young men many of whom undoubtedly committed acts of crime that did not require reading and writing as a prerequisite. Of course, Atlantic Equipment and Power Limited contributed to the school and its remedial reading program, and to Project Read—another community sponsored remedial reading program for adult Bahamians.

That experience in the Bahamas provoked me to investigate and come to understand what it takes to master the skill of reading. The first step for most people is to learn to speak. On a few brief occasions, I watched in awe as my granddaughter slowly mastered that major cognitive feat. It was something to behold. Then, after learning to speak, she slowly learned to read by associating the marks we call letters, then words with the sounds she made when she spoke—the meaning of which she already knew. That required that she grasp the discrete units of sound (called phonemes[78]), which, when put together represent words. Phonics is a method that breaks words down into their individual phonemes and then connects them to the symbols on the paper—that is, the 26 letters of the English alphabet or, in the case of the Chinese language, about 5,000 individual characters. Once the sounds associated with the letters of the alphabet are learned, a child can sound out each word. With phonics, reading becomes a manageable set of rules that enable a child to sound out—and read—almost any word. Reading soon becomes an enjoyable mind-opening experience.

That system is based on the philosophy that knowledge is gained objectively by perceiving the facts. Those facts are then used to teach children the abstract knowledge of the language and subsequently to read. I was taught using that system at Longwood Grade School during the 1950s and it successfully formed a solid foundation for my future learning—a foundation that is often missing from the modern educational system.

Unfortunately, a few years later, the so-called "progressive educational system" taught children to focus on the whole word, memorizing it as the teacher pronounced it—practically an impossible feat. Using that method, a child is

---

[78] Phonemes are the smallest phonetic unit.

completely lost when faced with a word she has not memorized. John Dewey is considered the father of "progressivism"—linguistic corruption, actually—which crippled the reading abilities of a whole generation of children. For years afterwards, I witnessed numerous university graduates who could generally read commonly used words, but struggled if they needed to put together a string of words in a sentence that conveyed a coherent message, and to combine sentences into a paragraph that conveyed a distinct idea. They were victims of that "progressive educational system." I recalled that Christiana, my Chinese secretary in Hong Kong, had to revise many reports—reports written by "educated" English-speaking westerners—to make them understandable to the reader. English was her second language, but she had learned it well using phonics. I went through several similar experiences during later years. Protect your children from the "progressive" system and make sure they learn the power and joy of the language with the phonics method.

It is generally accepted that most newspapers throughout the world are written at a grade six to grade eight reading level.[79] That means that—if properly taught—all students at that level should be able to pick up a newspaper, read it, understand it, and tell you the meaning of what they read in their own words. My ad hoc survey of children in many countries indicated that few of them could do that. Those who cannot read and write effectively will struggle with their learning for the rest of their lives. There is a high probability that they will be marginalized and dislocated by the global economy.

My definition of becoming educated is simply the ability to learn. Educated young people have a good future; most illiterate young people do not. The ability for higher learning first requires the ability to read and write well at an early age. This is a universal need and should be a vital priority of all educators. Unfortunately, social ability and graduating with a certificate is often given a higher priority in the public education system.

Atlantic's employees became excited and executed the game plan; the changes implemented were successful—revenue, operating profit, and shareholder equity steadily improved. Then 2001 happened. On July 23, 2001, the owners decided to divest of the business. There was a variety of good reasons for doing so, and I supported the decision. Ownership by a larger dealer would make more resources available to grow the business and to deploy the new marketing programs and business systems being introduced by Caterpillar. The employees understood and generally accepted the positive outcomes that were expected to

---

79 This book is written at a grade 11 reading level according to the Flesch-Kincaid Readability Test.

accrue from the decision. Many other significant events that occurred during 2001 affected Atlantic—the World Trade Center disaster on September 11; the fire that destroyed the straw market; and hurricane Michelle on November 5, to cite the most significant ones. In my report to the Board of Directors at the end of the year, I made the following comments:

> There are many opinions on what effect recent local and world events will have on the Bahamas, both short and longer term. These events include: the sagging U.S. economy, the Asian, European and Japanese recessions, the straw market fire, the World Trade Center disaster, OECD/FATF induced legislation, the new Bahamas Employment Act, recent layoffs and unemployment, construction slowdown, BISX difficulties, plummeting retail sales, and shortage of foreign reserves. Another major upcoming event that has put everyone on hold is the uncertainty of the pending election. The impact of these situations is likely to be negative in the short to medium term. However, longer term, the outlook for continued growth in the Bahamas is positive.

As expected, those events had a negative impact during 2002; however, Atlantic performed reasonably well as compared with many other Bahamian businesses. The divestiture activity lasted the entire year. Meanwhile a new political party came to power, new labor laws were implemented, tourism slowed significantly as a result of the 9/11 disaster, and the deteriorating economic conditions worldwide and the restructuring of the financial regulations created uncertainty in the financial community. Many small businesses were forced to close, which resulted in a growing level of unemployment.

While working in the Bahamas, I became involved with the Rotary Club and a variety of civic organizations to contribute to the betterment of the community and the Bahamian people. Consequently, I was caught up in many discussions concerning social issues. Aside from the serious issues of literacy and education, there was much debate within the government, the community, and the health care profession regarding the need for a new national health care system. During that time, the following statement was made: "We must introduce universal access to quality, affordable health care—not as a privilege, but as a right." Unfortunately, most people found nothing wrong with that statement, since, as a society, most have come to believe that everyone has a right to basic medical services. However, it is based on the false premise that "health care" is a commodity that the government has the right to seize and redistribute at its whim. The statement ignores the fact that without considerable mental and physical effort on the part of doctors and the other medical professionals, there is no health care in the first place. And it implies that doctors have a duty to support poor and sick patients, and teaches that those who "need" the medical services (the patients) are morally superior to the providers of the services (doctors, nurses, and other medical professionals).

The Management team at Atlantic Equipment and Power Limited restructured the business for sustainable growth and profitability.

In order for the government to control the distribution of health care, it must control the lives and minds of the individuals who provide it. That is exactly what happens in a socialized medical system. Doctors are told whom they can see, how many patients they can treat, how much they can charge, what their income shall be and the services they shall provide. Medical professionals are expected to become public servants and selflessly sacrifice their time, knowledge, ability, and resources to satisfy the alleged needs of their patients. The best, the brightest, and the most capable will not work under such oppression, and it is no wonder that there is a serious shortage of good professionals and top-rate services.

Similarly, for a socialized system to work, government must also control the patients—telling them which doctors they can see and when, and forbidding them to freely seek the services of medical professionals of their own choosing. A socialized medical system takes away the individual freedom of both the medical professionals and their patients.

Medical practitioners, like the rest of us, have a right to work for themselves and for their own enjoyment, and to make as much money as they can through voluntary trade without the threat of coercion by government. Similarly, patients have the right to accept or reject the advice and services, and to shop around for the best value they can get. An "individual right" is the freedom to act within one's means; it is not an entitlement to the goods and services provided by others, regardless of the perceived need. We all have a right to life, but no one has a right to health care.

You may say, "What about all those poor people who cannot afford private services?" It has been my experience over many years that medical professionals are among the most benevolent and often help those who "need" help, according to their own free will. That is especially true when they can enjoy practicing their profession without coercion. In addition, all of us are free to offer assistance to those who deserve our assistance—according to our own judgment and means—many of us do by voluntarily supporting a wide variety of private charitable organizations.

The solution to the health care dilemma is a private medical system that respects and honors the heroic efforts of medical professionals, and leaves them free to offer their skills and abilities, the same as plumbers, technicians, engineers, lawyers, and architects. As one who has experienced a variety of health care programs throughout the world, I can say from firsthand experience that health care is much too important to be left in the hands of government bureaucrats. Quality care can only come from the hands of proud, independent, private medical professionals. Canada may be the world's best example of government's *failure* to manage and provide quality health care services in a first world country.[80] I can testify from personal experience that the system in Taiwan is far superior.

Eventually, the shareholders of Atlantic and the purchaser, General de Equipos de Columbia (GECOLSA), the Caterpillar dealer for Columbia, signed the Asset Purchase Agreement. Application was then made to the Bahamian Investment Review Board for approval, which eventually was granted in the spring of 2003. GECOLSA elected to bring in a new president for the business, and once again, I became unemployed. However, I am pleased to say it was a soft landing and a pleasant ending to a wonderful five-year relationship with the Crothers family. They were supportive and provided the capital and encouragement necessary to implement the strategy.

---

80 Nadeem Esmail and Michael Walker, *How Good Is Canadian Health Care? 2007 Report. An International Comparison of Health Care Systems* (Vancouver: Fraser Institute, 2007).

17

WARM WINDS AND CALM SEAS

(1993 — 2003)

> *There comes a tide in the affairs of men that, taken at the flood, sucks them swiftly away from the sea and the boats and strands them for the best part of two decades on the reefs of Marriage, Career and Bringing up Children. By the time they and their partners are ready to fulfill their dreams, they are forty or fifty and fainthearted. They no longer have that youthful zeal so many imagine [as] being a prerequisite for cruising. You see such people sitting disconsolately in RV parks all over the country. And they sit there unnecessarily because it is possible to start cruising in middle age. More and more couples are doing it. I've done it myself. So, if you've been tempted in the past, if you've dreamed of trade winds and desert islands, remember that it's not too late. All it takes is a bit of guts.*[81]
>
> —John Vigor

SAFE boating requires preparation. Serious boating adventures require serious preparation. Unbeknownst to me at the time, my preparations started while I was a member of the "OPB Club" in Hong Kong in the early 1980's— OPB Club being short for "Other People's Boat Club," a club that allowed one to enjoy boating without having to actually own a boat. Of course, one had to have friends and be sociable enough to be invited aboard. I occasionally received invitations to work as a crewmember in various offshore sailboat races, and to

---

[81] John Vigor is a freelance journalist based in Oak Harbor, Washington, USA. He has raced, cruised, and written about boats for more than 30 years. He is the author of *The Seaworthy Offshore Sailboat: A Guide to Essential Features, Gear and Handling* (2001); *Twenty Small Sailboats to Take You Anywhere* (1999); *Danger, Dolphins and Ginger Beer* (1993), a sailing adventure novel for 8- to 12-year-olds; *The Practical Mariner's Book of Knowledge* (1994); and *The Sailors' Assistant* (1996).

cruise the Chinese coast aboard the ever-present Chinese junks that were popular with the Hong Kong expats. The only previous boating experience I had was paddling a canoe on the rivers of northern Ontario as a boy—an experience that does not compare.

During my years in Hong Kong, I had became hooked on boating and decided to learn more. Months later, after much study, I obtained a Certificate of Competency (Master) and Certificate of Competency (Engineer) from the Marine Department in Hong Kong. Those certificates allowed one to operate a sail or power vessel up to 15 tons in and out of the Hong Kong harbor. Believe me, the training provided essential knowledge for safely navigating the busy commercial waters of Hong Kong harbor. The local captains gave no latitude to novice boaters and often ignored the rules to gain a small advantage.

Bonnie Skye

Much later, in 1993, while living near Toronto, we bought our first real boat—a 33-foot sloop named *Bonnie Skye*—and joined the Port Credit Yacht Club. Within a few weeks, Hélène had overcome her fear of the boat tipping over and was soon handling the helm as I tweaked the lines. Weekend racing around the buoys and pleasant cruising on Lake Ontario became a major pastime during the short summer seasons.

A few years later, while living in Montréal, we continued to enjoy boating from the Trident Yacht Club near Gananoque, Ontario. Although the seasons were short, sailing through the Thousand Islands group and on the surrounding waters of eastern Lake Ontario was idyllic. During the summers, Hélène and I steadily advanced our sailing skills and actually won a few of the local club races.

In the winter months, we furthered our knowledge of boating by completing most of the courses offered by the Canadian Power Squadron, including Basic Boating, Advanced Piloting, Marine Electronics, Celestial Navigation, Cold Weather Marine Survival Guide, Marine Weather Handbook, and Overboard Rescue Techniques.

In 1998, when the opportunity to work in the Bahamas came along, we took *Bonnie Skye* with us and looked forward to sailing in paradise. However, we soon discovered that the Bahamas is not an easy place to sail. It is predominantly powerboat country because of the shallow water and numerous coral heads. Of course, a sailboat is the vessel of choice for the annual "snowbird" cruisers from the north who have adequate leisure time to dodge the coral heads and explore the beautiful waters of Abaco and Exuma. Nevertheless, close observations revealed that they spent about as much time motoring as they did sailing.

We eventually decided that a powerboat would better suit our boating lifestyle, so we sold *Bonnie Skye* with much regret and bought a Grand Banks 32 named *Baby Grand*. She had a special character all her own and provided many hours of enjoyment on the waters around Nassau and the islands of Exuma. The main drawback was the wooden construction, which required hours of maintenance to keep her teak looking good under the hot Bahamian sun. That became a burden, so we decided once again to look for another boat that required less work and provided more enjoyment.

It seemed simple enough, but it was not—selecting the "Proper Yacht," that is. It was our third attempt, so we surely had to get it right this time. I was determined the search would receive a lot more study and consideration than had the previous two purchases. In fact, I devoted two years to intense investigation. We were already subscribers to half a dozen boating magazines, so perusing the ads became a regular pastime, as did surfing the Internet.

The YachtWorld site soon became our method of choice for narrowing down the possibilities according to brand, style, location, age, and price.[82] So wide was the selection and so vast were the choices that it became critical to narrow the search even further to vessels that met specific criteria. Therein lay our dilemma—I realized the search had to stop until we had identified those criteria.

One day we attended a boating seminar and listened intently to a veteran boater who said the most important question to ask before buying a boat is, "What are you going to do with it?" Do you need a fishing boat or a cruiser; a slow trawler or a high-speed boat; a boat for coastal cruising or for messing

---

82   www.yachtworld.com.

around the harbor; a boat to entertain friends or to be alone; a boat with lots of creature comforts or one for simple living; a sundeck or a cockpit; galley down or up; a flybridge or flush deck; two engines or one; diesel or gasoline powered; propane or electric stove; generator or inverter—or both? We had not done any serious thinking about the pros and cons of those alternatives, so it was no wonder we had difficulty making a selection. I finally understood the need to approach the task more rationally and systematically, and to first identify the important criteria to match our intended use. It became a mini Six-Sigma project.

Baby Grand

Eventually, we decided that we would mostly use the boat for coastal cruising and island hopping; we might also take the occasional overnight run out of sight of land but would not undertake long-distance, blue-water passages. With our purpose now established, our other requirements became clear and included such features as two heads, two private staterooms, two diesel engines, a sundeck, pilothouse, and both an inverter and generator. Solid construction and low maintenance, of course, were essential.

Having completed our homework, we felt much more comfortable continuing our search. Shortly thereafter, I stumbled across a book by Ed McKnew and Mark Parker called *The Powerboat Guide*. In its 1775 pages were descriptions of over 1600 models of boats of various sizes, shapes, and vintage. It also had III chapters representing the same number of manufacturers, each with a description identifying key features and attributes of each model, and provided average retail prices for models built since 1980. It was a fantastic resource for the powerboat shopper and most boat brokers have a copy, usually dog-eared, on their bookshelf.

Weeks of scrutinizing that information revealed interesting vessels that we had not previously considered. One that caught my attention was the Classic Chris Craft, which according to the *Powerboat Guide*, "was once the undisputed king of the worldwide pleasure boat industry." It was definitely a strong boat. Reports indicate that an early mistake converting from wood to fiberglass caused Chris Craft to delay their conversion to the late 60's and early 70's. When they finally made the conversion, their early fiberglass boats were thick, hand-laid solid fiberglass throughout—overkill.

Kassequa—a 47' Chris Craft Commander. In 2004, we lived on the boat for about 7 months leisurely cruising the Bahamas, Florida, the Intracoastal Waterway (ICW), Chesapeake Bay, and the Potomac River.

Investigation revealed the Chris Craft 47' Commander met most of our established criteria, especially the two-cabin flush deck model. A search began in earnest. Could we find one in decent shape at a decent price? We inspected a few and came away disappointed. Finally, after months of patient searching, we discovered one in New Bern, North Carolina, that was a very close match to our criteria. Although a 1970 model, she performed very well and gave us confidence. The only work required was routine maintenance and ongoing improvements as we got the time and the inclination. The systems worked well, and we felt very safe while underway and at anchor. The hull was entirely hand-laid fiberglass, about twice as thick and strong as hulls made 30 years later. The previous owner was a retired naval officer who had devoted several years to restoring the interior and various systems. Very clean and about 80 percent restored, it easily passed the marine survey. It came with the original 1970 sales brochure, a detailed service history, and names of all four previous owners. We took possession of the vessel in June of 2002 at Beaufort, North Carolina, and renamed it *Kassequa*.[83]

After provisioning and taking care of a few maintenance details, we spent most of the summer cruising down the Intracoastal Waterway (ICW), through Abaco and Eleuthera, and across to our home in Nassau, Bahamas. Early in 2003, my work assignment was approaching a conclusion so we slowly wound down our activities and commitments in the Bahamas and prepared for an extended cruise. We had no commitments and no desire to return to Canada in the middle of winter, so we decided it was time to go cruising—something we had talked about for years. However, before that could happen, it was necessary to go frolicking with the sharks.

※

> *They're sinister, cold-hearted, cold-blooded, ruthless eating machines who enjoy an occasional snack on shark experts, and people stupid enough to swim in the ocean when there are perfectly good swimming pools just a few hundred yards away.*[84]

We watched with rapt attention as the Stuart Cove diver carefully opened the lid of the bait box, skewered a piece of raw fish on the hand spear and slowly held it above his head. Instantly, an eight-foot reef shark swung its head sideways, turned upwards, snatched the bait off the end of the spear, and then swam a short distance away to enjoy its morsel. Meanwhile, a dozen other sharks swam over and around us as we sat, motionless on the sand, among the coral heads 50 feet below the surface. They appeared to be maneuvering into a favorable position as they stalked the bait box, knowing that another piece of food would soon be coming.

My stepson Andrew had only recently acquired his scuba certification and

---

83 During its history, the boat has been named *Patema II*, *Ann*, and *Bear Hug*. We decided to name it *Kassequa*, which was the Lucayan Indian name for chieftain.
84 http://www.cdnn.info/news/article/a020430.html.

was determined to do a shark-dive before ending his brief visit to the Bahamas. Once he had made up his mind, there was little I could do but go with the flow and try to make it a safe and memorable experience for him. I had already been intrigued by the possibility of doing a shark dive, but had not considered it high priority. However, sharing the experience with Andrew was a good excuse to make it happen.

The Bahamian Tourist Office takes every opportunity to promote the country's pleasant climate and beautiful clear waters. There is an extraordinary diversity of marine species thriving amongst the coral, caverns, and blue holes.[85] The diving possibilities are endless. Reef sharks are prohibited from being caught and harvested in United States waters. It is also forbidden to feed sharks in the waters off the coast of Florida, so you must go to Caribbean and Bahamian waters to participate in scuba shark-feeding dives.

You can find a shark dive in many parts of the Bahamas; however, living in Nassau, we decided the best choice for us would be Stuart Cove Aqua Adventures, located on the southwest side of New Providence Island. Stuart Cove landed a job as a stunt diver in the James Bond feature film *For Your Eyes Only* (1981). Subsequently, he bought his first dive boat and started his own dive business, which soon grew into one of the leading dive operations on New Providence Island. In 1983, Stuart and his partner, Michelle, became underwater film production coordinators on the island during the filming of another Bond movie, *Never Say Never Again*. He trained Sean Connery and Kim Basinger as certified divers, so they could complete their roles in the film. Stuart also choreographed the underwater shark wrestling. Later, the site was part of the set location for the movie *Flipper*, and by 2003, it had become one of the leading dive centers of the entire Caribbean. I figured that if Stuart's operation was good enough for James Bond, it was good enough for Andrew and me, so we booked the shark-dive event for a Saturday morning in July. It was to be an adventure of a lifetime—albeit a short one-day event.

We arrived early at Stuart Cove Aqua Adventures with eager anticipation and a good amount of butterflies in our stomachs. It was about a 45-minute ride out to the dive location—a flat sandy area called the Runway and Shark Arena—near the New Providence Wall and the Tongue of the Ocean.[86] The

---

85 Blue holes are usually circular, steep-walled depressions, so named for the dramatic contrast between the dark blue, deep waters of their depths and the lighter blue of the shallows around them. Blue holes were formed during past ice ages, when sea level was as much as 100-120 meters lower than at present. They are typically found on shallow carbonate platforms, exemplified by the Bahama Banks, as well as on and around the Yucatán Peninsula. http://en.wikipedia.org/wiki/Blue_hole.

86 The Tongue of the Ocean is the name of a deep oceanic trench in the Bahamas separating the islands of Andros and New Providence. The depth of the water drops from roughly 10 feet along Andros' offshore barrier reef to over 6,000 ft, and the drop is roughly 100 miles long. This channel and the Providence Channel

event was organized as a two-tank dive. The first dive—a routine exploratory dive along the Wall at a depth of about 40 to 50 feet—allowed time to relax and get used to seeing a few sharks in the vicinity. It also provided an opportunity to change our minds and return to the boat if swimming with the sharks suddenly seemed too intimidating. None of us opted out.

During previous years, I had dived in a variety of places throughout the Bahamas and had never encountered a shark. Nevertheless, by the time we dropped anchor, donned the dive gear, and entered the water, they were already swimming around at a distance, waiting for an easy lunch. The arrival of the boat and the anchor hitting the bottom must have sounded like a dinner bell to the sharks in the area.

While changing tanks for the second dive, we received careful instructions to follow during the feed. It was important not to panic or make any sudden moves, to sit still on the sand with our hands and arms tucked close to our bodies, and to avoid waving our hands or touching the sharks as they swam past. A professional underwater cameraman was present to take photos, so plenty would be available; it was not necessary to take our own. The internationally recognized "buddies" safety system was in force, and Andrew conceded to accepting me as his "buddy."

With tanks on and masks in place, we entered the water once again and formed a semicircle on the sandy bottom about 50 feet down. The feed took place at 11 a.m. every morning. Several sharks were already starting to gather in anticipation of the next feed—they obviously knew how to tell time. Soon the Stuart Cove feeder left the boat with the bait box and slowly drifted downwards to the center of the semicircle that we had formed. The sharks saw the bait box, knew exactly what it was all about, and immediately followed the feeder to the bottom. By then, plenty of sharks were on hand and they proceeded to swim closer, passing between us, over our heads and all around, several coming within touching distance. I watched a couple of members of our dive group struggle to get the correct negative buoyancy that would allow them to sit comfortably on the bottom, and hoped they would not provoke an attack with all their thrashing about.

The Caribbean reef shark (classification: *Carcharhinus perezi*) is not considered a threatened species and lives in abundance in the tropical western Atlantic and the Caribbean waters, from Florida to Brazil. Generally, they inhabit shallow waters near shore, cruising along the edge of a reef or continental shelf

---

are the two main branches of the Great Bahama Canyon, a submerged geological feature formed by erosion during periods of lower sea level. Taking advantage of the deep water close to shore, the United States has operated AUTEC (Atlantic Undersea Test and Evaluation Center) on Andros since 1965 to research antisubmarine warfare for the Western Alliance; see http://en.wikipedia.org/wiki/Tongue_of_the_Ocean.

over deep water, feeding on rays, crabs, and other small fish. The reef shark has six very keen senses to detect its prey, including smell, sight, sound, taste, and electric pulses. They are also able to pick up low-frequency sound vibrations, indicative of a fish struggling nearby. Many fishermen are often surprised to find that a reef shark had taken a big bite out of their catch while they were reeling it in, and they sometimes ending up with only a head left to brag about. The only known evidence of Caribbean reef shark becoming aggressive is apparently during moments of passion when males have been known to leave bite marks on the dorsal fins of possibly uncooperative, female partners.

They kept away from us unless they were being baited, in which case they became quite bold and made very close passes. The Stuart Cove feeders carefully presented the bait on the end of a stainless steel spear, about two feet long to keep the sharks a bit further away at the critical moment when they take the food. Each piece was small enough to be gulped easily in one bite; therefore, the other sharks did not attempt to fight over it. The feeders never removed the food from the bait box until the previous piece had been completely consumed and the sharks were calmly swimming about waiting for the next serving. That technique controlled the pace of the feed and prevented a feeding frenzy. When the energy level of the feed became excessive and the sharks became a bit unruly, the food was withheld until the situation calmed down. It was amazing nonstop action from start to finish as a few jockeyed for position waiting for the food to come out. Meanwhile, the other 20 or so sharks swam slow circles around the area within touching distance, anxious to take their place in line and receive the food.

At one point, the Stuart Cove feeder gently grabbed a shark and turned it over on its back as we all watched with astonishment. The shark suddenly went into a state of tonic immobility—a natural state of paralysis. I read later that sharks can be placed in that state simply by inverting them—provided one has the courage to do it. The shark can remain in that state of paralysis for an average of 15 minutes before it recovers, but in that case, it only lasted a few seconds, long enough for us to observe the paralysis. Scientists have often exploited that phenomenon to study shark behavior. So, if you ever find yourself being attacked by a shark, simply grab it and turn it over on its back…!

Suddenly, a shark peeled away from the group, flicked its tail slowly and headed straight toward Andrew and me. Its beady eyes, chipped teeth, and diabolical smile succeeded in frightening us for an instant as it passed over our heads like a silent submarine. As it turned and came back toward us, the photographer caught all three of us in a great pose—we stopped breathing shortly so that bubbles did not obscure the view. When the shark passed back over us, both Andrew and I instinctively violated an important rule and let our hand slide gently along its belly as it swam back toward the bait box. Only then did I notice a large fishhook caught in the corner of its mouth trailing a length of line. I was told later that this was a common sight.

Andrew and the author on a shark-feeding adventure organized by Stewart Cove Dive Center, New Providence Island, Bahamas.

At the end of the feed, the sharks all quickly disappeared to seek nourishment elsewhere. We remained until they had gone and then explored the area to look for the sharks' teeth that often fall out and settle to the bottom. Only a couple of divers were lucky enough to find one. Finally, we surfaced and made our way back to the boat.

The Bahamas offer some of the best shark encounters in the world today. Most are well organized, the waters are warm and crystal-clear, and you get excellent action. The experience was everything we had expected, and I highly recommend it as an experience to remember. Andrew would heartily agree. He was able to check it off his list and move on to other adventures while carrying with him great memories of this one.

The recent popularity of the shark dive spurred the Professional Association of Diving Instructors (PADI)[87] to offer a Shark Awareness Course, which is now available at several locations in the Bahamas. Those wanting a closer encounter can take one of the Assistant Shark Feeder Courses, which allows recreational divers to don a chain-mail suit and feed the sharks.

There are numerous sites on the Internet designed to instill fear and to emphasize the danger of participating in commercially organized shark encounters. One site ventured the opinion that no one had ever lost money underestimating the intelligence and judgment of scuba divers, especially those who dive with sharks, and that "shark feeding is to the Bahamas what sex and violence is to Hollywood." Another generally described dive operations as "overpriced and overdeveloped tourist traps." Several sites are replete with gruesome descriptions and photos of shark attacks, showing missing and mangled limbs of those foolish enough to go frolicking with sharks—blatant fear mongering. Several organizations are strongly opposed to the sport. On January 2002, the Florida Fish and Wildlife Conservation Commission managed to get a law passed that made it illegal for divers to feed marine wildlife in the State of Florida. A grassroots coalition of recreational divers, dive operators, fishermen, and environmental groups fought a two-year battle with the dive industry—most notably PADI and DEMA (Diving Equipment Marketing Association)—to get the law passed.

Statistically, shark attacks are both uncommon and less risky than many other ordinary activities on the water, especially considering the number of people in the world's oceans on any given warm summer day. However, shark diving does require preparation, common sense, and good scuba diving experience and expertise. Shark feeding events began in the Bahamas more than 20 years ago, and during that time more than 60,000 divers have participated with virtually no incidents of a respectful guest being bitten. I am certain the danger posed by the Bahamian drivers encountered on route to Stuart Cove that July morning would have been much greater than the danger posed by the encounter with the sharks. The risk associated with shark diving is reasonable and controllable, and I am glad we were able to share the experience.

---

87   PADI is one of the leading organizations to teach diving at all levels, and to certify both divers and dive instructors; see http://www.padi.com/padi/default.aspx.

18

KASSEQUA

COASTAL WATERS, EASTERN U.S.A.
(2003 — 2004)

Hélène and I departed the Bahamas in early December of 2003 and slowly headed across to Florida with pleasant relaxing stops at Chub Cay and Bimini. After only a couple weeks on the water, life already seemed timeless.

We waited for a good weather window before heading across the notorious Gulf Stream—a powerful ocean current that flows north along the east coast of the United States. That time of year the weather was unpredictable, and every few days, winds would blow south against fast currents flowing north, creating treacherous, heavy seas in the Gulf Stream. It was our third time across and we were hoping for pleasant, calm seas. Unfortunately, we were not so lucky. Although the wind was from a favorable direction, it was quite strong and built 8 to 10-foot seas on the port quarter most of the way to Fort Lauderdale. The crew and the boat did very well at a steady 9 knots with an occasional 13 knots on the downside of a wave. The autopilot did most of the steering, which gave us time to watch the waves coming at us. Occasionally we had to counteract broaching, but otherwise *Kassequa* performed well. It was a great relief to enter Port Everglades despite heavy rain, poor visibility, and confused seas.

We made our way up the New River and docked at the Lauderdale Marine Center, a new marina with good services and reasonable prices. We found ourselves surrounded by mega-yachts, but *Kassequa* was not the least bit intimidated and held her head high. Clearing-in through United States Immigration and Customs had become much more complicated after the destruction of the World Trade Center Towers, and security was understandably tight. All boaters had to go to a United States Customs and Immigration office and present themselves in person instead of just checking in by phone.

Once that was done, we began to explore the city. Back on the mainland, things worked and we could get whatever we wanted at reasonable prices. The fruits and vegetables were plentiful and fresh; the stores were well stocked and we saw products we did not know existed. Hélène walked up and down the aisles in awe.

While in Fort Lauderdale, we acquired cell phone service and had an Air Card installed in the laptop computer to get wireless email and Internet over the cellular phone systems while cruising. It worked great so long as we were in range of a cell-tower. We also installed a special antenna to watch DirecTV while on the boat. The antenna followed the satellite signal as the boat swung, yawed, and rocked at anchor. For us, being connected with satellite TV, cell phones, wireless email, and the Internet was a necessity.

Just before Christmas, we moved to Cove Marina at Deerfield Beach, about 30 miles north of Fort Lauderdale, and celebrated Christmas and New Year's with our family. After the holidays, we made our way north on the ICW to North Palm Beach, St. Lucie Inlet and up the St. Lucie River to the town of Stuart.

It was near the end of January when we awoke to a cool, sunny day, dropped the mooring line, and headed across the Okeechobee Waterway, which is 155 miles long, and stretches across South Florida from Stuart on the Atlantic Ocean to Fort Myers on the Gulf of Mexico. Its main segments are the St. Lucie Canal, Lake Okeechobee, Lake Hicpochee, and Caloosahatchee River. The shallow waterway has five locks for small commercial and leisure craft. At the center of Florida's heartland, Lake Okeechobee is the largest of the Florida lakes and the second largest freshwater lake within the United States—second only to Lake Michigan. Its name was derived from the Seminole Indian words meaning "big water."

We found the central part of Florida to be quite different from the hustle and bustle and sophistication of the Gold Coast—much more laid-back and easygoing, with country-style surroundings. It was easy to navigate and the diverse scenery ranged from cow pastures to orange groves, to desolate swamps, to backwater towns, to sugarcane plantations. The trip was one of the highlights of our entire cruise.

Boating offers many interesting challenges, often when you least expect them. Twice I tried to leave the dock with a line still attached to the cleat. Fortunately, the boat was moving very slowly, it was early in the morning, the audience was small, and the only thing damaged was my ego. Then there was the time I backed over the line on the mooring ball and wrapped it around the prop shaft. After donning the wet suit and holding my breath a few times, I freed it with no adverse consequences. Another time, while approaching the mooring ball, I failed to get the line on the cleat before the wind blew the boat past, causing the line to catch on the prop and rudder, and pull the mooring ball and lines completely underwater. So, once again, I had to dive under the boat a few times in an attempt to untangle the mess of lines and chain. It was getting dark and the wind continued to blow. After an hour of struggling, we were able to get out of the mud and attached to the mooring ball, with the help of TowBoat US. That one experience more than paid for our annual unlimited towing insurance premium. Next time we wished to pick up a mooring ball, we would seek help from a friendly boater. Almost every day we learned something new, and that day was no exception.

Another notable experience occurred when we suddenly lost all power on the starboard prop while maneuvering into a tight slip with high winds and a strong tidal current. With only one prop on the port side, and no bow thruster, *Kassequa* instantly became uncontrollable. It turned out the starboard tail shaft had pulled out of the coupling after the retaining bolts had loosened and fallen out. The next few frantic minutes seemed like an eternity as dockhands and fellow boaters rushed over to manhandle her into the slip. We managed to avoid hitting the multi-million dollar yachts moored nearby, although Hélène later said she lost 10 years of her life in about 10 minutes. The excitement continued as TowBoat US once again came to the rescue and gently inched us out of the congested marina and up the river to a boatyard. They hauled us out early the next morning for repairs. The work was performed efficiently and by noon we were back in the water and on our way again. They say there are two groups of boaters: those who have run aground and those who will run aground. We were the former. Events like those seem disastrous when they happen, but afterwards their significance seems minor in the overall scheme of things, and they improve one's seamanship.

Fort Myers lies on the western end of the Okeechobee Waterway. We decided to spend a few days moored at the City of Fort Myers Yacht Basin on the Caloosahatchee River opposite the old part of the city. It was quiet during our visit; however, the downtown and waterfront were being developed and one day it will undoubtedly be a busy spot if the town fathers have their way. A visit to the summer homes of Thomas Edison and Henry Ford was the highlight of our stop in Fort Myers. Edison was named the "Man of the Century" a few years ago—an excellent choice, in my opinion. Every time we turn on the lights, we should say a silent thank-you in his honor. It was disappointing to see the obvious deterioration of the buildings and grounds; however, renovations were finally underway using visitors' fees and private donations.

From Fort Myers we made our way north up the west coast to Charlotte Harbor, and spent five weeks moored at the Burnt Store Marina located eight miles south of Punta Gorda—a very peaceful and relaxing place, notwithstanding the numerous human snowbirds that flock there during the winter months. In fact, three such residents were old friends from the Trident Yacht Club near Gananoque, Ontario. We had a great time socializing, shopping, visiting, and cruising with them. The weather was near perfect. We enjoyed sunset cruises on Charlotte Harbor with side trips to the surrounding islands, including Boca Grande on Gasparilla Island (where the Bush clan regularly visits to relax and play golf), Cabbage Key (where the patrons had covered the walls of the local bar with dollar bills), and Venice, where we had a great visit with friends. Nearby Useppa Island was so private they chased you away unless you were a member. We did not feel deprived, anchored a short distance off the beach, sipping wine in quiet solitude as the sun went down.

Hélène on Kassequa, enjoying the ambiance of Burnt Store Marina.

We finally departed Burnt Store Marina to explore the west coast of Florida further. Our first stop was Sanibel Island, famous for shelling and beautiful sunsets. Obviously, during the past 50 years or so, millions of tourists had collected most of the shells. We had been spoiled by the beaches in the Bahamas, and here the beach seemed dirty and ill-maintained, and, with no good reason to stay, the next day we moved down the coast to Naples and found a very quiet and peaceful anchorage just inside Gordon's Pass. A pleasant dinghy ride two miles further up the river brought us to downtown Naples, a hangout for the rich and famous, with elegant condominiums, shops, restaurants, clubs, and parks—a beautiful place to visit.

At that point, we had a decision to make. From Naples, we could return to the east coast either by going south around the Florida Keys or back across the Okeechobee Waterway. After a careful study of the charts and discussions with other boaters, we decided to avoid the Keys. Most boaters did not speak well of the Keys, mainly because the place has a reputation of being quite unfriendly to transient boaters. It is a National Wildlife Refuge and one must follow the many restrictions and regulations. Merely touching the bottom can attract a stiff fine, and having to be towed off a sandbar can make a big dent in one's cruising budget. The waters are very shallow and touching the bottom is a not-infrequent occurrence, even for a meticulous boater. In addition, part of the Keys is a "No Discharge" zone and being so strict, it seemed like spitting in the ocean could subject one to visits from the environmental police. The environmentalists want to prevent private citizens from interacting with their own environment, but they conveniently ignore the communities, such as Key West, that dump raw sewage directly into it.

We had enjoyed the Okeechobee Waterway immensely the first time across, so with our new information, we decided to go back the same way we had come. The scenery, the wildlife, and the vegetation made it a very enjoyable journey, especially when traveling very early in the morning, which we were inclined to do. Two days later, we arrived back at Stuart and, once again, picked up a mooring ball at Southpoint Anchorage, intending to stay for a few days. It was a convenient location to catch up with our snail-mail, and stock up on a few provisions from Publix and the local farmers market.

On March 31, 2004, we departed Stuart and resumed our cruise north on the ICW. The plan was to follow the spring season, hoping to arrive at the entrance to the Chesapeake Bay in early May. So far, the arriving spring weather had been exceptionally good—pleasantly cool in the evenings and warming to 70–80°F during the day. We were able to travel whenever we felt the urge, with little concern for the weather. It was a bit disconcerting to deal with 8—12 foot tides in that area of the coast, but all the marinas had floating docks so it was hardly noticeable. A 12-foot tidal range can make anchoring quite tricky, so we did not try that, although many boaters did. During the next two weeks, we journeyed to Vero Beach, Cocoa Beach, and Daytona Beach. A major highlight was a full-day tour of the Kennedy Space Center at Cape Canaveral. The experience testified to the greatness of man and the can-do attitude of the brightest and best of America—food for the soul—a welcome contrast to the continuous barrage of depravity engulfing us every day from the mainstream media. The Dream is alive, and Mars is next. Thank God for pioneers.

We spent Easter of 2004 at St. Augustine, Florida. Strong winds that followed a cold front held us down for a few extra days, so we enjoyed more time to explore and it turned out to be a blessing. St. Augustine was established after the ruthless Spaniard Juan Ponce de Leon landed on April 2, 1513. Since the place was full of flowers, he named it "La Florida," the flower. St. Augustine is a small city, which a local tourist brochure described as being "the oldest continuously occupied European settlement in the United States." In 1917, Ring W. Lardner wrote a book called *Gullible's Travels*, in which he said the following about St. Augustine:

> First, we went to St. George Street and visited the oldest house in the United States. Then we went to Hospital Street and seen the oldest house in the United States. Then we turned the corner, went down St. Francis Street and inspected the oldest house in the United States. Then we dropped into a soda fountain and I had an egg phosphate, made from the oldest egg in the Western Hemisphere. We passed up lunch and got into a carriage drawn by the oldest horse in the Florida, and we rode through the country all afternoon and the driver told us some o' the oldest jokes in the book.

Clearly, Mr. Lardner was not impressed with things old, even though it seemed to be a place containing so much of the past in so compact an area. These days the city certainly takes full advantage of its history and aggressively goes after the tourist trade. The visit to the Castillo de San Marcos was a highlight. It is an unusual castle designed to funnel enemy assault troops into killing fields. On Easter Sunday morning, we visited the oldest Catholic parish in North America and enjoyed the Easter parade with southern belles, high school bands, and noisy floats. We walked the narrow streets depicting early Spanish architecture and colonial life, and concluded that at some future date it would be great to return and spend time learning more about St. Augustine and its people.

By April 14 the weather had improved enough for us to depart St. Augustine and continue north on the ICW. After an uneventful day of cruising, we arrived at Amelia Island only to discover that the water level was too low for us to enter the harbor, so we had to float around until the tide came in. Once again, the tidal range was about 12 feet, which created a significant current, even inside the harbor. The level was unusually low, apparently because of high winds and the alignment of sun, moon, stars, and any other celestial body that might have had an effect. Eventually, we were able to enter the Amelia Island Yacht Basin and then, after a few tense moments dodging other boats—all the while negotiating a strong wind and swift current—we managed to back into a narrow slip.

We spent a comfortable night and departed Amelia Island early on a perfect sunny, cool day, then made our way north past St. Mary's Inlet on the border between Florida and Georgia. Several United States Navy installations were in the area and we observed a submarine being escorted out to sea. Since

September 11, 2001, private vessels had to stay at least 500 yards away from all military vessels, so we had to move out of the channel and point the bow away from the submarine as it passed. Failure to do so provoked a quick response from the Coast Guard providing escort. That was not the time to dialog or ask questions about what was going on. The movement of military vessels was announced on the VHF radio in advance, so if a boater seemed ignorant and surprised, the Coast Guard knew they were not listening to the radio—a legal requirement while underway.

Many situations occur as one cruises, and staying alert is critical. It is important to know where you are, where you are going, and what to expect as you move along. Numerous publications are available that explain it all, if they are read. Many boaters have subjected themselves to risks they did not even know existed, simply because they were not prepared or exercised poor judgment. For example, it was not uncommon for skippers simply to follow the boat in front, assuming the skipper in front knew what he was doing. Often the followers were lucky—many times, they were not.

There is always new information to learn, especially when cruising in strange waters. Typically, I would spend one or two hours planning and organizing each new segment of the trip, but still encountered surprises along the way. Someone once described cruising as an idyllic experience interspersed with frequent moments of sheer terror. An overstatement, perhaps, but we found that five or six hours of cruising, even when everything went well, resulted in mental and physical exhaustion, albeit of a pleasant sort.

The next stop was at Jekyll Harbor Marina at Jekyll Island, Georgia. In the early 1900s, the island was a winter escape for the rich and famous, an exclusive community that Rockefeller, Vanderbilt, Morgan, Crane, Pulitzer, and others enjoyed. The state of Georgia bought Jekyll Island in 1947, and today it is both an upscale community and National Historic Site with 33 of its original homes and cottages remaining. The region is known as the "Land of Five Flags" because Spain (1540), France (1562), England (1736), the Confederacy (1860s), and finally the United States (1865) have all claimed it as their territory.

We borrowed the bicycles the marina provided and rode around the entire island, stopping to visit the sites. En route, we stumbled across an official government alligator hunter who had captured a large 10-foot male in order to relocate him to a more remote location. The alligator had grown too big for the small pond in which he was living and was feasting on the baby alligators. When we arrived, he was all tied up with duct tape while the hunter's eight-year-old son proudly sat atop him.

The section of the ICW in South Georgia immediately north of Jekyll Island was mostly miles and miles of shallow creeks and rivers bordered by nothing but swamp grass as far as one could see—boring. We had seen it all twice before and were not looking forward to seeing it again. Therefore, as we approached St. Simons Inlet, just north of Jekyll, we checked the sea. It was calm, and after a quick review of the charts, we decided to go offshore along the coast and then re-enter the ICW at Wassaw Sound near the Savannah River. It would be a long day—about 85 miles—but with sufficient time to return to the ICW before dark.

While offshore, we simply set a heading, engaged the autopilot, maintained a lookout and relaxed. During an offshore passage, solitude takes over. We usually sat on the sundeck reading, handling email, or surfing the Internet.[88] Despite the peacefulness, it was important to check the chart and be vigilant because shoals often extend out for many miles, knowing their location is critical. They are usually noted on the charts and sometimes marked with a buoy. Although there may be no land in sight, a dangerous piece of it could be lurking just below the surface. Traveling alone on the ocean, barely in sight of land, was always a welcome change from the stress and constant anxiety of navigating the ICW—checking the route, looking ahead for channel markers, dodging crab pots and fishing boats, watching for "No Wake" zones, overtaking, and being overtaken. We always preferred an offshore passage when the weather and sea conditions permitted.

We arrived at Wassaw Sound on schedule and proceeded to Thunderbolt, a small community on the outskirts of Savannah, Georgia. We were determined to allow adequate time to explore that famous city with its remarkable history, so we looked forward to an extended stop. Rumors had circulated up and down the ICW that the marina at Thunderbolt delivered Krispy Kreme donuts and a newspaper to each boat every morning. Sure enough, the next day we discovered the tradition was alive and well—a half a dozen donuts each morning.

There are three major cities along the southeastern coast of the United States that deserve serious exploring: St. Augustine, Charleston, and Savannah. They are similar in many respects—each offering excellent examples of good old southern hospitality, tons of history, and many interesting places to visit. Of the three, we preferred Savannah. All were interesting stops, each with their own personality and idiosyncrasies. I usually observed the bigger picture, while Hélène pointed out the details, such as the magnolia blossoms, the white rocking chairs on the large porches, and the stained glass windows in many of the homes. Although I may have been looking around, I always saw more through her eyes.

On April 21, we received the exciting news that we would finally be grand-

---

88 We could usually get a good cell phone signal connected to the wireless Air Card in the laptop so long as we stayed within five or six miles of the coast.

parents for the first time. My daughter and her husband were expecting! Two days later, we celebrated the event, along with my birthday, at Bubba Gump's Restaurant in Charleston, SC.

The next day, near the North Carolina border we approached the only floating pontoon bridge on the entire ICW and noticed congestion on the waterway. An officer informed us that the bridge was closed indefinitely while a truck was being salvaged from the middle of the channel. Apparently, a good ol' southern boy returning home from the bar the previous night had decided that with enough speed he could jump the gap from one side of the channel to the other while the bridge was open. Surprisingly, he lived.

Instead of waiting, we backtracked a short distance to go offshore at the Little River Inlet. About four hours later, we arrived at Cape Fear River Inlet and re-entered the ICW with good waves and 20 knots of wind on the quarter. The shelter of the ICW came as a welcome relief, although most of the trip was quite pleasant. We moored in Southport, another quiet, sleepy North Carolina village, and enjoyed a couple of days visiting longtime friends who had recently built a retirement home overlooking the ICW. It was unique with its "Widow's Walk" and panoramic view from the roof.

After an enjoyable and uneventful cruise north from Southport, we arrived in Beaufort, NC, just in time to ride out a nasty cold front that was approaching. Beaufort was a thriving modern boating center and an easy place to spend some time. It is a popular stop for cruisers heading both north and south, and it was easy to see why. Every conceivable maritime service is available there, and it is the home of the North Carolina Maritime Museum with its artifacts from *Queen Anne's Revenge*, the flagship of the famous pirate Blackbeard. The ship sank in 1718, and after a search that lasted many years, it was recently discovered in 20 feet of water near Beaufort.

After some downtime relaxing in Beaufort, we traveled to Belhaven, and on to Norfolk, VA, stopping overnight a couple of times along the way. Twenty miles of that section of the ICW goes through the man-made Alligator River-Pungo River Canal, and as we studied the chart, our attention was drawn to a "Caution Note C" that read as follows:

> Both sides of the canal were foul with debris, snags, submerged stumps, and continuous bank erosion was caused by passing boats and tows. Corps of Engineers controlling dimensions, published in the U.S. Coast Guard Local Notices to Mariners, was generally less than the 90-foot projected width; consequently, navigation near mid-channel was recommended. Mariners were advised to exercise extreme caution when navigating the canal.

Caution notices like that tended to cause a little puckering. My anxiety was further raised after chatting with a skipper who had hit a stump, thereby significantly damaging his propellers and struts. He readily admitted going too fast and not paying close attention to the center of the channel. There was no choice but to go, so we departed with confidence and successfully negotiated the entire distance by late that afternoon. There was no traffic and the canal was alive with plenty of wildlife and interesting scenery. Hélène was at the helm most of the time.

As we approached Norfolk, a long tug and tow came into view. It turned out to be a barge with a large dredge dragging pipes that stretched out far behind. Two small tugs kept the trailing barge in line and helped to negotiate the turns and narrow bridges. The skipper, Captain Ed, was only traveling about three knots, so after a brief radio conversation to establish communications and discuss strategy, we negotiated a safe pass. As it turned out, we passed each other five times during the next week. Captain Ed traveled around the clock and got ahead of us at night, and then we would catch up and passed them during the day. At the end of the week, we had become quite well acquainted. Commercial vessels will not change course or speed to avoid a pleasure craft, so one must pay careful attention when passing. The vessel being passed always has the right-of-way, no matter what—an important rule of the sea.

The shock of Norfolk hit us in the face as we came around a bend in the river. For the past several weeks, we had become accustomed to meandering through the quiet, laid-back, easygoing rural atmosphere of the countryside. Norfolk was the exact opposite. We were suddenly surrounded by large warships, commercial vessels, shipyards, dry docks, tall buildings, warehouses, airplanes, helicopters, bridges, railways, and busy highways—all seemingly intermingled and emitting a cacophony of noise. We eventually managed to navigate through it all and tied up at a marina next to the boardwalk, only two blocks from the center of town. Norfolk lies at the northern end of the Intracoastal Waterway at the mouth of Chesapeake Bay.

We celebrated having navigated the entire eastern ICW, as well as a western portion of it. A major milestone completed! As the sun set over Norfolk, Hélène and I toasted each other on the back deck and then went downtown for dinner. Norfolk is a heavily industrial city; however, we were impressed with the cleanliness and quaintness of the waterfront and downtown areas. We toured the battleship *Wisconsin*, mothballed and moored downtown as a tourist attraction. The *Wisconsin* saw duty in WWII, the Korean War, and in Operation Desert Storm. If was definitely worth a couple hours of our time—and it was free.

We explored Chesapeake Bay during the next month or so. The bay stretches over 200 miles from north to south and 40 miles across at its widest point. The average depth is only 21 feet, and strong winds can change wave conditions quickly. It is termed an estuary—a body of water in which fresh river water mixes with salty seawater—and Chesapeake Bay is one of the largest estuaries in the world. Its brackish water is an ideal habitat for the blue crab, and it was necessary to keep a sharp lookout for crab pots as we cruised about, especially in the shallower areas. Crab dishes are prolific at the local restaurants and the local folks definitely know what to do with them.

The first stop up the Chesapeake Bay was Deltaville on the west side of the Bay and the eastern side of Virginia, followed by Solomons Island, one of the top destinations for mariners cruising on the Bay. It was reported that the resident population of Solomons Island was around 1,000, and the boating population was about 3,000. Many people in Washington, DC, keep their boats moored at Solomons Island and enjoy them on the weekends. The marina was in a very sheltered bay and we enjoyed a very quiet anchorage in the harbor on Back Creek. We can personally testify that the crab cakes at Stoney's Restaurant deserve their renown.

From Solomons we proceeded north to Annapolis, described as another "deliciously overgrown small town." Annapolis is a very popular boating destination. It is the capital city of Maryland and the home of the United States Naval Academy, WestPoint. A finger of water extended into the center of Old Town, near a bronze statue of Alex Haley, the author of *Roots*. It was a startling reminder of the slave auctions, and purportedly the site where Alex Haley's ancestor, Kunta Kinte, was sold. Annapolis was definitely worth an extended visit—lots of history and places to see and appreciate.

It was then time to explore the Potomac River and visit Washington, DC, where we intended to spend the long Memorial Day weekend. I was especially taken with Mount Vernon, home of George Washington, the first President of the United States, and his wife, Martha. The British granted Washington's great-grandfather the property in 1674, and it remained in the family until the Mount Vernon Ladies Association purchased it in 1858. George Washington is buried at the site along with members of his family. The property has been under restoration ever since and it is a very impressive historical site. We anchored in the Potomac that night, and enjoyed a beautiful sunset and a perfectly calm evening.

It was Memorial Day 2004, and the just-completed WWII Memorial was being officially dedicated, so we decided to take advantage of the opportunity to see it. Although about fifty years too late, it was certainly an impressive memorial to all those who fought and died for our freedom. Fortunately, the Memorial Day celebrations ensure that we remember and honor those who died defending our way of life. It is important to note that they did not die for peace—they died defending our freedom. Hélène took advantage of our time there to visit

Arlington Cemetery with friends. They arrived early and were able to complete their visit by the time the security agents started preparing for the president's arrival. Meanwhile, I stayed on the boat and watched the Memorial Day ceremonies on TV while listening to the 21-gun salute in the background—a very moving and impressive event.

We left Washington and headed down the Potomac River on June 1, 2004, en route to Beaufort, NC. For the last seven months, our cruising adventure on *Kassequa* had met all our expectations, and in another month, we planned to have the boat in dry dock and listed for sale.

> *The benefits I derive from freedom are largely the result of the uses of freedom by others, and mostly of those uses of freedom that I could never avail myself of. What is important is not what freedom I personally would like to exercise but what freedom some person may need in order to do things beneficial to society. This freedom we can assure to the unknown person only by giving it to all.*
>
> —F.A. Hayek

It was about noon when the phone rang, just as we were passing Mount Vernon. For the past several weeks, we had speculated about what the future might bring as the next chapter of our lives opened up. Little did we know that that phone call would present an opportunity to live and work in Asia—Taiwan, to be exact. The new owner of the Caterpillar dealer in Taiwan was looking for a Managing Director to put the business back on the road to recovery after several years of neglect. It was another post-acquisition restructuring assignment.

Was the timing of the phone call serendipity, or did the gods know our cruising adventure was ending and decided to take charge of our destiny once again? I do not believe in manifest destiny and chalked it up to serendipity. Later the same week I received another phone call from SpencerStuart in Toronto, inquiring if I would be interested in an opportunity in Ontario with similar challenges. After having gone a year with no specific options on the horizon other than retirement, there were two alternatives to be considered in a period of one week.

It is usually better to have options from which to decide, even though it can make the decision more agonizing. And agonize we did. Going to live on the other side of the world was not an easy decision, especially at that late stage in our lives. Would it work out? Should we move that far away from our children, our family, and friends? Would the Toronto opportunity be a better, safer choice? Hélène had long dreamed of seeing Asia, never thinking that she might live there one day. But what better way to see Asia? And perhaps surprisingly, our children were quite excited for us.

We decided to learn more about the Taiwan opportunity. On June 20, 2004, I departed for Kuala Lumpur, Malaysia, and Hong Kong, China, for interviews. The discussions went well. I felt comfortable with the people and the organization. I knew the Caterpillar business was much the same worldwide, and working for another dealership would be much like putting on a comfortable old shoe. Since I had already spent time living in Hong Kong and traveling much of Asia, it would not be such a new experience for me. However, it would be for Hélène, and Asia is so different in so many ways from the Western world that trying to describe it is next to impossible. One must see it, experience it, and live it to understand its nuances. Nevertheless, Hélène was an adventurer, and game to go if I was comfortable with the business arrangements. We took a deep breath, suppressed our anxiety and doubts, and I signed the contract.

Having made the final decision, we became quite excited and began to look forward to the future with great anticipation. Over the next month, our belongings were either sorted, given away, sold, discarded, put in storage or packed for shipment. Many detailed arrangements were necessary to get our travel visas from the Taiwan Cultural and Trade Office in Toronto before we left. We had to prove we were married, that we were not a security threat, that our education was valid, that we were citizens of Canada, that we were in good health, and that we could support ourselves. After a final whirlwind tour to say good-bye to our family and friends, we boarded a plane on July 27, 2004, and took off for Taipei.

19

IHLA FORMOSA

(2004 — 2008)

Taiwan is part of the sacred territory of the People's Republic of China. It is the inviolable duty of all Chinese people, including our compatriots in Taiwan, to accomplish the great task of reunifying the motherland.

—Preamble of the 1982 Constitution of
the People's Republic of China

Taiwan is an island located about 100 miles off the coast of China. It is one of the most densely populated regions on Earth, hosting 23 million souls jammed into an area slightly larger than Massachusetts and Connecticut combined. The squeeze is accentuated by a chain of mountains (covering about half the island) that are incapable of supporting human settlements. Taiwan has more people than Australia and about two-thirds that of Canada in a fraction of the space.[89]

In the 16th century, the Portuguese explorers were so impressed by the beauty of the island that they called it "Ihla Formosa," meaning "beautiful island." The Tropic of Cancer bisects both Taiwan and the Bahamas; and the weather is similar in both countries. Taiwan has two distinct seasons—cool and damp, and hot and humid. Typhoons are frequent from July to October, although residents take them in stride and they do not disturb normal life for long. Earthquakes are frequent, too, but normally small. A major one in 1999 killed over 2,000 people around its epicenter, near the town of Puli, the geographical center of the

---

[89] There are about 635 people per square kilometer, compared to about 30, 3, and 2 people per square kilometer in the United States, Canada, and Australia, respectively.

island. Soon after our arrival, we experienced a significant earthquake measuring seven on the Richter scale at its epicenter, which fortunately was located 100 kilometers offshore at a depth of about 6 kilometers under the Pacific Ocean. It was only a force four quake in Taipei area, and lasted for about 30 seconds, but was reported to be the strongest one recorded in Taiwan within the previous five years. The office building shook and seemed to jump around as I held my breath and waited—30 seconds of that is a long time. With hurricanes, at least you know they are coming, whereas earthquakes are usually a total surprise.

The original inhabitants of Taiwan were members of indigenous aboriginal tribes. Around the 14th and 15th centuries, ethnic Chinese (pirates, traders, and fishermen) arrived from the Chinese mainland. Later, in the 17th century, farmers from southeast China began to migrate to Taiwan, displacing the indigenous people in the process. Of course, they brought their language, religion, culture, and family traditions. The Portuguese were the first foreigners to establish an outpost on the island, and thus began over 400 years of turbulence—as evident by the Dutch invasion and Manchu takeover in the 17th century, right down to the long struggle for democracy that only took hold when Lee Teng Hui became the first democratically elected president in 1996.

While democracy eventually prevailed, conflict and uncertainties about Taiwan's legal status have continued. In the late 17th century, the Manchu dynasty more or less controlled the island as a prefecture of the province of Fujian, although it was very much still a frontier. Subsequently, as a result of the Sino-Japanese War and WWII, Japan occupied Taiwan from 1895 to 1945. When Japan surrendered after WWII, the territories that Japan had taken during the Sino-Japanese War, including Taiwan, were returned to China. However, this reversion to China did not settle the fate of Taiwan.

In 1945, the Kuomintang (KMT) escaped to Taiwan after losing the civil war against Mao Tse-tung and established marshal law on the island.[90] Chiang Kai-shek ruled the island with an iron hand, imposed strict press censorship, and imprisoned political dissidents—secret police were everywhere. The violence and police action affected almost every family on the island. On February 28, 1947, the KMT put down anti-government demonstrations by massacring thousands of Taiwanese civilians, and that date is still commemorated as an historical event to be forever remembered. The harsh treatment was counterproductive because many people began to think of themselves as Taiwanese rather than Chinese. Some went even further and began to think that Taiwan

---

90 As Chiang Kai-shek's Nationalists lost political and military ground to the Communists in 1948, Taiwan became a refuge and the island was flooded with several million Chinese. Currently, about 80 percent of the people living in Taiwan are descendents from ethnic Chinese ancestors who came from mainland China, either in the early centuries or after 1948.

should be an independent country, separate from the mainland. Those events established the roots for what today is the independence movement.

During the 1980s, the U.S. government pressured the ruling KMT to implement political reform. Eventually, in 1987, Chiang Ching-kuo[91] lifted marshal law and spawned the beginning of the democratic process. The KMT ruled Taiwan from 1949 until the major opposition party, the Democratic Progressive Party (DPP), was elected in the year 2000. Subsequently, Taiwan became a legitimate functioning multi-party democracy without a civil war or bloodshed—a very rare accomplishment.

The DPP advocated formal independence and sovereignty for Taiwan, which antagonized the PRC Communist leadership in Beijing and they intensified their efforts to diplomatically marginalize Taiwan. They have succeeded; over the years, Taiwan's political allies slipped away one by one, as they bowed to China's wishes and treated Taiwan as part of China, granting official diplomatic recognition only to the PRC. By doing so, these countries benefited from trade, investment, and foreign aid from China. Both Taiwan and China "bribed" several countries with foreign aid to give them official recognition—called "checkbook diplomacy." China had much deeper pockets and usually won that economic contest. Although the United States also does not recognize Taiwan as a separate country independent of China, they continued to sell military hardware to Taiwan and reserved the right to defend the island if it was invaded by China.

The KMT Party advocated friendlier ties to China with ongoing dialogue, diplomacy, and closer economic and cultural cooperation. The KMT and the DPP tended to split the population. The Chinese in Taiwan, whose ancestors escaped from the mainland with Chiang Kai-shek after 1945, generally supported the KMT, while the local Taiwanese mostly favored the DPP. The ultimate outcome of the polarization is certainly not obvious; however, everyone seemed to agree on two critical points: a) the Taiwanese people have no stomach for conflict and do not want to go to war, and b) Taiwan's democratic system is sacrosanct.

The major dispute with China centers on whether Taiwan is a sovereign country or a province of the PRC. Long and detailed arguments have been put forth to defend both points of view. The issue must be resolved by long and intense negotiations—or a war. China intimidated Taiwan with about 1,000 missiles pointed at it from across the Strait, and concern has been expressed about how much control the Communist Party leadership has over the military to prevent them from prematurely firing off a few missiles. If domestic unrest

---

91   Chiang Ching-kuo was Chiang Kai-shek's son, and he took over after Chiang Kai-shek died in 1975.

continues to grow and China becomes unstable, party leaders may feel the need to rally the people around a nationalist cause in order to maintain power and control. Reclaiming Taiwan by force would be a perfect way to create national fervor and provide an excuse to clamp down on growing domestic unrest. Of course, if this happened, thousands of Taiwanese and Chinese people would die, and it would risk a serious war between China and the United States.

In 2005, the PRC passed legislation authorizing military action if Taiwan takes concrete action to change its constitution in order to officially declare independence and become a sovereign country. The communist leadership is determined to "reunite" Taiwan with mainland China, just as they did with Inner Mongolia, Tibet, Hong Kong, and Macau. Despite assurances to the contrary ("one country, two systems"), Hong Kong and Macau have so far not been allowed to develop a legitimate democratic system, so Taiwan has good reason to be skeptical about being able to maintain its democratic system if reunification were to take place.

China has been described as a country with a billion-plus people who do not like taking instructions and with a leadership who insists on giving them. As more and more of these billion-plus people experience economic liberties, their dislike for taking instructions will increase, as will their desire to participate in their own governance. Capitalism is a political system as well as an economic system, and it cannot coexist for long with a dictatorship. An objective glance around the world during the past few hundred years will demonstrate the truth in that—no matter what the theorists may say.

In my experience, the Chinese people are the hardest working capitalists and entrepreneurs in the world, even surpassing the Japanese. If a billion Chinese eventually combine political and economic freedom, they could become a world powerhouse, and our children would be well advised to learn the language. On the other hand, if economic and political freedoms do not converge, I predict China will eventually fall back into chaos and anarchy—heaven forbid. The outcome is not clear, and subject to much speculation.

Few Chinese would be old enough to remember as far back as 1912 when "about 20 million citizens walked, bicycled, or rickshawed their way to polling stations across the country to elect a national government." The process was considered a success.[92] Unfortunately, this budding democracy was soon destroyed by warlords, violence and corruption. Later in 1954, the Chinese again went to the poles to elect members of the local legislatures after Mao Tse-tung promised democracy. Then, for a second time, the opportunity for democracy vanished as Mao changed his mind, installed a dictatorship, and plunged the

---

92 Bruce Gilley, *China's Democratic Future, How it will Happen and Where it will Lead*, (2004).

country into a nightmare that killed about 50 million Chinese citizens.

In March of 2008 during the Taiwanese presidential election, it was reported that millions of mainland Chinese had their eyes glued to their television sets; one Chinese commentator enviously remarked, "Today we are all Taiwanese." China is not immune to the forces of social science, and these forces continue to chip away at the dictatorship. There is no doubt that the Chinese people desire freedom as much as anyone else does, and I predict that they will eventually embrace a democratic form of government—in fact, the process has already begun. Certainly, the remarkable economic progress that has taken place since my first visit in 1979 justifies that prediction.[93] The transition is already turbulent, but if they decide to follow the Taiwanese example, it could be relatively peaceful.

As the 21st century unfolds, Taiwan will have a greater influence on the future of China than China will have on the future of Taiwan—in fact, it already has. I am very optimistic about the future of Taiwan and cautiously optimistic about the precarious future of China—both are joined at the hip. We are in the middle of an unfolding drama with major geopolitical implications and consequences.

The future of the world will be greatly influenced by how events in Asia unfold during the coming decades. To understand and possibly help guide future scenarios, it is important to understand the history and culture of the region. Many excellent books have been written recently on these subjects, and they present a wide variety of interesting and valuable analyses, opinions and predictions. In addition to the plethora of books about doing business in the region, I encourage you to read the following:

- Richard C. Bush, *Untying the Knot: Making Peace in the Taiwan Strait* (2005); Bush, who worked on China and Taiwan issues his entire professional career, offers a detailed study of the relationship between Taiwan and China, exploring the significant differences and many similarities of the two sides and the difficulties that must be resolved;
- Richard C. Bush and Michael E. O'Hanlon, *A War Like No Other: The Truth about China's Challenge to America* (2007), which argues that America and China are closer to war over Taiwan than most realize;

---

93 Although over 100 million Chinese are still very poor, several hundred million have escaped destitution, and a middle class is developing rapidly in the urban and coastal areas. As the *Economist* recently described the situation, "*In China 25 years ago, over 600 million people—two-thirds of the population—were living in extreme poverty (on $1 a day or less). Now, the number on $1 a day is below 180 million.*" Obviously, there is still much room for improvement; however, China's recent economic development has probably been the most successful program in all of history to rescue people from extreme poverty. "Somewhere Over the Rainbow," *Economist*, January 26, 2008, 25

- Ted Galen Carpenter, *America's Coming War with China—A Collision Course over Taiwan* (2005), another interesting and thought-provoking point of view;
- Kenneth Lieberthal, *Governing China* (2004), a very objective analysis of China from the ancient imperial Chinese system to present day administration;
- Alan M. Watchman, "Why Taiwan? Geostrategic Rationales for China's Territorial Integrity" (2007), which describes Taiwan's increasing geostrategic importance to China, and presents a perspective from the imperial dynasties to Beijing's current government;
- Guy Sorman, *The Empire of Lies, The Truth about China in the Twenty-First Century*, (2008), in which the author lets the Chinese people "speak for themselves" and "presents the reader with a vivid portrait of the real China, revealing the dangers behind the illusions."
- Bruce Gilley, *China's Democratic Future: How Will it Happen and Where will it Lead*, (2004). The author predicts that an elite-led transformation rather than a popular overthrow will end China's communist government, and describes how democracy in China will be "Chinese" with fundamental liberal features rather than Western. He also considers the implications of this "Chinese" democracy for Asia and the United States.
- Jung Chang and Jon Halliday, *Mao: The Unknown Story* (2005), a groundbreaking biography of Mao Tse-tung, based on decades of research and interviews with virtually everyone inside and outside of China who had any dealings with him. Keep in mind that the current leaders are Mao's political heirs and his picture still hangs in Tiananmen Square.

After 14 hours on the plane, we landed at the new airport in Hong Kong on July 29, 2004.[94] Soon we were checked into the Mandarin Hotel in Hong Kong. It was one of the oldest and most elegant hotels in the city, and had not changed much since the last time I visited in 1986. Many good memories came flashing back. That short one-day stop in Hong Kong was necessary to complete some employment documents and open bank accounts. Showing Hélène around the city would have to wait until another time. The next day we landed in Taipei and set up temporary accommodations in a hotel while we searched for a place to live. Although we were still struggling with jet lag, we wanted to take advantage of the weekend to look around at possible locations for our new home. The real estate agent met us at the hotel and worked hard to find something we liked. She spoke excellent English and certainly knew the territory. There

---

94 For five years, from 2001 to 2005, over five million passengers voted Hong Kong the Best International Airport. It is modern, efficient, and connected to the city by a fast Airport Express railway with trains departing every 12 minutes for a 24-minute journey downtown.

were no multiple listing services, so the only homes we saw were those listed by the agent. For that reason, it was typical to use several agents to help with the search.

During the next two weeks, Hélène searched diligently. We had only brought a few personal belongings, and our accommodation expectations were relatively modest—furnished three bedrooms, modern appliances, parking garage, security, central air conditioning and heat, and a view of the mountains. I say "relatively modest" based on typical North American living standards. She soon found a nice condominium located in a northern suburb of Taipei called Tienmu. The condominium was on the second floor of a new four-story building. The unique design was taken right out of a Frank Lloyd Wright book, including furniture, windows, and moldings. All of our modest expectations were met except there was almost no view, since we were only on the second floor and surrounded by taller buildings. Our new home was very comfortable, and most Taiwanese would say we lived in luxury. Compared to many, I suppose we did, but compared to most North Americans, not true—there was limited space, no place to BBQ, no patio, no yard, and hardly any sidewalks. As a consolation, we were close to a nice park and hiking trails in the mountains.

Tienmu village lies at the foot of Yangmingshan Mountain where the air is clear, the weather cool, and breezes plentiful. Tienmu village has attracted many expatriate families because it is the home of the American International School, the European International School, and the Japanese International School. We discovered some English-speaking shopkeepers; a good selection of cafes, boutiques, and stores for all kinds of shopping; and readily available public transportation—a unique ambiance. The Community Services Center in Taipei offered many opportunities to help new expatriates become settled, and we took full advantage of them. Their monthly magazine lists more than 30 community services, sports, and social organizations to meet many different tastes in activity preferences. There was no reason to feel isolated and alone. Within a few weeks, we had created comfortable surroundings with friends, services, and activities to help make us feel at home in Taiwan. The best part was the beautiful, friendly, and welcoming demeanor of the Taiwanese people—a pleasant contrast to the past five years spent in the Bahamas, where many of the locals did not want us there at all.

Although our four children were all adults by that time, one never stops parenting. Living in Taipei meant that we would have to do it long distance. Phone calls and emails are great, but it is difficult to send a hug through the mail or cyberspace. Fortunately, our children did not make us feel guilty for pursuing our life on the other side of the world. Nevertheless, it required more effort and empathy to maintain emotional closeness. There is no doubt that the distance and the infrequent visits added to our emotional stress; however, at times it seemed our love for our children grew stronger as a result. Madelyn, our first grandchild, was born after we left Canada, and we were disappointed to miss that wonderful event.

Our first granddaughter, Madelyn

Pictures and phone calls and descriptive updates on her growth were poor substitutes for being there, but that was one of the important trade-offs we knowingly made at the time. Was it worth it, and for whom? Who really knows?

Our choice to come to Taiwan was thoughtful, deliberate, and based on the best information available at the time. Therefore, it was a good choice, and we hope it turns out to be the right one, too. We are confident the parenting we did during the past 40 years taught our children to know right from wrong, and how to think and make choices for better living. Of course, as adults, the structure of their lives is now mainly dependent on the choices they make, rather than those we make. They do not need much parenting; however, when given a chance, we do it mainly for our own enjoyment. Usually, they indulge us.

Moving around was an interesting challenge, but not a particularly difficult one. The domestic airline network was extensive, with four airlines providing regular flights to most cities throughout the island. It was very convenient and the fare from one end of the island to the other was reasonable. Taiwan's traditional rail network circled the island and we found it to be inexpensive, efficient, and complicated. A north-south high-speed railway was completed in 2007. It is fast (300 kph), smooth, comfortable, and not dependent on the weather. Travel time from one end of the island to the other is only 90 minutes. City busses are ubiquitous, comfortable, and cheap; however, to find out where they went, we had to get on and ride, or get the information from an experienced rider. The Taipei mass rapid transit system (MRT) is clean, fast, and comfortable, and passes most of the major destinations. Combining the MRT and the bus got us everywhere we wanted to go. Taxis are clean, modern, cheap, and abundant, but the drivers speak almost no English, so it helped us to write the destination on a card in Chinese characters. The downside was that most taxi drivers we encountered seemed to have a death wish—keep your life insurance paid up if you go by taxi very often. I soon learned enough Chinese to direct the taxis with basic instructions to turn right, left, go straight, and stop. We also became familiar with the local transportation systems and used them extensively.

Driving in Taipei required steely nerves and was nothing short of madness much of the time. Roads are heavily traveled; many road signs are not in English, and English-language road maps are hard to find. Impatient drivers routinely make death-defying passing maneuvers. It is utter chaos as scooters, cars, taxis, pedestrians, and busses all try to be the first to pass the one in front. The scooters are everywhere. Whole families, including small babies, hang on for dear life as they wind through traffic at high speed. In North America, the drivers would be arrested and jailed for child endangerment; but here, that inexpensive mode of transportation allows the average Taiwanese to enjoy some independence, commute to work, and support the family.

My driver, Johnson, drove like a typical Taiwanese, which raised my stress level significantly. After my coaching failed to have an effect, I wrote a detailed Job Description and sent him to driving school. He learned CPR, the Heimlich maneuver, and a few security tips; and he acquired an official Chauffeur's Certificate. Although he was overjoyed that someone cared enough, it was not evident that he learned any good driving habits. He continued to get in the left lane when turning right, and the right lane when turning left in an attempt to get one car length closer to his destination. His habit of passing on the shoulder of the road stressed me out, so no more of that. I became convinced that driving safely was considered a sign of weakness and a loss of face. Unfortunately, after three accidents, continuing bad driving habits, and conflict with the office staff, Johnson was encouraged to look for another job. Frankie, my new driver, was much more professional and understood that the safety and comfort of the passengers were more important than being the first across the finish line.

Typical street scene in Taipei—congested, but pleasant, safe and friendly.

Taiwan High Speed Railway—smooth and comfortable at 300kph.

IHLA FORMOSA

Living in Taiwan entailed some adjustment to accommodate the language. The Chinese language has about 50,000 highly developed ideographic characters, or pictograms. Early in the 19th century, the usual form of spelling Chinese words and names in English (Romanization) was called the Wade-Giles system. During the Second World War, a system called Yale was developed by the famous university of that name. In 1979, the *New York Times* developed a new method, known as pinyin, and that has been adopted as the most common method used in mainland China. Of course, Taiwan had to come up with their own system to counter China, so they developed a system called Tongyong. All methods of Romanizing Chinese characters are tools for pronunciation, not a language. They use phonetics and the roman alphabet to duplicate the sound of a Chinese word or character. Unfortunately, none of the methods is simple because they combine various letters of the alphabet in different ways to form the sound of the Chinese word. Even the pinyin words formed by the letters of the alphabet take on different sounds than are typically used in English phonetics.

It doesn't stop there. In Taiwan, the Taipei City Government adopted pinyin for their street signs, and the Provincial Government chose Tongyong. Some transliterations are so varied as to defy a logical connection. The signs on the freeway pointing to the same town may say Muja, Muzha, or Mujha. Unless the Chinese character describing a particular sound is written down, it is impossible to know what the sound means. For example, a professor at Beijing University wrote a coherent story about a hundred years ago using 95 Chinese characters all having the same sound.[95] When that sound was spelled in pinyin, it was "shih." The story demonstrated that transliteration, using pinyin or any other system, would never obviate the need for the Chinese characters. The language cannot be reduced to an alphabet, and therefore, the characters are here to stay. Nevertheless, pinyin has been used effectively as a method for learning to speak the language without necessarily learning what the characters mean.

Mandarin Chinese is considered a level III language, or exceptionally difficult, because it has four tones that all have different meanings and is not based on an alphabet—each character has to be memorized. Reading a newspaper and normal conversation require knowing about 3,000 to 5,000 characters. Nevertheless, shortly after we arrived, Hélène courageously undertook the challenging task of learning to speak some survival Chinese using the pinyin system. She persisted and made good progress. I decided that learning our home

---

95 Tim Clissold, *Mr. China* (2004), 136; that memoir is the true story of Mr. Clissold's collision with the Chinese as a venture capitalist during the period from 1995 to 2002. Highly recommended.

address and how to direct a taxi was sufficient, given the state of atrophy that my brain had reached. Dealing with the language was a handicap in almost everything we did. However, eventually sign language, a few key words, and persistence achieved a level of basic communication necessary to deal with the essentials, like shopping, ordering food, and getting directions. I was surprised to discover that English was much less common in Taiwan than in Hong Kong and Singapore. In our company, I was the only one of 150 employees who did not speak Chinese, and initially, that was a significant source of frustration at work.

※

Most expatriates experience some culture shock when trying to adjust to life in Taiwan.[96] The shock usually hits once the "honeymoon phase" has passed and the excitement of the move has worn off. That was normal and unavoidable, since one can never be fully prepared for what is different and unknown. Living in a foreign country far away from home, family, and old routines can be difficult. Never having been exposed to Asia and not having a job situation to keep her occupied, Hélène experienced a short period of stressful adjustment. We realized that our stay in Taiwan could only be successful if we both felt right, and we worked to achieve that goal.

It is important to understand the many ways in which Asian culture differs from North American culture. In some cases, the difference is dramatic. For example, Western Caucasians like a healthy-looking tan and often spend hours lying in the hot sun to get the job done. Asians much prefer a snow-white skin color. Milky-white skin is considered elegant and there is a Chinese saying that if your skin is white you can cover most of your ugliness. TV ads promote a wide variety of natural and artificial products to block out the sun and remove tiny facial hairs and dead cells to give the skin a clean, glossy—and whiter—look. That cultural preference supported a large and active cosmetics business.

When speaking to Taiwanese people, often what is not said is more important than what is. They usually speak indirectly. For example, the question, "Can you fix the TV?" probably means, "Fix it now, I need to use it." Communications are usually aimed at building relationships and preserving harmony within the group. There is usually implicit meaning in what is said, and one must learn to understand the unspoken message. Non-verbal communication often provides important clues. The Western tendency to "call a spade a spade" or "tell it like it is" or "quit beating around the bush and spell it out" is usually considered bad

---

96   I am indebted to Amy Liu and the Taipei Community Services Center for reference information about Taiwanese culture and customs. See www.community.com.tw

form. That presented a special challenge for me because I prefer to "tell it like it is."

Communication is further complicated by the importance Asians place on hierarchy. The hierarchical structure often determines what can be said and how it is to be said. Some people, based on their perceived position in the hierarchy, do not feel they are entitled to speak, or feel they should only voice their opinions and thoughts when they are individually solicited. The Chinese character for "good" and "obedient" is the same—pronounced "guai" in pinyin. It is a word often used when addressing children. From a young age, children are expected to listen and learn through memorization, never questioning their teachers. They are not taught or encouraged to think for themselves, or to argue and discuss issues. Taiwanese are taught to show respect and to engage in polite talk with elders and those in positions of authority. They learn not to take credit or be boastful. The downside of that is they often grow up with low self-confidence, and demonstrate insecurity and shyness. Consequently, it is often difficult for them to think critically, and step up and take charge of a situation, or to show initiative and take action when facing a problem or a crisis.

Another important cultural characteristic relates to being an insider or an outsider. An insider always enjoys special treatment. Family members, relatives, and close friends are insiders. Businesses and property are often owned by several family members—insiders. The local Caterpillar dealership bought a piece of property for a new branch office and the title was held by five brothers and an 85-year-old mother—all of whom had to sign and chop the documents.[97] Within an organization, employees on the same hierarchical level may be insiders, whereas others are considered outsiders and are often treated as strangers. It is unusual for Chinese to initiate interactions or to develop social relationships with outsiders.

Outsiders can work toward becoming insiders by building their individual "guanxi account." There is no good English equivalent for Chinese "guanxi." It is about relationships, connections, friendships, dependencies, and obligations. Guanxi involves ongoing reciprocal exchanges of gifts, assistance, services, references, and introductions. The Chinese mentality is very much one of "You scratch my back, and I'll scratch yours." In essence, that boils down to exchanging favors regularly and voluntarily. One's guanxi account gains when help is provided, and places an obligation on the other person to return the help at some unspecified future date. If one receives, then one incurs an obligation to give later on. Be suspicious when receiving a significant gift because it may indi-

---

97 In China, from ancient times to the present, your chop affixes your credit and your promise to all official documents, no matter how important or trivial. After signing your name, your chop is still required for a document to be legally binding.

cate a major favor will be expected in the future.

    The significance of guanxi became quite evident when I tried to get our sales representatives to make cold calls on new customers. New customers—strangers—were outside the salesman's guanxi system, and had no obligation to consider a purchase. The salesman waited for an opportunity to develop some guanxi with the new customer. One area manager worked long and hard to establish a relationship with a significant customer in the region—to no avail. Then it was discovered the customer went to school with his brother-in-law and they suddenly were members of the same guanxi system and could talk serious business. The basic concept of selling Caterpillar products is to demonstrate the benefit of the products and services; however, in Asia, guanxi is a fundamental component of doing successful business and may be the most important factor in a purchase decision. It also explains the frequency of nepotism and special favors—often thought of as bribery or corruption in the Western value system. In Asia, a conflict of interest is simply a competitive advantage, an effective way to keep one's guanxi account in balance.

    When it comes to giving gifts, the Taiwanese like to keep it simple: just give a red envelope—stuffed with money. It is called a "Hung-Bao." That is to help pay for the 12-course meal you will be served at the typical wedding. At the reception, someone will take out the money, count it, and record your name and the amount given. The Hung-Bao envelopes are always red—considered a happy and lucky color. Lacking discretion, I once asked, "If that's the case, why does the bride usually wear a white dress—a color associated with bad luck, tragedy, or death?" A mumbled reply included some mention of "Western influences." The negative implications of the color white often stood in the way of serving white wine. Many Chinese functions we attended only served red wine. There is a bit more to gift giving than what I've so far mentioned, and one must know what not to give as a gift. The following items should be avoided:

- Clocks: The sound of the Chinese phrase "giving a clock" (Song Zhong) is like the sound one says when saying good-bye to someone at their funeral.
- Flowers: White and yellow flowers are normally reserved for use at funerals, so they should not be given at other occasions.
- Gift-wrapping: Always use red, the color of good luck and prosperity. Avoid white, gray, or black—the funeral colors.
- Handkerchiefs and towels: They are given only to those attending funerals and are signs of sadness.
- Sharp objects: They symbolize bad luck and cutting off friendship. Umbrellas and fans also symbolize separation and termination of friendship.

Proper business protocol must be followed carefully. You must have business cards and always carry them with you. Exchanging business cards is a well-established ritual. At a Chamber of Commerce event, it would be typical to exchange about 10 to 15 cards—perhaps even with some of the same people you exchanged with at the previous meeting. Taiwanese business cards usually include titles and degrees because one's pedigree determines how they expect to be greeted. Cards must be presented right side up facing the recipient with both hands. That indicates you are giving a little bit of yourself when you give the card—a show of respect. And when given a card, you must look at it and read it in order to show respect. Since hierarchy and status are important, when in a group, you must greet people and stand in order of seniority. That also applies to social and business meetings; it is customary to wait to be told where to sit and then to sit only after the most senior person is seated. If you are escorted to your seat, you know you are an important guest.

Then the fun begins. At the typical Chinese banquet, you will soon hear the word "Gan-Bei." You will look up and see someone proposing a toast. You are not necessarily expected to drain your glass, but you gain a lot of face if you do. "Gan-Bei" means "bottoms up." You must respond to every toast throughout the meal to show respect. At a typical Chinese banquet, the Chinese hosts often work hard to get you drunk and sing Karaoke. It seems you are not really accepted until you have been out socially with them and they can see how you behave. It is what Westerners call "breaking the ice." Having experienced many social events in Asia, I would advise you not to get drunk, but to be very open and friendly and have a good time. After all, knowing how to sing is not a prerequisite to doing Karaoke—but a couple glasses of wine will certainly improve your singing ability; it did mine.

Understanding the concept of face in Asia is very important. Losing face is similar to the Western sense of "being embarrassed," but far more serious. Here, face goes far beyond oneself to include the entire family, ancient ancestors, and everyone who is part of your "group." If someone does something bad, he brings shame upon many people, causing him or her to lose face. It refers to a person's social image and self-respect—in other words, their entire identity. Children are taught that everything they do, good or bad, will affect the entire family. If they give the wrong answer on a school quiz, they are forced to stand up while the teacher lectures them about how they have shamed the school, their families, and their dead ancestors—and let everyone down.

It should be no surprise that the suicide rate is quite high. A 2005 survey of about 12,000 students from 21 schools across Taiwan indicated that 20 percent of the female respondents and 10 percent of the male respondents had contemplated suicide at least once during the past month. The local Taiwan newspaper reported an average of 12 suicides a day during 2006. From a very young age, students are taught to study hard and attend a good university, because high achievements bring face to the parents and the entire family. Thus, throughout life they try to avoid being in a position where they might give the wrong answers and lose face. In the office, the staff typically avoided speaking when with their seniors, and they never openly disagreed unless they had processed their thoughts, checked out the rules, and felt confident they were making the right comment.

In a Western business environment brainstorming is a common technique used to identify creative solutions and alternatives to solve problems. During these sessions, anything goes, and all comments, ideas, and opinions are welcomed and encouraged. However, in an Asian environment where face is important and the fear of giving a wrong comment is strong, brainstorming does not work well at all. That first became evident during a strategic development exercise. To be meaningful, a strategic plan should reflect the knowledge, experience, and input of all senior and middle management staff; however, that was very difficult to accomplish because of the reluctance of the Taiwanese staff to put themselves in a position of possibly making the wrong comment—and losing face—especially with a new and unfamiliar boss in the room.

Neither the people nor the cultural customs were going to change to suit our Western mind-set, so learning to understand and adapt was a priority. We quickly discovered that the Taiwanese people were very friendly and helpful, and just smiling would get us through most situations. After all, it is the most universally understood form of communication, and a lot easier than learning the language. Taiwanese smile very easily, which makes for easy living. In contrast, while traveling back to North America, I had to be careful not to inadvertently smile at strangers to avoid the risk of being thought a pervert.

IHLA FORMOSA

Many temples and cultural centers in Taiwan.

The main religions in Taiwan are Taoism and Buddhism. Many temples incorporate elements of both faiths. Many English-speaking places of worship are available in Taipei to satisfy a wide variety of religious beliefs. There is a significant Christian minority, with Protestants—mainly Presbyterians—making up about 80 percent of the Christian population. The remainder is Catholic. We discovered a small Catholic church located within about two blocks of our condominium, and Hélène found it quite comfortable—by that I mean it provided some spiritual sustenance without making her feel guilty for not having made a vow of poverty and given away all our worldly possessions to someone the church deemed more deserving. It was noteworthy, too, that no one complained or was offended when they put up a nativity scene at Christmas.

Confucianism is usually not considered a religion per se, but the philosophical thought and tenets of Confucius have endured since he died in 479 B.C. He believed that true pleasure came from generosity to friends, frequent social interaction, and obedience to hierarchy. For Confucius, harmonious relations between people always involved a superior and an inferior, such as ruler and subject, father and son, husband and wife, or older friend and younger friend. Accordingly, inferiors should always respect and obey superiors. Family obedience remains strong to this day, and fathers rule the home. Confucius preached the concept of guanxi—the force that binds people in a web of relationships and obligations. As Taiwan continues to modernize and internationalize, Confucian ideas will slowly loosen and become less important—probably not for the better. For now, Confucian ideas still play a central role in Taiwan society, and there is no doubt that they favorably influence lifestyles.

One day, my driver mentioned he wanted to present us with a gift. To appreciate that incident, one must first understand that the Chinese culture requires one always to accept any gift that is offered, but only after much protesting. The protesting from the intended recipient bestows esteem (face) on the giver for having successfully overcome the protesting—or something like that. After having protested vehemently, I said it would be okay, if he insisted. Johnson went on to explain that he was worried about whether he should give us the gift because of our Christian beliefs. I said not to worry, that our beliefs were quite accommodating. He also explained that the gift could only be presented on the "proper" day.

When the right day for gift giving came, Johnson presented us with a life-sized Buddha head carved in stone and resting on a round wooden base. It was not a bust, as one might expect, just the head. He proceeded to set it in a very prominent place in the living room, facing straight at us—but not staring, because the eyes were closed. That apparently was preferable because, if the eyes were closed, it meant Buddha trusted us and therefore did not have to watch us all the time. Buddha heads come with the eyes either closed or open, so if you feel the urge to buy one, be sure to get one with the eyes closed. This particular Buddha head allegedly came from mainland China and apparently was quite old, since such images have not been carved in stone for many years. After a few days, we moved it to a less prominent place, and it continued to watch over us.

The Buddha head.

Johnson assured us that Buddha would bring good health, happiness, and prosperity, and I have no reason to believe otherwise. According to Buddhism, if you do good deeds and help people, you can spend your second life in heaven; otherwise, you end up in hell forever. Where have I heard that before? Johnson was certain Hélène and I would end up in heaven, which was reassuring. In hindsight, I was happy to have protested so vehemently, because for Johnson it was a great and special gift. Questioning Johnson about why he felt the need to give it to us, he said, "You need it more than I do." I took it as a compliment. I am sure Johnson felt that employing and sending him to driving school was sufficient reciprocity for the gift. I hoped he gained a lot of face and that his guanxi account was once again in the black. One day the Buddha head may share space with another Buddha figure I acquired years ago in Burma (Myanmar) while making a road trip from Rangoon to Mandalay. That one was carved out of black ebony and covered in gold leaf. It took two years of negotiations to get it out of the country because the Burmese were certain that, as a foreign Christian devil, I would not show it the proper respect.

Taipei offered a variety of sightseeing alternatives. One weekend we ventured off into the mountains near the center of the country to visit a popular tourist area and meet some of Johnson's friends at a local aboriginal wedding. After four hours navigating the freeway and narrow mountain roads, we arrived at SunMoon Lake near Puli, the geographical center of the island. At one time there were two lakes, one called Sun and one called Moon. When a construction project brought them together, someone with a creative imagination suggested calling it SunMoon Lake. It was a beautiful area, nestled in the surrounding peaks, some of which rise to almost 4,000 meters. On September 21, 1999, the area experienced a major earthquake that killed thousands and caused much damage. A large temple in Puli that collapsed during the quake had not yet been repaired.

We arrived at the aboriginal wedding just in time for the reception. The people were mainly aborigines, the first inhabitants before ethnic Chinese (pirates, traders, farmers, and fishermen) arrived in Taiwan around the 14th and 15th centuries. He did not know the bride or groom well, but the local singer/emcee was a good friend, and that was good enough. Everyone enthusiastically welcomed us with a big round of applause as we tried unsuccessfully to sneak quietly into the back of the large tent where the meal was being served. We sat down and they started to bring the food…and bring the food. It would not stop coming. Embarrassing, really, until Johnson explained that a surprise visit by foreigners to an aboriginal wedding is a good omen. The bride and groom came by our table and made the traditional toast with red wine, so maybe he was right.

The bride looked like she might have been purchased and imported from Vietnam. Allegedly, there was a long waiting list of willing young Vietnamese girls looking for foreign husbands to give them a better life. Being a young wife in a remote mountain village with a Taiwanese aboriginal who could not speak your language would not be my choice, but it might be idyllic for some. The bride certainly displayed a smile of happy anticipation…or was that a reflection of terror and a call for help that I saw in her eyes when she glanced at me? I suggested to Johnson we should make a gift offering of a red envelope (money) to help with the food, and Johnson said, "Absolutely not…they would be very embarrassed for not having invited us!" Had we been invited, of course they would have expected a gift.

Aboriginal wedding reception.

That evening the PE faculty and students from the local university were having a celebration, and we were invited to join in once again. Elvis, a faculty member and a fan of the King of Rock and Roll, hovered around me all night practicing his English. The food was marginal at best but seemed to improve as we drank more beer. So did the performance of the local aboriginal dancers doing their traditional routine in the grass. They roasted a wild pig—the whole pig—on a spit over an open charcoal fire. They had finally caught it after much chasing through the woods. The toughness of the meat reflected the toughness of its physical condition from running up and down the mountains for a few years. Overall, a great experience.

IHLA FORMOSA

Yushan Mountain with a very rare dusting of snow — 3,952 meters.

After many interesting excursions through Taiwan, one in particular stands out in my mind. It was 7 a.m. on May 9, 2005. I was standing on the summit of Mt Yushan,[98] the highest point in Taiwan at 3,952 meters, and the highest mountain in Northeast Asia. The wind was blowing hard, visibility was down to about 20 meters and it was raining. We took pictures to record the event appropriately, ate some energy food, took a short rest, and started back down immediately. I had achieved my goal, although it was disappointing that we did not have a chance to see the surrounding panorama from the top of Taiwan. Maybe next time.

Two days earlier, nine avid trekkers, led by two guides from Freshtreks Taiwan,[99] had departed Taipei to attack the mountain. Day 1 started with a five-hour drive south along Highway #3 from Taipei to Taichung, then east on the narrow, winding mountain road that finally led to the mountain village of Dong Pu. By then we were all ready for dinner, relaxation, and some sleep. After some Taiwan beer and several interesting Chinese dishes at the local hangout, we were ushered to a hostel where we spent the night—five to a room, sleeping on the floor with large tatamis and pillows—not the Hilton, but clean and adequate.

Six o'clock the next morning (Day 2) the guides woke us for an early breakfast at the local open-air restaurant in Dong Pu. Everyone consumed the req-

---

[98] The Chinese word "Yu" means Jade, and the Chinese word "shan" means mountain. It translates into English as "Jade Mountain." Mt. Yushan, or Jade Mountain, is situated in the Yushan National Park. It is called "Jade" because the peaks are covered with snow in the winter, giving it a greenish-white appearance in the bright sunlight.

[99] http://www.freshtreks.com/termsofuse_eng.html.

uisite energy to start the day. Then, back in the van, we wound our way further up another narrow mountain road, rather pretentiously called the "New Central Cross-Island Highway," dodged rocks that had fallen off the mountain, and finally arrived safely in the small settlement of Tatajia 1½ hours later. Tatajia Visitor's Center is the entrance to one of the two trails to the summit of Yushan. Everyone passing the trailhead is required to register with the government authorities and get a permit. Freshtreks had organized the details a month before, so we had no problems checking in and finding our way to the starting point at 2,589 meters. We rechecked and adjusted our packs; each weighed about 10 to 12 kilograms with our clothes, personal items, and some food that was distributed equitably amongst the hikers according to perceived ability. The two strong, young guides carried the most.

At 10 a.m., we headed up the trail with a spring in our step and a smile on our faces, despite the cloudy weather and poor forecast for the rest of the week. Both guides contributed to our pleasant mood, since they had taken good care of us so far and certainly displayed a positive attitude as we embarked on the adventure. While on the trail, one guide would lead and the other would follow the queue. The trail was wide, well marked and maintained. There were about 84 "bridges" or boardwalks that had been constructed across areas where it would have otherwise been impossible to pass. In several areas, the trail was literally on the edge of a cliff that fell almost straight down to oblivion. One tends to be much focused when these precarious sections of the trail appear. In the more treacherous areas, chains were attached to the rock wall for security during the traverse; however, the fact that several anchor points had come loose and fallen out raised questions about their security. Acrophobia sufferers would be well advised not to look down.

Alpine ecosystems are highly variable and the weather changes constantly. The peaks and extreme variations in the landscape create their own weather zones. The rain we experienced added a significant measure of discomfort. In several places, the surface of the trail was comprised of loose stones about the size of a baseball. The rain tended to make them a bit slippery and I took extra care to avoid slipping and twisting my ankle. Raincoats are necessary, as well as waterproof covers for the backpack. Gloves are essential to protect your hands as you reach for support and to keep you warm, even in May. A good pair of trekking boots with ankle support and a firm sole is highly recommended. Wearing sneakers or running shoes would be a mistake. Walking on trails like that consumes far more energy than on a smooth, secure surface, and muscles become tired sooner than you would expect. Allowances must be made for these kinds of situations when the weather is bad.

On the way up, we passed through what is described as the "white forest"—a grove of trees burnt in a major forest fire had weathered to an ashen white color. For the most part, the slopes were heavily wooded and overgrown with grass and a variety of lush vegetation. Remarkably, many coniferous trees were very large, with trunks two feet or more in diameter. It was surprising that their roots could adequately grip the shallow topsoil over the steep rocky slopes. The precipitous slopes and the heavy jungle-like vegetation made it impossible to explore off the trail in many places.

The first day was arduous, but not dangerous. At about 5 p.m. we arrived at the Paiyun Refuge—altitude 3,402 meters. The refuge was a typical hostel with a kitchen for doing your own cooking, but do not expect any cooking facilities other than water and a table to work on. Park officials enforced one very good rule: you ate everything you brought with you, or you took it back down—no exceptions. At dusk, the generator was started to provide some light, and about two hours later, when dinner was finished, it was turned off—lights out! The sleeping accommodations consisted of very long bunks, one on top of the other. Each bunk accommodated about 25 to 30 bodies, laid side-by-side. In total, the refuge can accommodate about a hundred trekkers and is usually crowded during the peak tour period. Taiwanese like hard beds, but these were extreme. If you need a mattress and a pillow of some sort, bring it with you.

Day 3 started with everyone coming alive at about 3:00 a.m.—at least the fortunate few who had eventually managed to doze off. About that time the adrenalin kicked in, which more than made up for lack of sleep. From the Paiyun Refuge, it is a 2 to 2½ hour trek to the summit. In order to see the sunrise, climbers generally get up at 3 a.m. and, with the help of flashlights, start the final climb. That morning, however, the rain and fog ensured that we would have no chance to see the sunrise, so departure was postponed until 5 a.m.

The final stretch below the summit is much steeper than the trail up from Tatajia. After about an hour, we reached the tree line and broke out onto a steep, crumbling rocky slope devoid of any vegetation. The trail up that section was a series of switchbacks across the open, crumbling rock faces and areas of rockfalls. For safety, each person crossed these rockfalls one at a time so as not to dislodge rocks that might tumble down on climbers coming up from below. The higher we went, the stronger the winds became, especially at one area near the peak—named the "Wind Mouth." I confidently estimated the wind near the top of Mt. Yushan was gusting to about 40 or 50 miles per hour. We held on to fixed lines and scrambled up a very steep slope over broken boulders for about 100 meters to reach the top.

After a drink, snack, and brief rest on the summit, we headed back down the mountain—much faster than coming up. Later in the afternoon, the clouds broke and the sun shone through, allowing us to see the beautiful scenery in the lush valley below. After a lunch break and a few rest stops, we arrived back at Tatajia at 2:45 in the afternoon—exhausted and happy.

Generally, the mountain is steep and rocky. Rockfalls and crumbling cliff faces are prevalent. Climate at the lower levels is warm and humid; the mid-levels are cold and damp, and at high altitude, it can be quite frigid. Several mammals live on the mountain, including black bears, wild boar, water deer, longhaired mountain goat, flying squirrels, and monkeys. There are also about 151 species of birds, 228 types of butterflies, and several kinds of snakes. At such high altitude, there is no guarantee you will have good weather for the ascent, but local hikers generally agree that the fall (October and November) has the most stable weather for hiking anywhere in the central mountains. We traveled from 2,589 meters at the trailhead to 3,952 meters at the peak. The total surface distance traveled was about 22 kilometers. Average speed was 2.5 kilometers per hour when walking and 1.1 kilometers per hour overall, including resting time. There is good cell phone coverage most of the distance, including from the summit.

If you like a good hike, go to the top of Mt. Yushan. You do not have to be a highly experienced mountain trekker. However, we all have our limits, so don't underestimate the need to be relatively fit, especially aerobically, to deal with the thinner air at higher altitudes. Going up was mainly a challenge for the cardiovascular and pulmonary systems, whereas coming down was hard on the legs and knees in particular. Physical endurance is the primary challenge, so climb the higher peaks around Taipei (such as Seven Star Mountain in Yangmingshan) several times, to get prepared. It helps to have a desire to succeed and a determination to persist even when some physical discomfort suggests otherwise. Life should be lived to the fullest, and standing on the top of Mt. Yushan will definitely contribute. It will remain among the fondest memories of my stay in Taiwan.

20

A CAPITAL IDEA

CAPITAL MACHINERY LIMITED
TAIWAN, R.O.C.
(2004 — 2008)

In the early days of my career, I worked closely with dealers. Then I got into the logistics side of the business, and that's when I really began to appreciate the strength of our partnership. I've worked with automakers, big industrial companies and many other OEMs, and although they have dealers too, it's not the same. We have a very unique relationship—a deep commitment to each other that we should not take for granted.
—Steve Wunning, Caterpillar Group President

For many years, Taiwan had been predominantly a market for used construction equipment imported from Japan—mainly Komatsu, Hitachi, and Kobelco products. An estimated 8 to 10 imported used machines were sold in Taiwan for each new machine purchased—a very unusual situation. The market for new machines was a small fraction of what it would normally have been if the number of imported used machines had been typical. The main reason for the atypical situation was that most Taiwanese customers had a short-term horizon when making a purchase decision, so the lower initial capital cost for a used machine was more important than lower life-cycle operating costs for a new machine. High productivity and utilization were not important factors in the purchase decision—they were sacrificed in favor of low initial capital cost.

During my years in Taiwan, the worldwide demand for energy- and manufacturing-related commodities—coal, petroleum products, and all types of minerals—was very strong. The rapidly developing economies in China and India were driving the demand, as well as the strong economies in North America and Europe. Commodity prices were at an all-time high; the price of oil hovered around $100 a barrel for several months. High commodity prices drove the mining and energy-related industries, which in turn created a strong demand for construction machinery and engines to provide power and electrical energy. The strength of the demand surprised everyone and exceeded the manufacturers' ability to supply. Consequently, several of the most popular products were on allocation—"managed distribution"—and most manufacturers lost sales because they could not meet delivery expectations. That situation made it important to carefully manage the supply chain and inventory levels.

Since the supply of new equipment was limited, used equipment became a substitute and the demand for used construction machines increased substantially. That drove up the prices for used machines so some customers that traditionally bought used decided they might as well buy new, which in turn, further drove up the demand for new machines—a vicious circle. Consequently, and remarkably, the size of the industry for new excavators in Taiwan doubled from 2003 to 2008, even though the overall economic growth in Taiwan, as measured by GDP, was essentially flat.

The strong worldwide demand and higher prices meant that many used Caterpillar machines were exported to areas where petroleum and minerals were being extracted and produced. Consequently, it was difficult to build population in Taiwan, and the after-market parts and service business suffered accordingly. The company was a victim of that situation particularly because of the strong preference for good used Caterpillar product outside Taiwan. In business when the demand is high, the bar is usually low and everyone can get over it—everyone did. All equipment manufacturers participated in the strong growth that took place. I had experienced a similar situation working in Africa and the Middle East during the late 1970s when investment in petroleum exploration and development was strong; however, it did not match the strength of the worldwide demand during the middle of the first decade of the 21st century.

Although I complained to Caterpillar about not being able to get enough products to satisfy our customers, I tried to see the "glass half full instead of half empty," and was careful to reminded myself that strong demand was preferable to economic stagnation and weak demand. Boom times do not last forever and the economic trough can suddenly arrive with a vengeance, as it has once or twice every decade since the panic of 1819—the first financial crisis in the United States. However, in the meantime, equipment manufacturers and their dealers were "making hay while the sun shone."

※

When Lei Shing Hong Limited took over the dealership in 2004, they changed

A CAPITAL IDEA

the name to Capital Machinery Limited and it became the sole authorized dealer for the distribution of Caterpillar products in Taiwan.[100] The main industries were marine power, electric power generation, general construction, and quarry and aggregate mining; in addition, there was a variety of petroleum and industrial applications.

The power systems products and the construction machinery products were operated as separate business units. The Power Systems Division was doing better than the Machinery Division—it was particularly successful selling large turnkey electric power plants, especially for use in the high-tech industry for standby applications. The Division also enjoyed a high share of the propulsion engines used in the custom-built mega-yachts manufactured in Kaohsiung. Although the pleasure craft OEM industry represented a good engine sales opportunity, there was almost no after-sales product support business, since all vessels were exported out of Taiwan. The relatively successful state of the Power Systems Division allowed me to devote most of my time turning around the Machinery Division.

The head office of Capital Machinery was located in Ta Yuan, near the Taiwan Tao Yuan International Airport—about 75 minutes from our home in Taipei. I was not looking forward to the daily commute, but the 2 ½ hours in the car every day provided an excellent opportunity to read, and I soon began to appreciate the quiet time. This was a major change from the previous year of cruising and relaxing on the boat, but it was challenging, interesting, and enjoyable. As Managing Director, I had a significant degree of independence to do what I thought was necessary to grow the business.

During my first week on the job, I took a whirlwind tour of the six branch offices. To my dismay, I did not encounter a single customer the entire week. Never had I experienced such customer abandonment in 35 years working with equipment dealers throughout the world. The problems were intuitively obvious: the organization had atrophied; facilities, tools, equipment, and inventory were lacking; there was almost no sales force; market share was at an all-time low; people needed training and there was no evidence of a recovery plan. The trader's mentality seemed to permeate the organization as illustrated by the following attitude: "Since we have the exclusive franchise for the territory, customers have no choice but to come and buy from us. Therefore, why waste a lot of money hiring expensive salespeople to go out and bring in the business. If customers want our products they will come and see us."

It was no wonder market share was at an all-time low. To my shock, I discovered a few weeks later that Komatsu was often able to sell new excavators

---

100 www.lsh.com and www.CapitalMachinery.com.tw

at premium prices over Caterpillar—primarily because customers judged their product support services to be superior—Taiwan may have been the only place in the world where that occurred, and I was not about to let it continue.

In all fairness, the worldwide SARS epidemic the previous year had hurt business throughout Taiwan; however, the state of neglect that I observed took many years to develop. Clearly, it was another restructuring and growth challenge. My experience and knowledge of the business gave me confidence about what needed to be done. The first and obvious task was to get the organization focused externally on the customers; we had to be proactive and demonstrate a desire to earn their business.

A senior management team was formed to develop a Strategic Plan along the lines of the business model described above. The Plan was built on a comprehensive analysis of the current situation and the need to respond quickly to the patterns of change that was taking place. The facilitation process took key members of the organization through a systematic exercise using an interactive bottom-up and top-down approach. At the end of that process, the participants had developed Vision, Mission, Common Values, Goals, Objectives, and Action Plans. Subsequent sessions took the process further down into the organization until all employees had individual work plans and clearly understood that we expected to achieve excellence in areas of strategic significance and set the company apart from competition. Recovery actions included restructuring management and operations, hiring additional staff to improve sales coverage, and focusing the entire organization on serving customers.

With a clear idea of where we were going and how to get there, we set out to achieve profitable growth and continuous improvement. We worked to achieve compatibility between the organization's culture, characteristics, management styles, and employee aspirations. In addition to the budget numbers, specific Key Performance Indicators (KPI) tracked sales coverage, such as call reports, call frequency, quotations, orders, lost sales, and follow-up. I knew that "what gets measured gets done"—either for better or worse—so individual performances were tracked weekly and monthly, and results were fed back to the managers and the sales representatives. Incentive schemes were based on achieving quantifiable goals.

The first two years required significant investments in inventory and capital assets to improve after-sales service and responsiveness. The two major full-service facilities in Ta Yuan and Tainan/Shanhua underwent renovation and added many new tools, equipment, and vehicles. A much larger facility was acquired to improve service and sales coverage in Taichung and the central part of the country. Lei Shing Hong also built a new facility in Kaohsiung, the home of a major shipping terminal and several important industrial and marine customers. The organization was restructured and personnel added to grow the business and provide improved after-sales service.

Although I was the only "Westerner" in the entire company, and the only one who could not speak the local language, the Taiwanese staff was very friendly, welcoming, and accepting—I felt comfortable among friends. My direct reports communicated reasonably well in English, but the lower levels of the organization did not, and I regretted not being able to drill down into the guts of the organization to learn firsthand what was really going on in the trenches, as was my normal hands-on style. Communications often required an interpreter and a lot of "managing by walking around." After asking questions two or three different ways in order to overcome my language handicap, acceptable answers were usually forthcoming.

As the new leader, the staff expected me to be an overpowering boss who gave orders and criticisms in the traditional Chinese autocratic style. I was expected to know all the answers to all the problems—or at least act as if I did. We had an objective to empower the people, but most did not want to be empowered, since it brings responsibility, accountability, and the possibility of making a mistake, losing face, and being punished. That attitude—embedded in the Chinese social order—reflected the Confucius philosophy and the consequences of living and working under military rule and marshal law for over 500 years—beginning with the various Dynasties, and not ending until the 1996 election of Lee Teng Hui. Consequently, most Taiwanese people were accustomed to an autocratic style of leadership; they preferred to be told what to do rather than be asked what should be done. Add to that the Confucius emphasis on hierarchy and the shame of making the wrong comment and losing face, and one can appreciate why it was difficult for the staff to adapt to the new participative management style. Some managers—in keeping with the traditional style—still believed workers must be threatened, constantly supervised, and told what to do, or they would bungle the job.

In contrast, my Western social order followed the participative, decentralized management style—that is, put the right people in the right job, train them well, empower them, reward them for performance, and focus all their efforts toward satisfying the customer. In other words, be a coach, not an emperor. It was my firm belief that, although business is not a democracy, it must strive for a consensus and give employees an opportunity to participate in decisions affecting their work. Most did not take advantage of the opportunity to participate, but I felt obliged to give it. That was the Caterpillar way, and it had served me well for 30 years. Therefore, with that approach firmly embedded in my psyche, I presented myself as the "coach" of the Capital Machinery Team, and made it clear that my primary job was to establish a game plan and create

A CAPITAL IDEA

an environment that allowed the team to score and win—remember, the coach never scores; only the players do.

Although outwardly Taiwanese people appeared to be a close-knit, harmonious society, it was essentially a façade—a fierce competitive spirit lied just below the surface. Cooperation and teamwork did not come naturally, and with everyone looking out for himself or herself, it was not easy to build a smooth functioning team. During meetings and discussions, there were smiles all around and cooperation and harmony at the surface, but back on the job they often disregarded guidance, direction, rules, and company policies with which they did not agree. Extensive and continuous follow-up was required to keep the organization focused. However, they performed. The Taiwanese employees were bright, intelligent, and quick to learn; they demonstrated a strong work ethic and desire to succeed—they did not come to work to fail—they came to work to win, and they were a pleasure to work with. The organization accepted my leadership and direction, and eventually came to embrace the participative, coach/team management style in preference to the traditional Chinese autocratic command-and-control style. My experiences have convinced me that Chinese people are the most entrepreneurial, individualistic, and capitalistic of all.

During these years, Caterpillar and its dealers were deeply involved with implementing the Six-Sigma program.[101] I refreshed my knowledge of Six-Sigma and once again began to provide leadership for its implementation within Capital Machinery. However, our task was to apply it to sales and marketing problems, whereas, at Crane Canada, we used Six-Sigma to lower costs in manufacturing operations. At Capital Machinery, it was a constant struggle to convince management to "buy in" and become committed to using Six-Sigma—they could not see the benefits. Moreover, the Six-Sigma practitioners seemed to have been trained to apply the all statistical methods and tools unwaveringly, whether or not they were needed for a particular project. That too often resulted in people sitting in meetings discussing miscellaneous analytical techniques ("killing flies with a sledge hammer"), instead of just getting on with the job of defining and fixing the problem. The methodology was used as an excuse to put off action if there was any doubt about what to do, or if there was hesitation in making a decision. Those who were inclined to be activity-oriented, instead of results-oriented, would study the problem using Six-Sigma instead of just taking corrective action—"paralysis by analysis." Nevertheless, we persisted and slowly made progress, although it was difficult to identify tangible savings and benefits. I believe Six-Sigma can be used to improve any process;

---

[101] You will recall that I was first introduced to that methodology in 1996 while working for Crane Canada—see Chapter 15.

however, it is better suited to manufacturing operations than sales and marketing processes.

Many companies have implemented the Six-Sigma methodology, with varying degrees of success—Bank of America, Caterpillar, Honeywell International (previously known as Allied Signal), Raytheon, Merrill Lynch, and General Electric. Recently, however, it has been reported that some are scaling back their involvement in Six-Sigma, saying that it stifles innovation and undermines individual contributions. The skeptics argue that squeezing the last ounce of efficiency out of an organization was never a guarantee of success, that success requires taking risks and investing in research and development, and allowing freethinking innovators to make individual contributions. Personally, I believe Six-Sigma is the best decision-making methodology to have come along in the past 40 years, and it would be a shame if it fell by the wayside like so many other programs that have come and gone over the years. In those organizations where it does not survive, it will be due to improper and undisciplined implementation rather than weaknesses in the methodology.

Hundreds of good books have been written on the subject of management and they all say about the same thing in different ways—"Pay attention to the customer!" It is true—they pay your salary and your benefits and your heat and your light and provide shoes for your kids and food for your stomach. Take care of the customer and he will take care of you. We were fortunate—many customers wanted Caterpillar products, as well as our after-sales service. They wanted to do business with us, and our challenge was to convince them that we also wanted to earn their business. Customers soon realized the attitude of the organization had changed: We were visiting them, so they soon began visiting us, looking for solutions. When you talk to customers, sales go up—a remarkable concept!

It was a proven formula for success and the business started to pick up and grow profitably at a rate that surprised even the most optimistic. The organization became customer-focused in everything it did. During the first four years, machinery sales more than doubled and profit contributions increased accordingly. In addition, market share improved significantly, despite an anemic economy.

We did not win simply by showing up; to capture market share, we had to claw back business from established competition—specifically, Komatsu and Hitachi. Early on, growth came more easily by "picking the low-hanging fruit"; but as competition fought back, growth slowed and price competition became intense. We fought to hold the gains, to maintain margins, and to win the high-opportunity business.

The team performed and the results were better than expected. By mid-2008, Capital Machinery Limited achieved market leadership in Taiwan for the Caterpillar construction equipment products that represented the vast majority of the opportunity. That growth in market share started from an all-time low point that existed at the time the business was acquired four years before. Maintaining that leadership position into the future will not be easy, but I believe with Caterpillar's support, effective leadership, and a continued laser-like focus on meeting customers' needs, the Capital Machinery team can make it happen. Having the opportunity to work with that group of dedicated employees was perhaps the most satisfying period of my entire career.

I must emphasize that the progress would not have occurred without consistent support from the parent company, Lei Shing Hong Limited. Significant funds were made available for investments in fixed assets, operating equipment, and working capital for inventory and additional staff. The main principal, Datuk C. K. Lau, met the financial needs of the organization without hesitation—he had confidence we could perform. In addition, Paul Ferris, Marianne Lim, and David Park provided guidance as needed with the development and implementation of the strategy from time to time. I very much appreciated their support, which made a significant contribution to the growth and prosperity of the organization.

With management and growth strategies implemented, I started to pay more attention to a problem I had discovered in my first weeks on the job: the fact that Komatsu enjoyed a much better reputation in the marketplace than did Caterpillar. A former salesman we hired from a competitor confirmed that Komatsu was often able to command a premium price for new machines, and several customers told me Komatsu's service was better than Caterpillar's.

How had that situation been allowed to develop? First, as already mentioned, most Taiwanese customers had a short-term horizon when making a purchase decision, so the lower initial capital cost for a used machine was more important than lower life-cycle operating costs for a new machine. Consequently, the demand for second-hand used equipment was unusually high, and for years, equipment traders had met the demand with machines from Japan, mainly Komatsu, Hitachi, and Kobelco—and over the years, these manufacturers built up a large active population of machines.

To provide after-sales service, Komatsu and Hitachi relied primarily on numerous free-lance service technicians scattered throughout the country—in addition to their own exclusive dealer organizations. They willingly provided these free-lance technicians (as well as many customers) with technical information and training to develop their in-house expertise. Gradually, a large number of free-lance technicians close to customers were able to perform low-cost maintenance and repair work on Komatsu and Hitachi products. Naturally, these technicians encouraged customers to buy new Komatsu or Hitachi instead of Caterpillar, since they were not familiar with Caterpillar products and could not provide after-sales services.

Locally available low-cost services appealed to many smaller customers, and in Taiwan, we struggled to overcome that Komatsu advantage—with little success. Consequently, we concentrated on winning back the larger, better-financed and more sophisticated customers that understood the importance of productivity, utilization and life-cycle costs, and who were in a position to accept and pay for our more modern and technically sophisticated services.

Thinking about that situation, I recalled a time early in my career when customer service was an obligation and a commitment to customers—an integral part of what the customers paid for when they bought the product. In the early days, service was not an important profit center. Then a change took place. In the 1960s, William Lambie, Caterpillar's Vice-President of Parts and Service, observed that a "service gap" existed—a gap between the dealers' service capabilities and the technical sophistication and complexity of the products. He also observed that simply fixing the machines when they broke was no longer acceptable—regular preventative maintenance and repair-before-failure was essential in order to optimize total product value—rightly so.

Therefore, Lambie launched a major initiative to close the gap. A series of seminars with dealers worldwide aimed to convince them they had to improve their service operations to meet the needs of the more technically sophisticated products. Dealers were told to develop more modern service methods and invest in specialized tooling, diagnostic equipment, and training to improve technical skills.

To make the investments more palatable, Caterpillar decided that service should be a marketing opportunity, rather than an obligation. The service challenge was no longer one of fulfilling an obligation; the new challenge was to capture the customer's service work—to do as much of their maintenance and repair work as possible. Marketing efforts were intensified; maintenance and repair options were developed and promoted in an attempt to convince customers to let the dealers do the work. Service became a wide range of "products"—maintenance and repair options—to be marketed, and CatPlus® became the marketing symbol. Speakers at "Cat Care Meetings" explained the added benefits of the modern, sophisticated products and attempted to convince customers they could not effectively service these new products themselves. Sophisticated time-and-motion studies were conducted to improve dealers' service efficiencies—I participated in several.

Some dealers became overly zealous in response to the initiative and were reluctant to help customers help themselves—elements of the service function were considered proprietary and not to be shared with customers. After all, if the customer would not let the dealer do the work, he became a service competitor. It was a new service paradigm and represented a fundamental change in the way Caterpillar and their dealers approached their service responsibilities.[102]

There was no doubt that since the beginning, superior after-sales-service played a key role in differentiating Caterpillar products—whether one considered service either an obligation or a marketing opportunity. The focus on service has been a major factor in the company's long-standing reputation for quality and reliability and for lowering life-cycle operating costs. Collectively, these advantages have justified premium prices and generated repeat sales. However, even in the twenty-first century, surveys continued to show that many customers think Komatsu's basic services are as good as or better than Caterpillar's, and I began to wonder if William Lambie's new paradigm had produced the benefits envisioned. Was it strategically wise to position the customers who wished to do their own work as service competitors?[103]

It was amusing to hear Caterpillar preach the service message to dealers during a seminar in 2006. The message was identical to the one I preached to dealers 30 years ago except for a few of the buzzwords and the visuals used to communicate the message. Although many improvements have been made to product design and performance during the last 30 years, I saw no significant progress in the way dealers provided service to customers—no breakthroughs in methodology, no innovative approaches. Perhaps it is time to investigate another new paradigm.

---

102 A paradigm is a new pattern or model that forms the basis of a methodology, in that case the methodology for providing service.

103 Remnants of that thinking still prevailed in the 21st century, although now, service customers are being categorized as *"Do-it-for-me," "Help-me-do-it,"* and *"Do-it-myself,"* and strategies are being developed for dealing with each category.

The management team at Capital Machinery Limited, along with a few Caterpillar District Representatives. With good support from the parent company, Lei Shing Hong Limited, the team restructured the business and achieved a market leadership position in Taiwan during the period from 2004 to mid-2008.

The vital force in business life is the honest desire to serve. Business, it is said, is the science of service. He profits most who serves best. At the very bottom of the wish to render service must be honesty of purpose, and, as I go along through life, I see more and more that honesty in word, thought and work means success. It spells a life worth living, and in business, clean success.

—George Eberhard

21

ETHICS, MORALITY, AND SOCIAL RESPONSIBILITY

The reason that a person should exercise integrity is the same reason that he needs to adhere to rational principles in the first place. Irrational action works against his life. Only the consistent loyalty to rational principles that integrity prescribes enables a person to reap the rewards of the other virtues and to achieve objective values. Breaches of integrity defeat a person's purpose of achieving his happiness [104]

—Tara Smith

WHILE working and traveling in the international business community, I encountered a wide variety of cultures and beliefs that produced a similarly wide variety of conflicting ethical standards and behaviors. I was determined to understand, to reconcile, and to deal with these diverse standards in a way that would be most beneficial to both the organization and to me. My journey toward that goal continues, but I am comfortable sharing some experiences and observations. My treatment of the subject is certainly not comprehensive, and I do not presume my views will be widely accepted. However, I share them with you, hoping they might provoke thought and help clarify your own views on the subject. Some will say, "Simply follow the Ten Commandments." For me, that guidance was certainly not sufficient for dealing with diverse cultures and social systems throughout the world, many of which do not even recognize the

---

[104] For an excellent examination of ethics and morality, see Tara Smith, *Ayn Rand's Normative Ethics* (2006). This book explains the fundamental virtues considered vital for a person to achieve objective well-being: rationality, honesty, independence, justice, integrity, productiveness, and pride. Tara Smith also discusses traits such as kindness, charity, generosity, temperance, courage, forgiveness, and humility. And she writes in a way that makes life's important issues easily understandable.

ETHICS, MORALITY, AND...

Ten Commandments.

Libraries are replete with volumes on the subject of business ethics; it is easy to explore the opinions of a wide variety of self-appointed experts. In North America, a significant industry has developed around corporate social responsibility—consulting firms, conferences, magazines, and scholarly journals. Awards have been offered to companies exhibiting the best "corporate conscience." Many large companies now have Corporate Ethics Officers, and there is an Ethics & Compliance Officer Association (ECOA).[105] There is no doubt that the role that business plays in society has become an ethical issue, and there are frequent debates about what role that should be. Often these debates suggest that the choice is simply one between money and morality—as if they were mutually exclusive.

It seems to me that the first ethical principle of business is to survive, to maximize the long-term value of the firm to its owners. Without survival, the subject of business ethics becomes irrelevant. Long-term survival can only be achieved by focusing on profit (the lifeblood of a business), by being a good corporate citizen, by making choices that benefit customers and other stakeholders, and by practicing ordinary decency and building trust through honesty and fairness. Unfortunately, the public often embraces an anti-business mentality and blindly accepts that any pursuit of profit is evil. In fact, the profit motive is a highly moral imperative for success and economic well-being. Long-term profitability requires honesty and integrity; practicing fraud destroys a company's value, as has been amply demonstrated by the recent examples of Enron, WorldCom, Global Crossing, and Arthur Anderson. To succeed, businesses must offer high-quality products, not shoddy goods; they must maintain a reputation for fair dealing and maintain accurate accounting statements; otherwise, they loose the trust of the bankers, the credit rating agencies, and the investing public. Even suspicions of wrongdoing can destroy a company's stock price and, therefore, its ability to borrow money. Creating wealth requires offering goods and services that satisfy customers' demand for value. The profit motive has given us cheaper, safer, and better products. The vast majority of business leaders—just like their employees—strive to earn honest profits as they work for their own rational self-interest. They should be rewarded for their success, not condemned. Defend the profit motive and your rights as a businessperson and do not accept unearned guilt.

---

[105] http://www.theecoa.org/

ETHICS, MORALITY, AND...

☙❧

The second ethical principle of business is to balance the pursuit of profit with social responsibility. It is not a matter of focusing on one to the detriment of the other—the two are not mutually exclusive, although without profitability, it is not possible to practice much social responsibility for very long. My experiences have convinced me that doing productive work that improves the human condition is the best way to practice social responsibility. By that, I mean doing work that, in the end, improves the lives of people who, in the 17th-century words of Thomas Hobbs, can anticipate a life that is "poor, nasty, brutish and short." How does business make a contribution?

The first and perhaps the most important contribution is the work the products do. One of the greatest rewards of my life has been playing a small part in projects that contribute to economic development throughout the world. Examples include the construction of roads, airports, railways, canals, dams, reservoirs, levees, sewers, and waterways; the development of sites for homes, factories, and stores; the clearing, forming, and terracing of land; the production and harvesting of crops; the excavating of coal and ore; the reclaiming of wastelands for useful purposes; the exploring for oil and gas; the constructing of pipelines; the disposal of waste materials; and the supplying of power for trucks, boats, industrial equipment, hospitals, and factories. Such work improves living standards and quality of life throughout the world. Developing countries always benefit the most from these projects—if their leaders care about the welfare of the people.

The second way in which business contributes to social responsibility is providing employment to people by establishing manufacturing facilities and marketing organizations in the various geographical areas they serve. Caterpillar's products and components are manufactured in 50 facilities in the United States and in over 50 other locations. Caterpillar has had a presence in over 40 countries around the globe. Each of its facilities has generated significant employment opportunities for the local people, so that they could look forward to improving their "poor, nasty, brutish and short" lives. Contrary to media reports, these facilities did not displace manufacturing capacity in the United States; quite the opposite—they strengthened market position and captured new business in new locations that would not have otherwise been available. In addition, in almost every instance, they stimulated exports from the United States.

Take China as an example. Caterpillar sold its first product to China in 1975, and shortly thereafter, I roamed the country helping to provide service support to our customers. Local production began in the early 1990s, and subsequently, several joint ventures and wholly owned facilities were established in China, together with a network of independent dealers. During the past few years leading up to 2006, exports to China increased 40 percent and, as a result, some 5,000 new production jobs were created in the United States, making a major contribution to the health and strength of the U.S. economy.[106]

The third contribution business makes to social responsibility is transferring and sharing technology. Each time a new facility is established somewhere in the world, a certain amount of technology transfer and information sharing takes place. Caterpillar first launched technology transfer agreements with the Chinese in the 1980s, at which time the Chinese began building licensed products. Technology transfers help people help themselves, which they must ultimately do in order to climb up the economic ladder and out of their poverty and attendant illiteracy. For decades, Caterpillar has shared its technology related to management, product design, application, service support, and a variety of other business functions with many countries.

Those are the predominant ways in which business fulfills its social responsibility and helps billions of people participate in the global economy and acquire jobs, knowledge, and a better quality of life. Since the beginning of the Industrial Revolution, business has been the primary engine driving the improvement of the human condition.

The third ethical principle of business deals with integrity. In our Western culture, rewards offered after services have been provided are generally considered gratuities; they are characterized as appreciation for services already rendered. On the other hand, rewards offered before the services are given are often considered bribes, a form of corruption; they are characterized as payments to influence preferential treatment in the future. According to these definitions, the timing of the payment is the main characteristic that distinguishes between what is ethical and unethical. Others believe the form of the payment is the most important distinguishing characteristic, arguing that paying for entertainment is okay, but just handing over money is not. Some believe the amount of the payment is the important distinguishing characteristic. I found all these definitions to be oversimplified and have come to believe that several factors must be considered together, and that the deciding factors—not always easy to evaluate—are whether the transaction violates the rights of other parties not involved in the transaction, and/or whether anyone has been unfairly disadvantaged.

It is quite common in the business world to entertain important customers

---

[106] James W. Owens, "The Realities and Rewards of Globalism—Caterpillar's View Toward China" (Keynote Address at Manufacturing Week, Chicago, March 22, 2006).

on all-expense-paid trips to sporting and other events, and I have participated in several. They were generally considered good public relations and rewards for customer loyalty; however, they were also invariably expected to influence preferential treatment when future procurement decisions were made—often called customer retention programs. In these situations, I asked myself, "Were anyone's rights violated, and was anyone unfairly disadvantaged?"

Most large companies have attempted to deal with the ambiguity by publishing a code of conduct. Caterpillar was one of the first companies to define a corporate ethics policy in a Code of Conduct[107] as early as 1974 and, over the years, has established an enviable reputation for ethical behavior. Rather than merely being a broad philosophical statement of little practical value, the Caterpillar Code acknowledged global reality and addressed ethical issues encountered in day-to-day business activities. It included statements like:

> We will keep our word. We won't promise more than we can reasonably expect to deliver; nor will we make commitments we don't intend to keep. We won't seek to influence sales [...] by payment of bribes, kickbacks, or other questionable inducements.

Caterpillar's Code also discussed the involvement of people in decisions affecting their work; aspiring to high standards in human relationships; stewardship of the Board; protection of the environment; relationships with suppliers, dealers, and public officials; financial reporting; inter-company pricing; public responsibility; and a variety of other ethical issues. Employees were expected to follow the Code, and each year had to sign a document that reported on their compliance to it. Caterpillar's Code was written to accommodate those differing business practices without compromising its basic principles. The Code recognized that there is not necessarily "one best way," because different cultures hold varying views about practices related to dealing with competition, information disclosure, international mergers, inter-company pricing, safety standards, intellectual property and trademark protection, and so on.

Shortly after the Caterpillar Code was first published, I was assigned to work for the company in Africa and the Middle East, and later in Southeast Asia—geographical regions where cultural practices and ethical standards are often significantly different from those in North America. I once joined a group of Saudi Arabian customers on an all-expenses-paid trip to a product demonstration and seminar in Malaga, Spain. Both existing loyal customers and potential new customers were hosted by the local dealer who entertained them all with the finest champagne and Spanish women that money could buy. It was a way

---

107 http://www.cat.com/ .

to show appreciation for customer loyalty as well as to influence future business decisions.

Occasionally, difficulties arose during normal commercial transactions and routine dealings with public officials. For example, our Chinese employees from Hong Kong periodically traveled to Indonesia to work with the local dealer. The longstanding antagonism of the Indonesians toward the Chinese periodically resulted in deliberate harassment of our Hong Kong employees. Occasionally, while passing through immigration at the airport in Jakarta in the 1980s, their passports would mysteriously disappear until a $50 gratuity was paid to expedite them through the immigration approval process. Consequently, I approved expense reports that claimed "Gratuities to Indonesian immigration officials—$50." Caterpillar's Code of Conduct clearly stated that we were strictly forbidden to pay (that is, bribe) public officials to avoid doing what they were expected to do; however, payments of "customary amounts" were allowed to "facilitate correct performance of the officials' duties" when deemed unavoidable. Paying the gratuity to the immigration official was not considered a violation, because the payment was to facilitate the performance of their official duties. However, one could debate the virtue of the immigration official who demanded a gratuity.

While working for the dealer organizations, I encountered intermediaries (consultants or brokers) who routinely handled the procurement of goods and services for government entities. If these intermediaries were not on board to facilitate commissions (kickbacks) to the purchaser, their role was otherwise difficult to explain. The intermediaries could usually issue an invoice to show transparency when scrutinized by the auditors. Few experienced people are fooled in such situations if the invoice exceeds what would be considered a reasonable amount for the "services rendered"; but then, what consultant is going to accuse another of fraud merely because they charged "too much" for their services? In some situations, the invoices may have been fictitious, in the sense that no legitimate identifiable services were performed. During the years that I was involved in the retail end of international business, there was occasional perceptible evidence of that practice. Caterpillar's Code strictly forbade its employees from participating in such activity, or in such activity engaged in by others. The Code also strongly discouraged its dealers from engaging in such practices.

Globalization produced some lively debates about corporate ethics. For example, is it sufficient that businesses meet local laws regarding safety and environmental standards if they are lower than are those in more developed countries? The explosion at the Union Carbide plant in Bhopal, India, in 1984, killed about 8,000 people and brought that environmental issue to the attention of the world community. Subsequently, most multinational companies (including Caterpillar Inc.) have established minimum standards for health, safety, and the environment that exceed the local requirements.

Cultural norms often determine whether a particular behavior is considered bribery and corruption, or simply customary practice in appreciation for customer loyalty and cooperation. I have listened to many self-righteous Western business people condemn behavior that on the surface is essentially the same as North American practices, except the rewards may be in the form of a gift or money rather than entertainment at sporting events. The difference between a gratuity and a bribe is often ambiguous, and one's judgment usually depends on the cultural perspective of the beholder.

I believe that each of us should strive to develop our own individual personal code of conduct based on what we identify as our own individual ultimate standard of value. Moreover, our personal code should go well beyond just gratuities, bribes, and corruption. It should include important issues, such as the proper role of business and the proper role of government, as well as corporate and individual social responsibility.

My ultimate standard of value is my life on Earth lived at a high level of self-actualization (as opposed to basic biological subsistence). Based on that standard, my individual code of conduct provides a good level of comfort without contradictions. However, I accept that my code may not be "right" for you, and quite likely, your code will not be "right" for me. The debates about what should constitute the proper absolute moral code for all human beings will go on indefinitely because we do not all share the same cultural and ethical values, and most people are not yet ready to accept that their own life on Earth should be the ultimate moral standard of value.[108]

---

108 In fact, many believe death and martyrdom represent a higher level of exaltation than life on Earth. I diagnose that belief to be an illness caused by the epidemic of mysticism throughout the world. Mysticism is the belief in intuitive spiritual revelation, the belief that personal communication or union with some divine entity is achieved through intuition, faith, ecstasy, or sudden insight. All organized religions would fall under that definition, as well as the many forms of superstition, tribalism, and witchcraft still prevalent throughout the world.

22

MYSTICISM: A WORLDWIDE EPIDEMIC

Faith is believin' what you know ain't so.

—Mark Twain

Religion is based, I think, primarily and mainly upon fear. It is partly the terror of the unknown and partly, as I have said, the wish to feel that you have a kind of elder brother who will stand by you in all your troubles and disputes. A good world needs knowledge, kindliness and courage; it does not need a regretful hankering after the past or a fettering of the free intelligence by the words uttered long ago by ignorant men.

—Bertrand Russell

Throughout my youth, Mother exposed me to Protestant Christian theology, doctrines, beliefs, and rituals. We attended church, Sunday school, and summer church camps. As a young adult I taught Sunday school and Bible Study groups, and my brother, Curtis, eventually became a pastor in the United Church of Canada. For the first 30 years of my life, I was immersed in Christianity and its teachings. I read the Bible, sang the songs, and performed the rituals.

It was distressing. According to the Christian message, I was condemned as a guilty sinner from the moment I emerged from the womb—and no one could explain how I had earned that condemnation.[109]

They said I had been fashioned out of clay or dust by what seemed to be an ill-tempered and threatening God who would not even show himself. I was to prostrate myself before that God with an attitude of submission, fear, and eternal gratitude—gratitude for what?

I was told my life on this Earth was only a brief interval during which I was

---

[109] According to the Christian belief in the concept of original sin.

to prepare for some unknown eternal life after death that I might earn if I sacrificed myself sufficiently for the benefit of others.[110] The so-called "eternal life" was never much of an incentive because no one could describe it in a way that sounded attractive. At least Allah promised a gaggle of virgins simply for dispatching a few infidels to hell during the transition to paradise. (I wondered what the women could earn—perhaps the opportunity to be the virgins?)

I wanted a productive, rewarding, and prosperous career; a comfortable and interesting life—yet Christianity upheld deprivation, humility, and self-sacrifice as virtues, and those who practiced these virtues were held in high esteem. Mother Theresa is admired for her sacrifice and charitable work much more than is Thomas Edison; yet, in my judgment, Thomas Edison contributed far more to the good of humanity than Mother Theresa ever did.

They said I should bow down and kneel on the ground with humility. I wanted to stand up and reach for the sky with pride, yet Christianity ranked pride as one of the seven deadly sins; and the Bible says, "Pride goes before destruction."[111]

At a young age, I instinctively loved and admired some people, but certainly not all—yet Christianity preached agape love—indiscriminate love for everyone. According to the Sermon on the Mount, I was to love my neighbors regardless of their character. That seemed to suggest it might be okay to disagree with Hitler's behavior, but I should nevertheless give him a big hug, forgive his actions, and invite him over for lunch with family and friends.

From earliest childhood, Christianity taught me to share, once again, indiscriminately—yet there were those who clearly had not earned or deserved my sharing.

The Christian doctrine contradicted my aspirations and sense of life in every way. Those contradictions gnawed at me as I studied Christianity on Sundays and struggled to live a secular life the rest of the week. The religious leaders were no help; they became irritated with my persistent questions and told me just to "have faith"—that God was beyond the power of comprehension.

At first, like most, I smiled, practiced self-deception, repressed the contradictions, and maintained superficial harmony to avoid the risk of alienating others. However, self-deception did not work; the contradictions continued to nag at me and created a level of anxiety that ebbed and flowed. I wanted clarity, understanding, consistency, and resolution, so I continued to search for answers. Was I the Devil incarnate?

Later I came to understand that the doctrines of all three great monothe-

---

[110] I always wondered: if that was my purpose in life, what was the purpose of the others? Were they to be my slaves and sacrifice their lives for me, even though I was a total stranger?
[111] Proverbs 16:18.

isms were essentially the same—Christianity was not unique. The common thread running through all forms of mysticism was the admonition to practice submission, obedience, and self-sacrifice. They differed only in the details—the purpose and the beneficiary of the sacrifice, the choice of which deity to worship as the true and legitimate one, the rules of behavior handed down by the prophets, and whether the messiah has come or is coming. Remarkably, tens of millions of people have died fighting over these trivialities and they continue to die every day.

At a relatively young age—after a naïve existence in North America—I was suddenly immersed in the tribalism and mysticism pervading Africa and the Middle East. My sense of contradictions became particularly vivid as I gained exposure to the many different cultures, religions, witchcraft, tribal beliefs, and superstitions firsthand—and observed their dire consequences on people's lives. The many faiths and practices I encountered bombarded my brain, shaped my thinking, and validated my notions about the significance and consequences of mysticism in all its forms.

It started in Nigeria. During the official ceremony to open a new training center in Kano, we discovered that several students from other regions of the country would not attend classes for fear of being attacked by competing "tribesmen" who were also attending classes. These tribesmen were students, educated young men from Nigeria's middle class beginning their new career as service technicians. They were not savages; however, members of each tribe practiced different customs and mystical rituals according to the teachings of their tribal leaders, warlords, and witchdoctors.

Typically, these warlords were educated at leading institutions in North America and Europe. They had experienced the freedom and prosperity of Western civilized societies, yet despite that knowledge and understanding, they returned home and promptly set about oppressing their own people and bankrupting their nations. They used mysticism and witchcraft to instill fear, and elicit loyalty and obedience from their tribal members.

According to the *Economist*, corruption has cost the Nigerian people over $400 billion—about two-thirds of all the aid given to all of Africa since the 1960s.[112] During the past 25 years, per capita income has fallen significantly. It is a poor country only because military warlords plundered the oil revenue for their private gain, instead of using it to improve living standards for the people. Nigeria is just one of several countries in Africa that are slowly working their way back to the Dark Ages in that manner.

In Zimbabwe—formerly called Rhodesia—Robert Mugabe assumed the

---

112 "The Good, the Bad and the President," *Economist*, January 5, 2008, 36.

MYSTICISM: A WORLDWIDE EPIDEMIC

reins of power after independence and ruled the country with brutality, trampled on human rights, and created a disastrous economic situation the World Bank has called "unprecedented for a country not at war." Over the years Mugabe has displaced almost a million Zimbabweans from their homes, disrupted the education of thousands of children, forcing many of them out of school, and confiscated the passports of those considered "injurious to the national good." Mugabe's brand of mysticism has brought the country close to collapse.

The Congo is no better. Dictator Mobutu Sese Seko launched a comprehensive nationalization plan in 1973 and subsequently plundered business for personal enrichment. During the past three decades, neglect, corruption, and tribal mysticism by Mobutu and his "kleptocratic" parliament—made up of former warlords—have left the infrastructure in shambles. In a 2005 survey, the World Bank rated the Congo as having the world's worst business environment.

In 2007, several African countries had the audacity to ask the World Bank and others to forgive their international loans and help them climb out of their primitive existence. Leaders of the civilized world have shown empathy to that request, and are likely foolish enough to fall for the swindle and give more of the worker's money to the plundering warlords. Like the oil revenue, most of that money, like the money that should have gone to pay the forgiven loans, will undoubtedly end up in private foreign bank accounts.

When my colleagues and I traveled to Saudi Arabia, Libya, and Sudan, immigration and customs officials invariably searched our luggage looking for an excuse to harass us; we were "infidels" and "non-believers"—therefore, the enemies of their God. *Time*, *Newsweek*, and *Playboy* magazines were routinely confiscated—these publications were considered too risqué according to the established religious rules. However, our local contacts assured us these publications got well read as they were surreptitiously passed from one official to another. They especially searched for copies of *Playboy* to study, and occasionally glanced at the others for news about the free world.

In Saudi Arabia, the wives of our employees could not go out alone to shop or visit their friends. They could not drive cars or wear clothes that showed bare skin. In Jeddah, I witnessed men being whipped in the public square for drinking alcohol, and women being persecuted for not being sufficiently covered, or for violating one of the many other rules of behavior. The Wahhabi mystics and the Saudi Ministry for the Propagation of Virtue and the Prevention of Vice—the Kingdom's religious police—enforced the Islamic (sharia) law and punished the non-believers and infidels. [113]

---

[113] Robert Fisk, *The Great War for Civilization: The Conquest of the Middle East* (2005). Wahhabism is the strict conservative Sunni Islamist religion of Saudi Arabia and Qatar, founded by the 18th-century cleric Mohammed Ibn Abdul-Wahhab (1703—1792). The Taliban clerics are products of the Wahhabi madras-

MYSTICISM: A WORLDWIDE EPIDEMIC

Fast-forward to 2007: Saudi authorities sentenced a married woman from the town of Qatif, who had been gang raped by seven men, to six months in jail and 200 lashes—yes, she was the victim of the rape, not the perpetrator. What did she do to deserve that barbaric treatment? She was in a public parking lot to retrieve a photo from a male friend. According to Islamic (sharia) law, women are not allowed to go out in public with men unless they are with their male relatives. The Islamic mysticism of Wahhabism still enforces strict laws on segregation of the sexes.[114] Obviously, nothing significant has changed since I first traveled the region 25 years ago.

Of course, the ruling classes—the political leaders and religious clerics—exempted themselves from these rules when the situation made it convenient to do so. Saudi businessmen were very hospitable, and during visits to their private homes, we shared cocktails and hors d'oeuvres at bars well stocked with a wide variety of alcoholic beverages—notwithstanding that the country officially banned alcohol in accordance with Islamic law.

Saudi customers attending a product seminar in Malaga, Spain, were entertained with the finest champagne and Spanish women that money could buy—despite the Islamic (sharia) rules of behavior. I was there; it was an unforgettable experience.

One day while I was flying from Jeddah to London on British Airways, my seatmate, wearing a full burka, quietly retreated to the bathroom.[115] A few minutes later, that Arab woman returned looking like a model out of *Vogue*, wearing a short skirt, sheer nylons, four-inch heels, long flowing hair, and plenty of jewelry and cleavage. It was a transformation. No doubt, she would arrive in London and meld into the fashionable crowd at Piccadilly Circus unnoticed. Of course, on the flight back to Saudi Arabia, she would change costumes again and disembark wearing the burka. Quite obviously, the mystical rules of Islam are flexible when necessary—at least for some. I suppose that if one has the power to make the rules, one has the power to ignore them.

The entire Middle East is dysfunctional—a boiling caldron of mysticism—and it has been for more than 2,000 years. Three of the world's dominant religions originated in the Middle East. The city of Jerusalem is claimed to be sacred to all three in their quest to reach eternal salvation.[116] It is not possible to

---

sas—religious schools for Muslims—funded primarily by Saudi Arabia.
114   *Economist*, November 24, 2007, 52
115   Burka: An all-over garment with veiled eyeholes, worn by some Muslim women.
116   It is worth noting that King David founded Jerusalem. For over 3,000 years, Jerusalem was the Jewish capital. There are no indications that Mohammed ever set foot in it. It was never the capital of any Arab or Muslim entity. Even during Jordanian rule, Jerusalem was not made the capital. Jews pray facing Jerusalem; Muslims face Mecca.

explain the human slaughter that has occurred in the name of these religions over the years. The fundamentalists of all three contributed to the slaughter, including the Christians. All three share a common idea—that they, and they alone, have the one "true" religion and will therefore have exclusive passage to the "life hereafter." They each believe their God is the only true God and their faith must reign supreme. The human slaughter will continue so long as the masses continue to accept the teachings that their version of the truth is the "exclusive" version.

Although the world's attention is focused mainly on the Arab-Israeli conflict, the majority of the slaughter has not involved Israel. For example, Syria killed 20,000 Arab Muslims while crushing an uprising in Hama in 1982; Saddam Hussein killed more Arab Muslims than the Israelis ever have and many consider him a hero; the 10-year Iran-Iraq war killed well over a million Arabs and Persians;[117] and over 2 million Sudanese have died in the ongoing civil war. The outrage over Israel and the Palestinians continues, while Arabs killing Arabs and the weakness of their society and political systems are overlooked.

Obviously, the suicide murders are more about money and power than supreme acts of genuine religious beliefs. The Muslim clerics have not strapped on bombs and committed suicide murders to martyr themselves or their sons for the glorious benefit of going to heaven with 71 virgins. Instead, they send their sons to the United States or the U.K. to get a good education. The suicide bombers are the outcasts, the orphans, the retarded, and the young hotheads. Suicide murder is simply a vicious form of terrorism, a weapon used by those seeking personal affluence and power, and mysticism is the tool used to make it happen.

India is particularly rife with mysticism. Hinduism, Buddhism, Jainism, and Sikhism were all born there, and the country has more Muslims than any country other than Indonesia.[118] Religion is an essential part of the nation's character. I found the Hindu brand of mysticism particularly astonishing. According to the *National Geographic* magazine, the ranks in that society come from a legend in which the main groupings emerged from a primordial being. One group—called the Untouchables—is considered too impure, too polluted, to rank as worthy human beings. Prejudice defines the lives of these 160 million people, particularly in the rural areas. Untouchables are shunned, insulted, banned from temples and higher-caste homes; made to eat and drink from separate utensils in public places; and in extreme cases, are raped, burned, lynched, and

---

[117] Persians are people born in Iran and are descendents of people who lived in ancient Persia and who founded an empire around 550 BC. Their language is Farsi, and they are not Arabs. Their dominant religion is Islam.

[118] Edward Luce, *In Spite of the Gods: The Rise of Modern India* (2007).

MYSTICISM: A WORLDWIDE EPIDEMIC

gunned down.[119]

The religious mystics of the Hindu persuasion expect these people to accept their misery and practice the self-sacrifice that might get them into a higher class of society when they are reincarnated—provided, of course, that their sacrifice is sufficient. I watched children from that caste begging for scraps of food outside the four-star hotels in Bombay, Calcutta, and Madras. Meanwhile, cows freely roamed through the market, eating whatever they wanted and generally destroying whatever got in their way.[120] Where is the virtue in a brand of mysticism that values cows over children and preaches the basic precept that all men are created *unequal*?

Further illustrating the shocking nature of Hindu mysticism, fast-forward again, to 2005, and read about the story of a girl whose grandfather arranged her marriage at the age of three to a neighborhood boy who was five years old. The marriage was blessed by the caste panchayat—the caste council, a powerful group of local leaders. In 2005, the girl, now 22 years old, broke the rules of marriage and refused to move in with her husband. By persisting, she could be stripped naked, persecuted, ostracized, and perhaps tortured to death. Once again, the Hindu mysticism of the caste panchayat ruled over the lives of the people. Her religious affiliation became a matter of life and death.[121]

After relocating to Hong Kong in 1979, I had occasion to visit China shortly after the death of Chairman Mao. In China, it was not a religious mystic that had been calling the shots for 30 years; it was a mystic of muscle—Chairman Mao. He had created his own divine persona, the altar at which the Chinese people were expected to worship. He even provided them with a "sacred" text—the *Little Red Book*. Under Mao's monotheism, the people had to confess their sins to the regime and sacrifice their lives to the Communist ideology with as much fervor and submissiveness as the followers of any religious mystic. Chairman Mao's mysticism of muscle resulted in the death of over 50 million of his own ethnic Chinese people through mass starvation and persecution during his reign of terror. Mao was not unique; many other strongmen down through history understood the power of mysticism and fear to control the masses—Adolph Hitler, Lenin, Stalin, Saddam Hussein, Pol Pot, and Fidel Castro, to name a few.[122] Like Chairman Mao, they held total control over people's lives and demanded unquestioning obedience to the dogmatism and doctrine of

---

[119] *National Geographic*, June 2003.
[120] The governments of India offered to import and protect the cattle facing slaughter because of the "mad cow" disease that swept through Europe in the 1990s.
[121] *Washington Post*, September 6, 2005.
[122] See Robert Gellately, *Lenin, Stalin and Hitler: The Age of Social Catastrophe* (2007); and Andrew Nagorski, *The Greatest Battle* (2007).

MYSTICISM: A WORLDWIDE EPIDEMIC

their ideology and cult of divinized personality.

In Beijing in 1979, the engineers attending our training seminars were not allowed to enter the hotel without a permission slip from the Communist Party. Nor were they allowed to inspect our equipment in the field without travel documents giving them specific permission. Control over individual choice and personal behavior was so extreme, it was difficult to tell the men from the women because they were all forced to wear the same drab blue Mao uniforms. Fortunately, several economic liberties have been granted since then; however, political freedom in China is still practically nonexistent.

The epidemic of mysticism is not limited to the lesser-developed countries. In Northern Ireland, the Catholics and the Protestants killed each other for years over differing beliefs, doctrines, and rituals. The same occurred in the Balkans during the dissolution of the Federal Republic of Yugoslavia where a once-modern society crumbled into chaos. To be Croatian is to be Christian Roman Catholic, and to be Serbian is to be Christian Orthodox. Here, Slobodan Milosevic—a Christian Orthodox Serb—led the Holocaust-like practice of ethnic or religious cleansing against the Croatians during the battles over religious, cultural, and ethnic differences—Christians killing Christians.[123]

Radical mysticism is also starting to rear its ugly head in the United States, specifically in the ranting of the right-wing Christian fundamentalists as they advocate breaking down the constitutional separation of church and state and converting the government into a Christian theocracy. Madeleine Albright, the former United States secretary of state, advocates mixing politics and religion to help solve the world's problems,[124] and President George W. Bush, as well as Osama bin Laden, firmly believes "God is on our side."

In Canada in the 1960s, the Federation de Liberation de Québec (FLQ) used violence and intimidation in an attempt to extend their control over the Québec "infidels" who were not of the same "tribe," who frequently did not share the same religion and did not agree with the FLQ's plan of "salvation" for the province. Fortunately, Prime Minister Pierre Trudeau declared marshal law and brought out the army to restore order before the situation got out of hand.

My wife tells stories of her persecution as a young girl while being educated by the Catholic Church in Québec. The religious mystics of the Christian faith told her what to read, what to think, and how to live her personal life. Young students under the nuns were not allowed to read the Bible independently until they were about 20 years old, for fear they would not be sufficiently brainwashed with the doctrine and the dogma to resist the contradictions and temptations

---

123 In the 1940s, the Catholic Croatians slaughtered thousands of Orthodox Christians or put them in concentration camps.
124 Madeleine Albright, *The Mighty and the Almighty: Reflections on America, God and World Affairs* (2006).

they might encounter. Meanwhile, the Catholic priests were having a heyday sexually abusing the young boys in the local orphanages—tragic events no one spoke about until 20 years later. Today, my wife is a recovering Catholic. She personally experienced methods of intimidation and mind control similar to those used to brainwash Muslim children to become suicide bombers in the name of Allah—the supreme mystic of the Muslim faith.

It is not an accident that free societies are relatively prosperous and enjoy a good standard of living, whereas totalitarian theocratic societies breed fear, ignorance, and hate as they struggle to meet the basic needs of survival—even those nations that enjoy bountiful wealth from oil. The cycle of desperation is not caused by poverty; it is caused by repression and ignorance, which creates vulnerability to fanatical beliefs in ancient tribal mysticisms. Mystics do not want their followers to be educated, independent thinkers; they want them to be ignorant and fearful so they will blindly follow the tribal leader who promises to take care of them in return for loyalty and self-sacrifice.

Israel is the only country in the Middle East that has a legitimate multiethnic, pluralistic form of government that protects individual freedoms to a significant degree. Israel has only 1/1000 of the world's population, and yet its $100 billion economy is larger than all its immediate neighbors combined. Israel has the highest average living standard in the Middle East, and in the year 2000, the per capita income exceeded that of the U.K. In contrast, its neighboring countries practice religious totalitarianism in one form or another and large numbers of the population are functionally illiterate. Totalitarianism and illiteracy often seem to go together—a coincidence, perhaps? I think not.

India has about 150 million practicing Muslims who are generally productive and quietly go about making better lives for themselves. It is the second largest community of Muslims in the world, yet we do not hear about them trying to kill us or destroy America.[125] Perhaps it's because, like Israel, they live under a political system (a form of democracy, perhaps) that, although fragile, messy, and corrupt, is also multiethnic and pluralistic. In addition, a basic secular education is widely available and most have economic opportunities and a political voice open to them. In addition, most individual liberties are acknowledged, which allows grievances to be expressed and addressed, usually without having to resort to violence.

So what is the point? The point is that mysticism in all its many forms is a worldwide epidemic. Whether it is a self-appointed mystic of muscle or a mys-

---

125 Indonesia has the largest Muslim community of any single country.

MYSTICISM: A WORLDWIDE EPIDEMIC

tic of religion, both share a common thread—they both demand self-sacrifice, submission, and unquestioning obedience. The outcome of that epidemic is always the same: millions of people living and dying in ignorance, poverty, conflict, and desperation.[126] I fail to see the virtue in that altruistic morality. My experiences have convinced me that only under a secular political system—one protecting individual freedom and maintaining an independent judiciary to enforce the separation of church and state—can people with differing beliefs and value systems enjoy freedom and co-exist peacefully.

The epidemic of mysticism desperately needs a vaccine. It is available—it starts with a quality, secular education that teaches all children they are sovereign individuals with inalienable rights to life, liberty, and the pursuit of their own happiness. A worldwide inoculation program should be implemented to wipe out that epidemic before it destroys the societies that are still mostly civilized.

> *Good people will do good things, and bad people will do bad things. But for good people to do bad things—that takes religion.*
> —STEVEN WEINBERG

---

[126] Christopher Hitchens, *God Is Not Great* (2007); the author provides detailed documentation of how mysticism, religion, faith, and superstition destroy civilized societies.

23

AS I SEE IT

> *Freedom is never more than one generation away from extinction. We didn't pass it on to our children in the bloodstream. It must be fought for, protected, and handed on for them to do the same, or one day we will spend our sunset years telling our children what it was once like in the United States where men were free."*
> —Ronald Reagan, 40th president of the United States

America is the greatest country in the world. I state that conclusion after having experienced and studied several different societies, cultures, and political systems in the regions where I have lived, traveled, and worked for the past 50-plus years. America is great because of the foundation on which it rests—the U.S. Constitution—a document unlike any other in the world because it was designed to protect the intrinsic rights of the smallest minority: the individual, specifically the individual American. The U.S. Constitution protects the individual American from the tyranny of both his own government and foreign governments, and enables him to pursue his own life, liberty, and happiness. (Note: it was not designed to protect the individual rights of every Iraqi or Canadian.)

Many Western countries approximate the American political system to a degree, but most prefer to emphasize multiculturalism instead of individual rights, naively believing that all cultures are essentially equal and that they can coexist peacefully and harmoniously, be they illiterate primitive tribesmen or citizens of an advanced, free industrial civilization. Multiculturalism does not recognize the sovereignty of the individual; rather, it considers the individual merely as a member of the religious, cultural, or ethnic group to which he/she belongs and gives priority to protecting the diversity and the "common good" of the group. Multiculturalism does not encourage the members of those immigrant groups to amalgamate or assimilate into a unified society. In fact, it does the opposite: it encourages the host society to accommodate and assimilate with the diverse cultures of the immigrant groups—a nation of diverse nations. The multicultural approach promotes ghettoization, discrimination, and ethnic animosity. Canada and Europe, in particular, pride themselves on their multiculturalism, refusing to see the inherent ethnic problems that are rapidly developing.[127]

As a casual observer traveling the Middle East, Africa, and Asia, I found it easy to see that American culture was far superior in every way to that of the Islamic world in terms of individual liberties, fair treatment, legal protection, personal security, and opportunities for a better life. Most Muslims I met envied us these advantages, although they considered American secularism inferior to Islam, demeaning to their faith, and an attack on their God. The idea of the separation of church and state is an anathema to devout Muslims, whereas many Americans and Europeans value the concept. In the Islamic holy lands in particular, devout Muslims take their religion seriously as an important part of everyday life, and some that I met were prepared to defend it to the death, although many were not. While traveling the Islamic nations, I heard the muezzin call Muslims to pray at regular intervals throughout the day, and for devout Muslims, stopping to pray was not an option. On the other hand, most Christians in North America and Europe may attend church occasionally, if it is not too much of an inconvenience. They certainly do not consider Christianity important enough to die for.

Although devout Muslims generally took their own religion seriously, they did not show much interest in the particular God I believed in, if any. They showed no animosity toward my beliefs and way of life, even though the differences between our cultures were enormous. They never tried to convert me to Islam and I never proselytized about the advantages of our secular way of life or about the importance of the separation of church and state, because I knew it would be tantamount to asking them to reject their God and their entire belief system. It was clear to me then (and it still is today) that our secular political system is fundamentally incompatible with Islam, notwithstanding the Bush

---

127 In February 2008, Rowan Williams, the Archbishop of Canterbury, primate of the Church of England suggested that, given the recent increase in the Muslim population, Britain should adopt elements of the Islamic (sharia) law in order to foster social cohesion. This is a good example of how a multicultural attitude can allow special interest groups to opt out of the established culture and systems—in that case the judicial system and the centuries-old British principle of one law for all with its insistence of tolerance and free speech. He was suggesting that theocrats should be in charge of the law and that religion should be given shelter behind special privileges. Of course, Reverend William's suggestion provoked outrage and ethnic animosity instead of social cohesion. It will be interesting to see if the sovereignty of the individual can fend off the multicultural movement—so far, it is losing the contest. See the *Economist*, February 16, 2008, 13. See also Mark Steyn, *America Alone: The End of the World as We Know It* (2006).

administration's determination to instantly democratize the Islamic societies.

The sum of my experiences employing, working, and dealing with Muslims indicated they were generally friendly and accepted a "live and let live" relationship. We mutually respected an unspoken truce based on the following understanding: "Of course, we have our differences, but if you don't mess with us, we won't mess with you, and we can get along and work together. If you don't tell us how to treat our women, we won't tell you how to treat yours."

That helps to explain the relatively peaceful relationship Americans and other Western nations have had with most of the Islamic nations for decades. In fact, during the Afghan-Russian war in the 1980s, the United States sided with the Afghan mujahideen who defeated Russia's Red Army in 1989 after 10 years of bloody fighting. During that war, the CIA covertly supplied billions of dollars in cash, military equipment, and ordnance to support the Afghan mujahideen. In addition, the ethnic Muslims inside Soviet Central Asia (for example, Uzbeks, Turkmen, Tajiks, and Kazakhs) were already becoming a problem for the Russians, and the CIA helped covertly to stir up that rebellion with the hope of pushing the Afghan jihad into Russia. The CIA arranged for the Koran to be published in the local Uzbek language, and worked with Pakistan's Intelligence and the Afghanis to distribute thousands of copies of the Koran to the mujahideen in Soviet Central Asia. The Muslims in these border republics were also provided with propaganda Islamic texts and Islamic sermons on tape.[128]

Of course, much earlier, in the 1970s, Islamic radicalism was becoming evident—most notably in the overthrow of the Shah of Iran and the attempted violent seizure of Mecca in 1979—but these acts were targeting corrupt and failing totalitarian Middle Eastern governments, not America.

So then, what broke the truce? Why did 9/11 happen? Why do we hear so much today about Muslims trying to destroy America and Western civilization? Why is Islamic militancy and radicalization increasing around the world? Why did Osama bin Laden decide to wage war against America?

The bipartisan Washington elite, the intellectuals, the academics, and the mainstream media would have you believe that our Islamist enemies despise us and wage war because of our secular lifestyle, our liberties, our democratic system, and our religious beliefs. That is what President Bush said in an address to Congress after the 2001 terrorist attacks. In effect, that message suggested

---

[128] Those were not the only actions taken by the United States government to foment the Islamist radicals, and I will leave it to you to decide how much these actions might have contributed to the backlash of Islamic radicalism against the West, and the increasing Islamic militancy and radicalization around the world. If you are interested in the full story, see the Pulitzer Prize winning book by Steve Coll, *Ghost Wars* (2004), 103–104; and see also Michael Scheuer, *Marching Toward Hell* (2008), 37–38.

that the Muslim faith turns people violent. I found that explanation hard to accept because it did not resonate with my personal experiences and observations while living and working with Muslims; it was not consistent with the attitude: "If you don't mess with me, I won't mess with you"; and it did not explain why the jihad against the West started only recently. I was anxious to reconcile the contradiction between my own experiences and the rhetoric coming out of Washington, London, and CNN.

When one is at war, it is prudent to know and understand your enemy, so I decided to investigate what the leader of al Qaeda, Osama bin Laden himself, said about his motivations for waging war against us. Surprisingly, I discovered he was very precise in explaining his motivations well before September 11, 2001. During a long interview in May 1998, he said:

> The call to wage war against America was made because America has spearheaded the crusade against the Islamic nation, sending tens of thousands of its troops to the land of the two Holy Mosques [Saudi Arabia] over and above its meddling in its affairs and its politics, and its support of the oppressive, corrupt and tyrannical regime that is in control...They rip us of our wealth and of our resources and of our oil. Our religion is under attack. They kill and murder our brothers. They compromise our honor and our dignity and dare we utter a single word of protest against the injustice, we are called terrorists. This is compounded injustice.[129]

Notwithstanding the fact that Arab nations are paid very well for their oil, the motivation to wage war was stated very clearly. Yet Washington's elite refused to understand that simple message that America's foreign policy of intervention and occupation was the real grievance—it was not our lifestyle, our liberties, or our religion. Osama bin Laden's motivation to wage war had nothing to do with how we lived or what we believed—it had everything to do with what he perceived we were doing to his holy land, to his fellow Muslim brothers and to Islam. Al Qaeda was waging a worldwide war against America primarily because it "messed" in the holiest countries of Islam—Saudi Arabia and Iraq. Although America had been "messing" around the Middle East for many years, Osama bin Laden emphasized that its most serious offense was establishing military bases in Saudi Arabia in 1990.

Although al Qaeda's original motivation for the jihad against America might have been to drive them out of the holy lands, there is some evidence to believe that the initiative has morphed into something much bigger and out of control:

---

[129] Transcript of a May 1998 interview with Osama bin Laden by his followers and ABC reporter John Miller. He goes on in detail to elaborate on how America and its allies have meddled in Muslim's affairs and its politics. See http://www.pbs.org/wgbh/pages/frontline/ shows/binladen/who/interview.html.

AS I SEE IT

a fluid, multinational jihad to kill infidels wherever they may be, simply because they are infidels. For example, the former head of Hezbollah, Hussein Massawi, said, "We are not fighting so that you can offer us something. We are fighting to eliminate you."

Did our leaders in Washington deliberately distort the truth because the need for foreign oil prevented them from reconsidering America's foreign policy in the Middle East? The mainstream media knew Osama's motivations, as stated—why didn't they challenge the administration and report the truth? Eventually, in September 1996, Osama formally declared war against America and its allies.[130] History will record that World War III began on that day. Moreover, Osama bin Laden had already demonstrated he was serious. Recall a few examples of his seriousness…

- 1993—Feb. 26: Bomb exploded in basement garage of New York World Trade Center, killing six and injuring at least 1,040. Al-Qaeda involvement was suspected.
- 1995—April 19: Oklahoma City. Car bomb exploded outside federal office building, collapsing walls and floors; 168 people were killed, including 19 children and 1 person who died in the rescue effort.
- 1995—November 13: Riyadh, Saudi Arabia. Car bomb exploded at United States military headquarters, killing five United States military servicemen.
- 1996—June 25: Dhahran, Saudi Arabia. Truck bomb exploded outside Khobar towers military complex, killing 19 American servicemen and injuring hundreds of others. Thirteen Saudis and a Lebanese, all alleged members of Islamic militant group Hezbollah, were indicted.
- 1998—August 7: Nairobi, Kenya, and Dar es Salaam, Tanzania. Truck bombs exploded almost simultaneously near two United States embassies, killing 224 (213 in Kenya and 11 in Tanzania) and injuring about 4,500; 22 men indicted, including Saudi dissident Osama bin Laden.
- 2000—October 12: Aden, Yemen. United States Navy destroyer USS Cole was heavily damaged when a small boat loaded with explosives blew up alongside it; 17 sailors killed. Attack linked to Osama bin Laden and members of al-Qaeda terrorist network.
- 2001—September 11: New York City; Arlington, Virginia; and Shanksville, Pennsylvania. Hijackers crashed two commercial jets into twin towers of

---

130 In 1996, Osama bin Laden wrote a "Declaration of Jihad against the Americans Occupying the Two Sacred Places." In that document, he made it very clear why he regarded the United States as his enemy.

World Trade Center; two more hijacked jets were crashed into the Pentagon and a field in rural Pennsylvania. Total dead and missing numbered 2,749 in New York City, 184 at the Pentagon, 40 in Pennsylvania. Islamic al-Qaeda terrorist group blamed.

- 2002—June 14: Karachi, Pakistan. Bomb exploded outside American consulate in Karachi, Pakistan, killing 12. Attack linked to al-Qaeda.
- 2003—May 12: Riyadh, Saudi Arabia. Suicide bombers killed 34, including 8 Americans, at housing compounds for Westerners. Al-Qaeda suspected.
- 2004—March 11: A series of train bombings in Madrid killed more than 200 people. Abu Hafs al-Masri Brigade, a group linked to al Qaeda, claimed responsibility for the attack.
- 2004—May 29–31: Riyadh, Saudi Arabia. Terrorists attacked the offices of a Saudi oil company in Khobar; they took foreign oil workers hostage in a nearby residential compound, leaving 22 people dead, including 1 American.
- 2004—June 11–19: Riyadh, Saudi Arabia. Terrorists kidnapped and executed Paul Johnson Jr., an American, in Riyadh, Saudi Arabia; two other Americans and a BBC cameraman were killed by gun attacks.
- 2004—Dec. 6: Jeddah, Saudi Arabia. Terrorists stormed the United States consulate, killing five consulate employees.
- 2005—July 7: Four suicide Islamist extremists detonated three bombs on three different underground trains in London during rush hour, and a fourth bomb an hour later on a bus. The explosions killed 52 people and injured 700. That series of suicide bombings constituted the largest and deadliest terrorist attack in London's history. Abu Hafs al-Masri Brigade, a group linked to al Qaeda, claimed responsibility for the attack.
- 2005—Nov. 9: Amman, Jordan. Suicide bombers hit three American hotels, Radisson, Grand Hyatt, and Days Inn, in Amman, Jordan, killing 57. Al-Qaeda claimed responsibility.

And the list goes on...

Unfortunately, Osama's declaration of war was not taken seriously, and the responses to these attacks have been insignificant. How many more attacks are we going to tolerate before defending ourselves against our enemies? When will we decide enough is enough? Do we wait until al Qaeda detonates a nuclear device

AS I SEE IT

in Manhattan or Los Angeles, a weapon we know they are trying to acquire?[131] As I write this, America's sons and daughters have been fighting and dying in Afghanistan and Iraq for more than five years, and yet the administration in Washington has still not issued a formal declaration of war or even explicitly identified the enemy.

It is foolish to think of it as a "War on Terror," as George W. Bush would like us to believe—terror is simply a weapon, a technique used to kill people. The war should be against the leaders of al Qaeda and the states sponsoring and funding the terrorist networks—those supplying the guns and the money and the safe havens and the training and the travel documents and the secure communications. To achieve victory, that support must be stopped.

But some suggest that achieving victory may not even be the goal. Paul Pillar, a 28-year veteran of the CIA, and a longtime deputy director of the Counterterrorist Center, viewed terrorism as "a challenge to be managed, not solved," and said: "it is a war that cannot be won..."[132] And Senator John McCain had the audacity to say that America needs to remain in the region and continue messing around for perhaps another "hundred years." This is moral cowardice... an admission that the United States cannot provide national security for its citizens...an admission that America's military might is neither able to defeat Osama bin Laden's al Qaeda networks nor the NGOs and the Arab states supporting them...an admission that the war has no end and we must learn to live with terrorism.[133]

There are four fundamental errors in the United States foreign policy. The first error was (and still is) failing to free America from its dependence on foreign oil during the past 35 years. In 1973, Saudi Arabia led an OPEC initiative to shut down our oil supply because of the Yom Kippur War. The embargo was a sudden, dramatic event that affected all Americans and should have been a serious wake-up call for our bipartisan elected leadership. Obviously, they continued to sleep, so now 35 years later, adversarial foreign governments still con-

---

131 In 2006, ballistic missile fuses were sent from a United States Air Force base in Utah to Taiwan by mistake. The U.S. military was unaware of their absence for 18 months. This is just the latest in a series of accidents and glitches that illustrates how vulnerable we are to nuclear material getting into the hands of terrorist groups. The Nuclear Threat Initiative (NTI, http://www.nti.org) reports that more than 40 countries have nuclear weapons materials; some of it is secured with only a chain link fence. See Sam Nunn "The Mountaintop: A World Free of Nuclear Weapons," Presentation to the Council on Foreign Relations, June 14, 2007, http://www.nti.org/.
132 Paul Pillar, *Terrorism and U.S. Foreign Policy*, pp. vii, 217—218 (2004)
133 Louis Richardson, *What Terrorists Want: Understanding the Enemy, Containing the Threat* (2006), 237.

trol America's economic lifeline, and the United States must continue "messing around" in Islam's holiest lands and supporting Arab dictatorships (particularly Saudi Arabia and Egypt) in order to ensure that the oil continues to flow.

I was personally "messing around" in the Arab nations in the late 1970s, and the main reason we were there was to support the petroleum exploration and development projects throughout the Middle East and North Africa. Americans needed the oil then and the need is even greater now, 30 years later—great enough to pay $100-plus a barrel for it, knowing that much of the proceeds are used to buy armaments that kill their sons and daughters in Afghanistan and Iraq. This shocking and morally unacceptable situation could have been avoided had American leadership given first priority to maintaining domestic energy security for the United States. Of course, the leaders of other Western nations are equally guilty, as are the radical environmentalists for fear mongering about clean, safe nuclear energy and for caring more about preserving a few acres of remote woodlands and wetlands than for the security of Americans. Capitulating to the environmentalists, Congress has placed some of our own most plentiful sources of oil "out of bounds"—for example the Alaska wilderness (potentially 1 million barrels a day), most of America's coastlines (estimated at 100 billion barrels), and oil shale in Colorado (estimated to be 1.5 trillion barrels). Becoming independent of foreign oil within a few short years would be a cakewalk compared to the national initiative that President Kennedy launched to get an American on the moon almost 40 years ago.

Given the conflicts in the region, the supply of oil from Saudi Arabia is less reliable now than it was at the time of the embargo in 1973. Without warning, the supply chain could be violently disrupted or curtailed for religious reasons, as happened in 1973. Nigeria and Venezuela are similar examples. Venezuela is intensely adversarial toward the United States, and in Nigeria, violence is escalating between rival Christian-Muslim factions in the Niger Delta, the oil-producing region in the south. Radical Islamists and al Qaeda are already active in that area too, and America may soon have to send in its military to secure its oil supplies from the region.

The sooner America becomes independent of foreign oil, the sooner it can withdraw from Muslim holy lands and stop sacrificing America's youth to prop up Middle East dictators. In the meantime, while becoming self-sufficient in energy, America should use the full capability of its military to eliminate its enemies (instead of trying to "win their hearts and minds"), establish national security for the United States, and ensure a steady supply of foreign oil—a matter of economic survival for the country.

The second foreign policy error is to believe that America has a duty and responsibility to police the world, to impose international "stability," and intervene every time ethnic or religious differences result in conflict or suffering, whether or not the situation represents a threat to the United States. Those altruistic acts of self-sacrificial intervention consume enormous resources that should be spent solving domestic problems and making sure Americans are safe at home. Invariably, instead of making the world safer, American intervention often makes more enemies and generates animosity, even from our so-called friends and allies.

The third foreign policy error assumes that diplomacy will achieve lasting peace in the Middle East. Diplomacy and compromise are only effective between nations that have common interests. They will not achieve a mutually beneficial agreement with someone determined to kill you. For example, the Taliban, Hamas, al Qaeda, and Hezbollah's stated policy is to push the Jews into the sea and wage war against America. Those radical groups are openly supported and encouraged by Iran, Syria, Egypt, and Saudi Arabia.[134] None of these states has any intention of compromising and making peace, since Hamas, al Qaeda, and Hezbollah serve as useful proxies for their own undeclared war against Israel.

While campaigning to be elected, the leaders of Hamas proudly declared to fellow Palestinians and the entire world that their objective was to destroy Israel in a holy jihad. Palestinian citizens supported that goal and voted to put Hamas in power—it was a landslide victory in a "democratic" election. Clearly, the priority for the Palestinian people is not to establish a Palestinian state; it is not to coexist peacefully with Israel and build a better future for their children. If it were, Hamas would have been soundly defeated in the election and serious talks would be underway.

Why do the world's leaders refuse to hear and accept what they say and do? Why do they continue to send hundreds of millions of dollars to support their terrorism? Why do they hang on desperately to the myth that diplomacy and appeasement can suddenly overcome thousands of years of religious and ethnic conflict? Peace will come only with the utter defeat of either the Palestinians or the Israelis—and it won't come soon; such is the nature of that centuries-old conflict.

The fourth error in America's foreign policy is to believe that instant democratization is a panacea. George W. Bush read Natan Sharansky's book, *The Case for Democracy*, and latched onto democracy as a cure-all for the ills of the world. Subsequently, the Lebanese, the Iraqis, the Palestinian Authority, Hezbollah, and Hamas acquired legitimacy from being democratically elected. A spokesperson for Hamas, after it won the election, said, "I thank the United States

---

134 Michael A. Ledeen, *The Iranian Time Bomb* (2007)

that they have given us the weapon of democracy…It's not possible for the United States to turn its back on an elected democracy." Those terrorist groups embrace democracy because it gives them legitimacy and disarms America. Democratically elected terrorist groups do not advance the cause of freedom.

Democracy is unlimited majority rule—the idea that the government is free to do what it wants, so long as its behavior is sanctioned by a majority vote—by the "will of the people." George W. Bush and his entourage seemed to think that if people vote, its okay—regardless of whether or not they value freedom. Therefore, it is difficult to object when democratically elected tyrants dispatch suicide bombers to execute civilians, or plant roadside bombs to terrorize the population, or indiscriminately fire missiles at the "infidels." After all, they were elected by the people and simply carried out the "will of the people."

Be it known, democracy—majority rule—was *not* the foundation of the American system. The Constitution did *not* establish the United States of America as a democracy where the majority makes the rules; it was established as a Republic under which the state protects individual rights, no matter what the majority thinks or how many people wish to take them away—the "will of the people" be damned. The U.S. Constitution declared the rights of the smallest minority—the individual—to be inalienable. It is time the U.S. elected leadership based its foreign policy on that principle. Protecting individual rights requires objective laws and an independent judiciary—a concept that is completely contrary to Islamic (sharia) law.

As I have pointed out, any attempt to impose secular democracy on a predominantly Islamic culture, typical of Saudi Arabia, Afghanistan, and Iraq, is asking the people to reject the Koran and to turn their backs on their God. It is, therefore, doomed to failure. Advocates of America's current foreign policy seem to think that by improving the living conditions of the Iraqis and the Afghanis—better roads, schools, health care, and drinking water—they will suddenly set aside their ancient Islamic culture and deep ethnic differences, reject their God, embrace Western secular democracy with open arms, and live happily ever after. They seem to forget that even in the United States, it took over 100 years of relative stability and development before the Constitution was first drafted. It took another 100-plus years of bitter elections and domestic and foreign wars to achieve relative calm throughout the nation and implement most of the basic tenets of the Constitution.

Unfortunately, the bipartisan crowd in Washington was blind to that reality and ignorantly marched off on a crusade to save the world with unrelenting political and military intervention, appeasement, compromise, and instant democratization. Instead of securing the borders, improving domestic conditions, eliminating its enemies, and protecting its own citizens, American leadership

AS I SEE IT

chose to sacrifice its young men and women in foreign lands—lands where they were often not even welcome—seemingly, to win the admiration of the world's audience for their sacrifice, benevolence, and altruism. Appeasement, along with compromise and diplomacy, does not win the hearts and minds of those who wish to kill us—it never has and it never will.

&c&

During the last century, the free world demonstrated the will, determination, and bravery to win two great wars. Our enemies were defeated in four short years while fighting on several fronts in those two important conflicts. Consequently, our freedom and security were preserved. Since then, however, the United States has hardly won or finished a conflict. Nor has it mounted a serious response to the many terrorist attacks during the past 20 years. How is it possible that the United States, with an enormous military might, with missiles, aircraft carrier groups, and stealth bombers that could strike any target within a day, be stymied for over seven years by a few ragtag militia running through the streets of Bagdad or Basra or the hills of Afghanistan?

It is possible when our fainthearted leadership fails to declare war and refuses to identify and eliminate our enemies—choosing instead to call it a "Global War on Terror," foolishly suggesting there are no nation-state enemies. The United States Congress has even refused to declare the leadership of al Qaeda and the Taliban our enemies, deciding instead to treat them as individual common criminals and let the American judicial system determine their guilt or innocence. As Americans die, our bipartisan elected officials debate whether the concept of "enemy combatant" should still be acknowledged.

It is possible when America and its allies adopt a morality of self-sacrifice in an attempt to spread secular democracy and persuade our enemies to like us in order to win some inconsequential international popularity contest.

It is possible when squeamish, misty-eyed government leaders adopt the whining attitude expressed by a senior Western diplomat recently, when he asked me, "But what about the cost of winning?" I responded, "What about the cost of losing? Freedom is not free."

It is possible when indiscriminate compassion and "proportional and discriminate response" hamstring our soldiers with self-sacrificial rules of engagement designed to avoid offending the sensibilities of our enemies, instead of protecting the safety of the soldiers. Be thankful the "just war" theorists were not around during the First and Second World Wars.[135]

---

[135] "Proportional response" refers to using force proportional to the nature of the threat, and "discriminate response" refers to the need to differentiate between combatants and non-combatants. The "just war" theorists

AS I SEE IT

It is possible when we *fail* to proclaim loudly and proudly that our freedom, prosperity, and way of life are morally superior to the primitive desperation and morality of death brought about by religious fundamentalism.[136]

If American foreign policy does not change, I am fearful that future attacks will make 9/11 seem trivial. America may have the strongest and most powerful military in the world, but its bipartisan moral weakness and lack of will empowers its enemies.

The mainstream liberal media and intellectuals continually emphasize peace, when it's freedom that's important. Freedom requires courage, commitment, bravery, determination, and the willingness to risk one's life, whereas all that is necessary to achieve peace is to wave the white flag and surrender to our enemies. For me, surrender is not an option. To maintain our freedom and security, we must have the conviction, self-esteem, and pride to believe that our political and economic system is worth protecting. It is time to reaffirm the superiority of our way of life based on rational self-interest. It is time to abandon the self-defeating strategy of appeasement and sacrifice. It is time to quit messing in other people's lives when America's national security is not clearly at stake, and stop draining the treasury and sacrificing the lives of brave young men and women in an attempt to buy the love of those who wish to destroy us. It is time to conclusively and unequivocally defeat our enemies and win.

America's proper role in the world is to set a good example of how an enlightened political and economic system can protect individual freedoms and create opportunities for people to live life on Earth at a higher level of self-actualization. It is up to other societies to decide on their own whether they want to follow that example; it is not America's duty to impose it upon them.

For the sake of our children and our grandchildren, it is time for America to put America first. Otherwise, there will be no example to follow, and the U.S. Constitution will be a relic in the archives for our ancestors and future historians to marvel at and wonder about.

---

believe it is better to risk the lives of one's own combatants than the lives of the enemy's non-combatants. Clearly, it weakens the effectiveness of the military's response, sacrifices American soldiers, emboldens the enemy, and prolongs the conflict. See Scheuer, *Marching Toward Hell* (2008) 75.

136 A Taliban spokesperson said: "Americans are fighting so they can live and enjoy the material things in life, but we are fighting so we can die in the cause of Allah." And a taped message from one of the Madrid bombers, Shehzed Tanweer, included the following statement: "We are 100 percent committed to the cause of Islam. We love death the way you love life." And in 1999, Ramzi Binalshibh, a member of al Qaeda who helped bin Laden with recruiting, wrote, "I come to you with men who love death, just as you love life…" Steven Coll, *Ghost Wars*, 2005, p.476.

AS I SEE IT

Wake up America!
Where have all the leaders gone?

Nearly twice as many Muslims live in Indonesia, Pakistan, India and Bangladesh as in the entire Arab world. Thus the 'struggle for the soul of Islam' must inevitably be fought and won not only in the Arab heartland, but on its periphery as well—a fact which offers a unique, little known opportunity for those wishing to promote moderate and progressive interpretations of Islam. Non-Arab Muslim populations have the power to help define Islam, and to discredit Wahhabism as a heretical fringe movement financed by oil-rich extremists.137

---

137 Kyai Haji Abdurrahman Wahid and C. Holland Taylor, "A Tradition of Tolerance in Indonesia Offers Hope," *Foreign Service Journal*, April 2008, 35. Kyai Haji Abdurrahman Wahid was president of Indonesia from 1999 to 2001. Prior to that, he headed Nahdlatul Ulama, the world's largest Muslim organization. C. Holland Taylor is chairman and chief executive of the LibForAll Foundation (www.libforall.org), a nonprofit organization he co-founded with Wahid, which works to reduce religious extremism and discredit the use of terrorism. The world's population of Muslims exceeds 1.3 billion people, and Indonesia has the largest population of Muslims. Only 300 million Muslims live in the Arabic-speaking countries that represent the heart of the radical Islamist movements. The authors argue that Indonesia has the potential to help define Islam as moderate and progressive.

24

LIFE IS FOR LIVING

To be, or not to be, that is the question.
—Shakespeare, Hamlet

Life is a continuous series of choices and everyone must make them. The ability to think, to evaluate, and to choose is the supreme characteristic that makes us human. Every choice leads inexorably to right or wrong, good or bad, success or failure—according to how one defines those terms. Every choice is a building block of the structure of one's life, and every one counts, whether large or small. We have the free will to either create destructive social environments through ignorance and maliciousness, or, through enlightened self-interest, to create a free and civilized society in which we can achieve our values and flourish.

My choices were not always rational or based on the best information available at the time, and in those cases, they inevitably turned out to be the wrong choices. However, at a young age I knew instinctively that life was for living and therefore tried to make conscious, deliberate choices that enabled me to achieve my values and enjoy life—in other words, to live.

At the young age of about 25, I became a student of Objectivism after reading the book *Atlas Shrugged*, by Ayn Rand. It has had a significant impact on my thinking, my values, and my life for over 40 years. Objectivism has been my beacon shining the way through the blizzard of confusions, uncertainty, and contradictions that have continually bombarded me from a young age. It offered a positive vision that my life on this Earth mattered—to me. It offered a rational alternative to what I saw as a socialist agenda aimed at hindering progress, industrialization, capitalism, and even Western civilization. Therefore, it should not be surprising that Objectivism has significantly influenced my life and my story.

Many have attempted to discredit Ayn Rand's ideas; nevertheless, I am confident that in time Objectivism's ideas and philosophy will prevail and have a positive impact on humanity as a whole, perhaps the greatest impact of any philosophy in the history of modern man—precisely because it is a philosophy "for living on Earth."

The Ayn Rand Institute reports that more than 6 million copies of *Atlas Shrugged* have been sold, and more of Ayn Rand's books are being sold now than at any time since *Atlas Shrugged* was first published over 50 years ago.[138] Objectivism is being taught in more than 30 universities, and it is projected that before long more than a million high school students will be studying Ayn Rand.[139] I am not surprised. Her ideas offer the positive values that young people are looking for as they struggle with their contradictions. I continue to be a student and an advocate.

∞⊂≥

As I write this, most of my contradictions have been resolved and I live life without anxiety about its purpose, its values, and its virtues. Although I am a student of Objectivism, I also remain a student of mysticism and spirituality and share my views on these subjects:

What is God? Does he/she/it exist? For centuries, there has been ambiguity about what the word "God" means and how it should be interpreted. Dictionary definitions make it sound as though God is human, using words such as "supreme being," "all-powerful," "all-knowing," "creator," and "ruler." They imply the personification of something big, complex, and mostly unknowable. Certainly, God means different things to different people, and to suggest that there is but one "true" God is the height of arrogance. Some personify the "Great Spirit" of love and harmony that seems to bind us to friends, humanity, and nature as God. Most join a convenient and popular religious group and blindly accept its "supreme being"—whatever it may be—and then (fortunately) proceed to behave in ways that usually contradict the values they profess to believe. Others reject all divine concepts and call themselves atheists. A few others walk the middle of the road, accepting that God may exist, but remain skeptical until they have more evidence—calling themselves agnostics. Lately, it has become popular to join a fundamentalist group and become a member of "God's Warriors"—be it Jewish, Christian, or Muslim. Most religious authorities would call me a "secular humanist" or an atheist.

A recent attempt to explain the complexity of the universe was called "Intelligent Design." This hypothesis argues that the "design" of some organisms

---

[138] www.aynrand.org, November 12, 2007.

[139] Marc E. Babej and Tim Pollak, "Atlas Shrugs Again," *Forbes Magazine*, September 28, 2007, http://www.forbes.com

seem too complex to be explained by evolution and therefore concludes that there must have been a "designer" with higher intelligence. Proponents seem to ignore that, following their own logic, that "designer" must have been more complex, which would suggest the need for another "designer" of even higher intelligence or a "supernatural designer" that transcends scientific study and evolved intelligence—in other words, God. Therefore, after these obscure mental gymnastics, we are right back to where we started. The "Intelligent Design" hypothesis is nothing more than a feeble attempt to give mysticism a superficial and fraudulent appearance of being scientific.

For years I studied, deliberated and, at times, agonized about the God that should or should not fit into my life. For me, the universe has always been my "God," and here I use those two terms interchangeably. Call it nature if you prefer. It is convenient to personify the universe as God to aid visualization and I have done that here; however, it should be understood that I do not worship any god.

How do you describe God? Standing on the top of a mountain, scuba diving in the ocean, watching a sunset, experiencing an earthquake, or living through a hurricane—it is obvious that God is big, complex, all-powerful and mostly unknown, but not unknowable. By using our minds, we learn more about the universe every day—planet Earth is not flat and the sun does not revolve around it. Each of us is an integral part of nature and the universe, as is a tree, an insect, and a distant star.

The universe often seems malevolent—is yours a malevolent God? Many believe life is a hopeless struggle, and the most we can expect are a few moments of comfort along the way as we prepare for "everlasting life" after death. Bertrand Russell wrote an essay that made that argument:

> *The life of man is a long march through the night, surrounded by invisible foes, tortured by weariness and pain, toward a goal that few can hope to reach, and where none may tarry long. One by one, as they march, our comrades vanish from our sight, seized by the silent orders of omnipotent death. Very brief is the time in which we can help them, in which their happiness or misery is decided. Be it ours to shed sunlight on their path, to lighten their sorrows by the balm of sympathy, to give them the pure joy of a never tiring affection, to strengthen failing courage, to instill faith in hours of despair. Let us not weigh in grudging scales their merits and demerits, but let us think only of their need—of sorrows, the difficulties, perhaps the blindness, that make the misery of their lives; let us remember that they are fellow sufferers in the same darkness, actors in the same*

tragedy with us.[140]

Bertrand Russell was wrong. In fact, the universe is benevolent. Man has the capacity to meet his needs in the environment in which he operates. The mind—if we choose to use it and its ability to reason—provides us with the capacity to learn about the world, our environment, and the universe. We have the free will to either create destructive social environments through ignorance and maliciousness, or, through enlightened self-interest, create a free and civilized society in which we can achieve our values and enjoy life. Of course, pain, suffering, and loss occur in life, but they are not the core of life. They serve a useful purpose to alert us to conditions that may be a threat to our lives so we can act accordingly to change that condition. There are no guarantees of success; however, by making good decisions (that is, rational decisions) it is man's natural state to be successful and to enjoy living. That is the essential core of human life and represents the benevolent view of the universe. If we adopt that view, and act accordingly, the universe will be benevolent toward us.

Is God a creator? Yes, in the sense that new creatures are born every day, the universe is ever changing, and her creatures have been continually adapting to their environment since the beginning of time—if time had a beginning.

Does God "rule" the universe? The laws of the universe exist, so in that sense, God rules. And one of God's laws is the Law of Probability, which means some people will be more fortunate than others. I was fortunate to have been born to parents living in Canada; 160 million "Untouchables" were not so fortunate—they were born to parents living in India who accepted the teachings of the Hindu mystics who told them that misery was their destiny in life. Anyone who has studied science knows about God's laws, as does anyone standing under an apple tree who thinks about it when an apple falls on his head.

Does God demand obedience? If we can agree that living well is a virtue (and many would not agree), then making choices to enhance the quality and structure of one's life would suggest obedience. Conversely, making irrational choices that bring unfortunate consequences that threaten, harm, or destroy the structure of our well-being suggests disobedience. However, God does not demand obedience; he gave us the choice to obey or disobey—that is, essentially, to live or die; to be, or not to be. Moreover, there is no forgiveness for our disobedience; its consequences are not removed. That might prompt some to say, "It's a cruel world out there." I would say, "It's a just world."

---

140 Bertrand Russell, *A Free Man's Worship* (1903).

LIFE IS FOR LIVING

Does God demand worship and sacrifice? Although I have known many demands for worship and sacrifice from mortal human beings, I have known none from God—only respect for his power and his laws.

Is God supernatural and imaginary, or is he real? He/she/it is real. I see and touch him every time I see and experience the universe and all its many elements—both good and bad. The sonnet "High Flight," written by John Gillespie Magee, says it well. He was an American pilot with the Royal Canadian Air Force and was killed in World War II, at the age of nineteen, on December 11, 1941.

HIGH FLIGHT

Oh! I have slipped the surly bonds of earth
And danced the skies on laughter-silvered wings;
Sunward I've climbed, and joined the tumbling mirth
Of sun-split clouds – and done a hundred things
You have not dreamed of – wheeled and soared and swung
High in the sunlit silence. Hovering there
I've chased the shouting wind along, and flung
My eager craft through footless halls of air.
Up, up the long delirious, burning blue,
I've topped the windswept heights with easy grace
Where never lark, or even eagle flew —
And, while with silent lifting mind I've trod
The high untresspassed sanctity of space,
Put out my hand and touched the face of God.

Are we sinners in the eyes of God? No. The human species enjoys one unique and profound characteristic—our mind, with its ability to reason and choose. That one characteristic distinguishes us from all the other species. It provides the opportunity to exercise significant control over our lives and our future—to make life-and-death choices. *If there were sins, the choice to resort to faith instead of using our God-given, all-important faculty to reason, to think, and to live well would be the greatest of all sins, because to do so would be to reject the supreme characteristic that makes us human.* In addition, the foolish idea that infants are born sinners (the concept of original sin) is so immoral, disgusting, and shameful that it does not deserve serious discussion.

Do you think about death? No…not much.

Why? Because death is not important. Living is important. I think about living. Freya Stark, perhaps the most remarkable woman adventurer of the 20th century wrote, "One life is an absurdly small allowance," and she lived to be 100 years old. Whether or not our life on Earth is a small or a generous allowance, it deserves our primary attention and focus to make the best of it. Yet the mystics of the world want us to focus primarily on sacrificing our life on Earth in order to prepare for death. They demand that we reject our mind and subordinate reason to blind faith in the supernatural.

As a young boy, I attended a small church in the country with my family. I still remember being frustrated when the pastor gave the weekly benediction at the end of the service: "May the Peace of God that passeth all understanding be with you as you go forth." At that young age, my mind was exceedingly curious, and I was frustrated at being told that it was incapable of understanding the Peace of God. The pastor—supposedly a role model—was telling me I had to reject the use of my mind and resort to faith—in other words, to nullify my consciousness. I was to trust his guidance more than my own, even though he had already given up trying to comprehend. Since then, I have observed mystics throughout the world commanding their followers to trust in them instead of their own mind and to follow the teachings of some fabricated supernatural entity beyond their power to conceive. Fortunately, I did not grant obedience to these authorities and fought against their admonitions; I trusted my own mind and later understood the "Peace of God." It does not passeth all understanding; it is evident every time I interact with the realities of nature and the universe and enjoy its benevolence.

The realities of the universe must not be confused with the many synthetic mystical structures of the mind aimed at controlling one's life and limiting one's ability to understand and enjoy the benevolence of the universe. There is no need to embrace mysticism in order to give life meaning. Our life on Earth should not be subordinated and sacrificed in order to possibly gain entrance to some other unknown supernatural life hereafter that transcends the universe—existence beyond existence—or to possibly avoid being banished to some unknown life hereafter in eternal hell.

So is that all there is, then, just a brief life on planet Earth? Yes, and it's enough if you made good use of it, and if you didn't, why do you think you deserve more, not having taken full advantage of what God gave you? God has more creating to do; your time is up; you had your chance; go in peace. Maybe you will be reincarnated and have another chance, as some believe.

Then what is the purpose of our existence? Each of us exists to enjoy life on that small piece of the universe called planet Earth. We are offered many great and wondrous things—from the furthest planets to the deepest matters of the spirit—and they are there for us to accept and enjoy, or to ignore. A significant portion of one's enjoyment should come from matters concerning the spirit, such as experiencing and studying nature, art, literature, and music; the enjoyment of family, friends, romantic love, recreation, and honest, productive work. These fulfill the human spirit, engender happiness, and validate our existence for as long as it may last. Matters of the spirit can prevent the certainty of mortality from being a threat to the value and meaning of our existence.

Material values and spiritual values need not compete with each other—both should exist together in harmony. The material world is there to enhance the spiritual, to allow a greater appreciation and enjoyment of the spiritual—not the other way around—and we must be careful to use the material world for that purpose. When the desire for material abundance displaces spiritual values, moral numbness takes hold and the material values lose much of their significance. Spiritual values are the antidote for that numbness and can sustain us as enlightened human beings. The spiritual allows each of us to live in society with value and meaning—and die peacefully when the time comes.

※

The enjoyment of poetry was an important spiritual value for my mother; she particularly admired Rudyard Kipling (1865–1936)—a prolific poet. From a very young age, I recall a needlepoint of one of his poems, called simply "If," hanging on the wall of our home—it went with us as we moved from place to place. Mother said very little about it, but I know she admired it greatly and encouraged us to read it. The message was powerful and each time it evoked inspiration and motivation. Mother knew I enjoyed the poem, too, and eventually gave me the wall hanging, although I left it in her room until she died at the age of ninety-two. Now a prized possession, it reminds me of my mother and her great guidance, quiet coaching, and intense devotion to her family:

IF

If you can keep your head when all about you
Are losing theirs and blaming it on you;
If you can trust yourself when all men doubt you,
But make allowance for their doubting too;
If you can wait and not be tired by waiting,
Or being lied about, don't deal in lies,
Or being hated, don't give way to hating,
And yet don't look too good, nor talk too wise:

LIFE IS FOR LIVING

If you can dream—and not make dreams your master;
If you can think—and not make thoughts your aim;
If you can meet with Triumph and Disaster
And treat those two imposters just the same;
If you can bear to hear the truth you've spoken
Twisted by knaves to make a trap for fools,
Or watch the things you gave your life to, broken,
And stoop and build 'em up with worn-out tools;

If you can make one heap of all your winnings
And risk it on one turn of pitch-and-toss,
And lose, and start again at your beginnings
And never breathe a word about your loss;
If you can force your heart and nerve and sinew
To serve your turn long after they are gone,
And so hold on when there is nothing in you
Except the Will which says to them: "Hold on!"

If you can talk with crowds and keep your virtue,
Or walk with kings – nor lose the common touch,
If neither foes nor loving friends can hurt you,
If all men count with you, but none too much;
If you can fill the unforgiving minute
With sixty seconds' worth of distance run —
Yours is the Earth and everything that's in it,
And—which is more—you'll be a Man, my son!

—Rudyard Kipling

Enjoy the benevolence of the universe; do not allow mystical structures of the mind limit your earthly enjoyment and happiness; maintain a proper balance between the spiritual and the material; and give your life its own meaning and purpose so you are satisfied when it is over. A flourishing life is possible without using mysticism as a crutch.

One cannot predict the future with any degree of certainty, but it has been a great journey so far, and I expect to be satisfied when it is over. Life is for living.

LIFE IS FOR LIVING

We hold these truths to be self-evident, that all men are created equal, that they are endowed by their Creator with certain unalienable Rights, that among these are Life, Liberty and the pursuit of Happiness.
—The United States Declaration of Independence,
July 4, 1776

Congress shall make no law respecting an established religion, or prohibiting the free exercise thereof; or abridging the freedom of speech, or of the press; or the right of people peaceably to assemble, and to petition the Government for a redress of grievances."
—First Amendment to the Constitution of the
United States of America

ACKNOWLEDGMENTS

The process of writing this story began, unbeknownst to me, in 1966 when I started keeping brief notes each day of where I was and what I was doing. I have continued the habit ever since. The actual writing of the story was a part-time project spanning 10 years, during which I began to appreciate the value of the contributions that others have made to the fullness of my life. I have benefited immensely from the wisdom and knowledge of so many people, that to acknowledge them all would be impossible. However, I ask your indulgence while I thank a few who stood out and touched my life in significant ways. They made my life rich, much richer than it otherwise would have been. Although the names may mean little to most, they mean a lot to me—for the association and experiences we shared, as well as for the moral and intellectual support they provided.

First, I wish to thank my mother who taught me the virtue of self-reliance and independence—she did so simply by allowing me to learn by myself the art of survival. She protected me with invisible boundaries that moved from time to time when she believed it was worth the risk to do so—sometimes even before I thought I was ready. She taught me right from wrong, and allowed me to use my own mind to decide which to choose. She did not try to protect me from the consequences of my choices, and therefore, I usually learned from my mistakes. Her love, guidance, and coaching helped me build the foundation for a flourishing life. Teaching a child to be self-reliant and independent is perhaps the greatest legacy a parent can leave. She made the greatest contribution of all.

I would also like to thank my father for supporting me during my formative years, for struggling to be a good father, and for insisting that I go to school. I regret being unable to share more of my life with him.

My first wife, Betty, shared many nomadic adventures with me and was a willing and supportive partner during most of my early life. Without complaint, she shifted from my shoulders to her own the responsibility for caring for our

ACKNOWLEDGMENTS

two young children when I was away. It was a contribution much greater than I appreciated at the time, and I wish I had thanked her once again before she succumbed to leukemia in 2003.

Although he survived for less than a year, our son, Gregory, made a significant contribution during his brief lifetime. Despite his discomfort and weakness, the easy smile and the bright, clear, and intense eyes silently helped me appreciate the special kind of transparent love and happiness only a child can experience and share. The purity of his brief existence positively confirmed that the concept of original sin is a myth—an evil designed by mystics to destroy the pride, self-esteem, and love of life with which every child is born.

I thank my other two children, Dale and Pamela, for sharing most of my nomadic adventures. I have many happy memories of watching them grow and mature into adulthood. Thank you for your love and for being there—then and now.

I want to acknowledge my teachers at Longwood Public School, Iroquois Falls High School, and Kingsville District High School. Although I can still see many of their faces, I cannot remember their names. Their instruction and discipline provided a foundation for lifelong learning. A special thanks to Charlie Campbell for being one of the few at that time who believed I "had good potential and would do well," and for launching me into an advanced education that opened the door to opportunities.

Professor Peter Southwell took over and ushered me through university and graduate school; he taught me the difficult task of using the language to communicate efficiently and effectively—perhaps the most valuable skill I learned at university. Most engineers are not taught that skill at all. Thank you, Professor Southwell.

I owe special thanks to literally hundreds of first-class, talented colleagues and outstanding executives at Caterpillar Inc. who taught me about business management and leadership—skills I seemed to absorb progressively, almost unconsciously. I feel especially privileged to have been part of Team Caterpillar, first on the inside of the organization for 20 years, and then while leading two Caterpillar dealer organizations for an additional 10 years. Many experiences with a variety of other corporations confirmed that Caterpillar people were preeminent. Thank you for your honest assessments, your coaching, your empathy, and for having the courage to challenge and criticize me when you thought I was wrong. I would like to name you all, but would surely forget someone. Nevertheless, I must mention Curt Caughey, Dev Keenan, Christiana Lee, Dan Olson, Hillary Watson, and Al Wickert whom I consider to be not only good colleagues but also special friends.

Special thanks go to a group of talented and dedicated professionals at

ACKNOWLEDGMENTS

Canadian Kenworth, Canadian Foremost, Robbins & Myers Canada Ltd., and Crane Canada who deserve most of the credit for the success we were able to achieve. In the story, I describe my 12 years with these organizations as "a frantic ride on an out-of-control roller coaster with many devious, conspiratorial, and insecure colleagues with marginal concern for integrity, teamwork, and good business judgment." The following individuals were not the only exceptions to that general characterization but were the most notable ones in positions of influence; they deserve special recognition and have my sincere gratitude for their professionalism and their contributions: Diane Bakker, Tom Banks, John Cecconi, Hill Clarke, Alan Cockrell, David Dickey, Stephen Jones, John Locke, Patrick O'Keefe, Chris Patterson, Richard Phillips, Bill Potts, Shari Pusch, William Pusch, Theresia Reisch, Stephen Russell-Hill, and Tom Stirr. I thank you all.

The key members of the management team at Atlantic Equipment and Power Limited deserve special acknowledgment for providing me with an unforgettable learning experience from inside a Caterpillar dealer organization for the first time. They provided full cooperation and support for the five-year restructuring and growth project that we went through together in the Bahamas. It would not have succeeded without them: Erma Cartwright, Raul Manzano, George McKenzie, Donnalee Roberts, Keith Roberts, and Richard Tremblay. Special thanks go to the principals: Frank J. Crothers, Michael J. Crothers, and Richard D. Evans—their support and encouragement were invaluable.

Perhaps the most enjoyable and satisfying part of my life's journey came near the end of this story, while at Capital Machinery Limited in Taiwan. It was another significant restructuring assignment designed to launch the business on a path of growth and prosperity. Although it was my second experience working inside a Caterpillar dealership, the Taiwanese staff made it a most unique and enjoyable one. Their desire and determination to succeed, their strong work ethic, their positive attitudes, and their pleasant and friendly personalities made it a special experience unlike any other. They did not just come to work, they came to work to win—and they did. I only had to show the way and provide some coaching from time to time. They made it happen at a rate that surprised even the most optimistic. The following individuals deserve special mention: Lucy Chen, Paul Chen, Tom Chen, Meisha Chang, Andy Chiu, Joann Chu, Tim Ferng, C.S. Horng, J.H. Hsu, Vincent Lai, C.J. Lee, S.H. Lee, F.I. Lin, C.Y. Lin, G.Y. Rau, Louis Tang, Dennis Wong and Peter Yiin. In addition, I would like especially to thank Datuk C. K. Lau for providing the financial support to the organization, and for having confidence that we could perform. The leadership at Lei Shing Hong—especially Paul Ferris, David Park, and Marianne Lim—provided guidance as needed with the development and implementation

ACKNOWLEDGMENTS

of the strategy. Their support made a significant contribution to the success that the organization was able to achieve. I thank you all.

I would also like to thank especially my brother, Everett, for offering suggestions based on his own experiences as a published writer.[141] All three of my siblings, Curtis, Francis, and Everett, shared most of the early years alongside me and helped refresh my memory and fill in details I had completely forgotten or did not know. Thank you.

Although this was not exactly a family project, my wife, Hélène, tolerated my frustrating hours at the keyboard, searching for the right words, and many more hours doing research and digging out information from a wide variety of sources. I thank you for your love, forbearance, encouragement, and constructive criticism. You have my love and gratitude.

Dr. Patricia Anderson and Mavis Andrews provided valuable assistance in helping to organize and structure the manuscript and, finally, in editing and proofreading it. Editing and proofreading assistance was also provided by Roger Mitchell, and Jane Rickards. There is no substitute for expert advice.

Finally, Sharleen Pasta and Kathleen Blondal at Trafford Publishing worked closely with me from the early stages to get the story published. Thank you for guiding me through that process and for your insights and suggestions.

One cannot predict the future with any degree of confidence, but regardless of future events, I expect to be satisfied with my life when it is over. It has been a great journey so far.

Maurice E. Marwood, 2008
professionalnomad@mmarwood.com

---

[141] Everett J. Marwood, *A Legacy Worth Leaving: Savoring the Past, Inspiring the Future* (2003).

ABOUT THE AUTHOR

MAURICE E. Marwood grew up after the Second World War as the son of a struggling, part-time farmer in eastern Canada. He eventually escaped the clutches of poverty and earned an MSc in engineering from the University of Guelph and an MBA from the University of Chicago. During his early career, he spent 20 years in increasingly responsible international positions with Caterpillar and, later, an additional 10 years managing two Caterpillar dealer organizations—first, as President of the dealership in the Bahamas, and most recently as Managing Director for the dealership in Taiwan. An expert in corporate turnarounds, he spent several years restructuring and renewing a variety of business organizations struggling for growth and profitability; his executive-level leadership has spanned manufacturing, distribution logistics, marketing, and international sales of industrial equipment and packaged consumer products.

Marwood has served as a Rotarian, Director of the Nassau Institute, Governor/Director of Chambers of Commerce, advisor to the University of Calgary Faculty of Management, and to the Conference Board of Canada's Operating Council for Business Excellence. He has been a frequent presenter and panel participant at university and industry association gatherings, and published articles on business management, leadership, and social issues in magazines, newspapers, and websites. In 2007, he was the first "foreigner" to receive a special annual award from the Council of Labor Affairs of the government of Taiwan, for innovation in the development of Human Resources.

From a young age, Marwood instinctively knew that life was for living and discovered an insatiable appetite for experiences and ideas. He worked hard to maintain a balance between life's critical success factors—the material and the spiritual—making time to raise a family and pursue such adventures as climbing the Matterhorn, trekking Nepal, marathoning, skiing, snowboarding, scuba diving, and cruising eastern North America and the Bahamas. Firsthand involvement in a wide variety of events and situations shaped his values, opinions, and philosophy of living that he shares with honesty and passion.

ABOUT THE AUTHOR

The author with his wife, Hélène.

ISBN 1425180353

Edwards Brothers Malloy
Oxnard, CA USA
September 8, 2014